T0267931

ALGORITHMS OF
ARMAGEDDON

domForestClassifier_from sklearn.metrics import classificat
racy_score, roc_auc_score_import numpy as np__np.random.
els]_WEAPON = np.random.rand(1500, 25) # 1500 samples, 25
_train, y_test = train_test_split(WEAPON, y, state=42)__s
dardScaler()_weapon_train_scaled =scaler.fit_transform(we

ALGORITHMS OF
ARMAGEDDON

THE IMPACT OF ARTIFICIAL INTELLIGENCE ON FUTURE WARS

ures.transform(WEAPON_test_scaled)__selector = SelectKBe
sform(weapon_train_poly, y_train)_weapon_test_selected =
sform(WEAPON_test_poly)__classifier = RandomForestClassifi
mators=150, maWEAPON_depth=15, min_samples_split=2, min_
les_leaf=1, random_state=42)__param_grid = {_ 'n_estimat
, 150, 200],_ 'maWEAPON_depth': [15, 20, 25],_ 'min_samp
t': [2, 5, 10],_ 'min_samples_leaf': [1, 2, 4]}__grid_s

GEORGE GALDORISI
SAM J. TANGREDI

SearchCV(classifier, param_grid, cv=5) grid_search.fit(WEA
cted, y_train)__best_params = grid_search.best_params__

sifier = Rando FOREWORD BY ROBERT O. WORK 2, **best_pa
mized_classifier.fit(weapon_train_selected, y_train)__pred
mized_classifier.predict(weapon_test_selected)__accuracy

e(y_test, predict **NAVAL INSTITUTE PRESS** auc_score(y_test, p
Annapolis, MD
i_class='ovr')_classification_rep = classification_report(
ictions) print("Accuracy:" accuracy) print("ROC AUC Sc

Naval Institute Press
291 Wood Road
Annapolis, MD 21402

Library of Congress Cataloging–in–Publication Data is available.
ISBN: 978-1-61251-541-0 (hardcover)
ISBN: 978-1-61251-566-3 (eBook)

♾ Print editions meet the requirements of ANSI/NISO z39.48-1992 (Perma-
nence of Paper).
Printed in the United States of America.

32 31 30 29 28 27 26 25 24   9 8 7 6 5 4 3 2 1
First printing

CONTENTS

FOREWORD

By Robert O. Work

ALGORITHMIC WARFARE IS warfare conducted through artificially intelligent means, where software superiority is the essential ingredient of military-technical superiority. We are well on the way toward algorithmic warfare. The joint force has essentially become an all-digital force.

Already we are beyond the point of incorporating artificial intelligence (AI) into the analysis of all-source intelligence information; as a tool for planning, war-gaming, and speeding human decision-making; and into weapons systems with some degree of autonomy.

To some extent, algorithmic warfare has been thrust upon us whether we are ready or not. Technology is constantly changing and growing in power; at the same time, knowledge is constantly expanding. The aggressive authoritarian countries that are our potential opponents have caught up with our previous military advantages, characterized by the development of guided weapons and the "battle networks" that employ them with exquisite precision. Now they are working on developing their own military applications of AI, threatening U.S. military-technical superiority.

We have been here before; in the late 1940s and 1950s, Western Europe was threatened with invasion by powerful Soviet forces with a significant numerical advantage over North Atlantic Treaty Organization (NATO) forces in the potential theater. The United States and NATO developed battlefield nuclear weapons to *offset* the Soviet advantages—in what is often referred to as the first offset.

After the Soviet Union developed its own powerful nuclear capabilities in the 1960s and 1970s while *expanding* its conventional military advantage, the United States embarked on the second offset, the development of nonnuclear guided weapons that could strike Soviet forces with greater precision and effectiveness than ever before.

Most fortunately, the Cold War ended without direct hostilities. However, the effectiveness of guided munition battle network warfare—what the Chinese call "informatized warfare"—was fully demonstrated in Operation Desert Storm in which Kuwait was liberated and significant territory was seized in Iraq after just 42 days of intense air operations and 3 days of high-intensity ground combat.

Operation Desert Storm spurred U.S. competitors to seek parity in this new way of war. Consequently, we now have the need for a third offset to neutralize the reconnaissance strike networks, guided weapons, and positional advantages of our potential opponents and preserve global deterrence. This third offset is built around AI-enabled autonomy—both at rest in intelligence, planning, and decision-making systems, and in motion on unmanned systems in every operating domain.

Algorithmic warfare, which takes advantage of the technical inventiveness and creativity of America's defense innovation base, will define this third offset. Our current advantage originates in the lead of the United States and its allies in developing commercial applications of AI. It is the responsibility of the Department of Defense (DoD) to translate this commercial activity into a military advantage in a responsible manner.

That was our objective during the time I served as deputy secretary of defense. We knew algorithmic warfare was coming, and we needed to adapt if we wanted to preserve a global environment in which democracy and prosperity flourish.

To those critically concerned about the future use of AI in military operations, DoD is trying mightily to pursue its application in a deliberate and safe manner. DoD is committed to using AI for the analyses of big data obtained by our intelligence networks and to utilize AI for human-machine teaming. In that effort, it has developed and promulgated principles for responsible AI. It has a policy on autonomy in weapons systems that preserves the use of *human judgment* over the use of force. That is why we have emphasized human-machine teaming in algorithmic warfare.

During my service as co-chairman of the National Security Commission on Artificial Intelligence with Alphabet/Google's former chief executive Eric Schmidt, I became even more aware of the capability of AI in transforming warfare and the alarming gap between the pace in which we are adopting applications of AI and the efforts of our potential opponents. We are clearly losing the initial technological advantage to which we have become accustomed. As Eric has publicly noted, we are not a decade ahead of our potential opponents, as some have presumed. We are perhaps a couple of years ahead. But we will soon be behind if we do not increase the speed at which we develop our algorithmic warfare capabilities. Being behind is not a good position in maintaining deterrence.

That is why I support every effort to bring public attention to this critical situation, and not just through official or academic reports. The last several years have witnessed almost a cottage industry of books on this subject, a few of which have discussed some aspects of the use of AI in military weapons systems. Most of these works fall into one of two categories: highly technical tomes targeted at a very small slice of policy and defense experts, or fictionalized accounts of future warfare where AI dominates the battlefield and humans are, at best, an afterthought.

What has been missing are factual books that explain AI in a way that any interested person can absorb in order to understand its impact on American national security.

Algorithms of Armageddon is such a book, and one produced by two experts in strategy and military technology. George Galdorisi and Sam J. Tangredi are national security professionals who have studied and dealt with AI in both the technical and policy arenas. They write clearly and convincingly. I participated in their previous collaborative book project, *AI at War*.

That is not to say that I agree with every one of their conclusions. But I am in full agreement with their concern that the true danger is not one of AI controlling humans, but of humans using AI to control other humans. That is the concern that prompted their writing of the book. Like them, I don't want to see the United States ever controlled by the algorithmic capability of an opponent.

This is a book that needs to be read by all who want to understand the importance of AI in military strategy, operations, and tactics, and why it is vital for American citizens to not only understand these issues by discussing the policy, legal, and ethical considerations, but also to address them based on evidence and analysis rather than speculation. The book's ultimate objective is to advance this critical dialogue in a thoughtful and durable manner so that choices can be made and action taken.

Algorithmic warfare is here, and the time for both discussion and action is now.

Following his career as a decorated U.S. Marine Corps officer, the Honorable Robert O. Work served as the undersecretary of the Navy from 2009 to 2013 and as the deputy secretary of defense from 2014 to 2017. In the latter capacity, he was the chief architect of the Department of Defense's Defense Innovation Initiative and its third offset strategy, designed to increase investment in cutting-edge technologies for the U.S. military to achieve and sustain the joint force's military-technical superiority. From 2019 to 2021, he served as co-chair (alongside former Google chief executive officer Eric Schmidt) of the National Security Commission on Artificial Intelligence.

INTRODUCTION
"The Ruler of the World"

IN 2017, FOUR YEARS BEFORE he invaded Ukraine for the second time, President Vladimir Putin decided to give the young people of Russia some advice about their future.

Meeting with students in Yaroslavl, a historic city 160 miles northeast of Moscow, Putin stood calmly but with his characteristic stiffness, the cause of which remains unknown: perhaps a serious illness, judo injuries, or, as one researcher speculates, a degree of autism. Another conjecture is that he was taught early in his career in the KGB (now called the FSB [Federal Security Service], the secret police that prop up all Russian dictatorships) to always keep his hand close to the place on his belt where a gun could be holstered.

Putin may not have been carrying a gun. However, this act of political theater allowed him an opportunity to make a forecast about another potential weapon. "Artificial intelligence," he intoned, "is the future, not only for Russia, but for all humankind. It comes with colossal opportunities, but also threats that are difficult to predict." He continued, ominously, "Whoever becomes the leader in this sphere will become the ruler of the world."[1]

THE PREDICTION, THE PROMISES, AND THE THREAT

Putin's predictions may not always be seen as particularly accurate; his 2022 expectations of a quick march on Kyiv, for example, were obviously wrong. Yet his view of artificial intelligence (AI)—with the exception of the "ruling the world" rhetoric—is in accord with the perspectives of enthusiastic technologists, upbeat investors, and the more sober analysts.

The first two groups can be seen as self-interested; their careers and economic success are dependent on the intellectually stimulating and profitable development of new technologies. They behold the promises that AI can bring to the processes that drive our economy. Scientific and engineering careers are being built, and fortunes have already been made through the application of AI to business. Some postulate that AI will completely change the nature of work. The most optimistic think it will bring all people more leisure by freeing them from the labor required to obtain basic needs.

However, a number in the third group—the analysts—have publicly advised prudence and caution in the assessment of the promises of AI. It may indeed revolutionize some of today's industries and create new ones. But the ultimate result of the widespread adoption of AI remains uncertain. It might make our lives easier, but not necessarily better.

Lurking within the promises of AI and those who create it are the risks and threats of its (perhaps very) harmful uses. Some of these uses will be unanticipated—perhaps completely unexpected—and some will merely be unintended, the results of known risks that were deemed implausible or initially inconsequential. But others will be intended uses by those who are most likely to bring human repression and war. Even Tesla Corporation's founder Elon Musk—whose company utilizes AI in its effort to build self-driving cars—dramatically maintains that AI poses a "fundamental, existential risk to the existence of civilization" and "needs proactive" government regulation.[2]

As concerned analysts, we are in the third group. This book is not intended to be merely a frightening polemic, a speculation designed to scare you. If you are indeed scared after reading the facts we will present, perhaps that is because you are prudently thoughtful. To some degree, we all should be a bit frightened of these unintended—and certain of the intended—usages of AI.

Our purpose, however, is to provide a detailed and impartial picture of the current state and potential evolution of *military* applications of AI. All technologies inevitably find a use in war. These applications include their intended, unconsidered, and inevitable uses. The term "evolution" is used deliberately; in order to give you a thorough understanding of military AI, we will also discuss the history of AI in everyday civilian life. Following our conclusion, you can decide for yourself as to the group in which you fit.

POWER RULES, AND AI WILL HELP IT

Whether justly or not, military force has historically been the decider of the fate of nations. Within the past thirty years alone, force has decided the conditions in Afghanistan, Armenia, Azerbaijan, Bosnia/former Yugoslavia, Chechnya, Colombia, Democratic Republic of the Congo, Georgia, Iraq, Israel/West Bank/Gaza, Libya, Nigeria, Rwanda, Sudan, Syria, Yemen, and Ukraine. Military stand-offs continue between the People's Republic of China (PRC) and Taiwan, North Korea and South Korea, India and Pakistan, Greece and Turkey (concerning Cyprus), India and the PRC (in the Himalayas), Iran and the Arab states (and Israel), and in other regions.

Thus far, the wars we have listed have not involved significant use of artificial intelligence to control weapons systems, analyze intelligence reports, assist in operational decision-making, or plan attacks. That is changing. The war in Ukraine has involved limited use of AI in choreographing drone attacks. Future wars, perhaps emanating from the current military stand-offs, will, beyond any doubt, involve significant use of AI, not simply for intelligence analysis and support functions, but throughout every aspect of actual combat.[3]

The question we will examine and answer in the upcoming pages is: What will be the full impact of this transformation on the lives, prosperity, and, particularly, security of Americans? Ultimately, the latter components of the question are the most important since without security and prosperity, life itself remains uncertain in a world in which—despite elaborate systems of diplomatic, moral, and ethical structures—power rules. And, despite those international laws, norms, treaties, humane feelings, promises, and protests, "ruling" ultimately includes the threat or application of military force. If that is a hard reality for idealists to stomach, they need but check the above list of wars or contemplate whether a conflict arising from one of the precarious stand-offs will inevitably drag in the United States.

Another aspect of power that is linked to force is the control of domestic societies. The United States came into being through the use of force to evict what was perceived as unjust British control of colonial society. Other peoples have taken similar actions. At the same time, most governments hold a monopoly of force within the bounds of their rule, ensuring their continuation, whether justly or unjustly. With AI, it is easier to suppress popular revolts. If the British had AI, would the United States be independent?

Authoritarian governments, such as those of the Chinese Communist Party or Putin's Russia, actively combine their monopoly of force with false information, propaganda, and other forms of information warfare to maintain their control of domestic society in the face of potential opposition. AI is already assisting them with the surveillance and information processing that facilitate their control. Moreover, it is assisting in projecting their forms of information warfare into other nations, including our own.

INTERRELATIONSHIP OF COMMERCIAL AND MILITARY AI

Most of the AI systems that are useful for domestic control are similar to those that can be used in modern warfare. Many are developed out of commercial AI applications. The nature of algorithm development is that the same methods used to track your Internet shopping choices and, in essence, surveil your decisions to predict your probable future purchases can be used to assess information about your other (physical) behaviors. When combined with state-controlled video cameras and biometric identification devices, practically every action in a public place (and many in private ones) can be monitored.

Privacy and human rights advocates and other critics of AI have already identified this threat. It is a threat with which the U.S. Congress and the legislatures of other democratic nations are grappling. It has become a day-to-day reality in China.

What is less publicly recognized is the degree to which commercial domestic security and potential military AI systems are entwined and entangled. Not only can one not exist without the others, but advances in one generally result in advances in all. The AI systems that might eventually control a commercial self-driving car will also control a main battle tank.

Your future car might not fire explosive tungsten or depleted uranium shells against an enemy. However, systems designed to target and fire weapons systems without humans actually pulling the trigger already exist, generally as fixed-in-place defensive weapons. When they can be combined with self-driving features now under development, such weapons systems will have high mobility. The U.S. Army has not yet attempted to apply AI to control autonomous battle tanks, but it is already investigating autonomy for lighter combat vehicles.[4] However, the Russian military has attempted to develop AI-controlled battle tanks.[5]

In the United States, many believe that we can keep commercial and military development separate through laws and codes of ethics. The U.S. Department of Defense has drafted and emplaced a number of instructions that are intended to guide "ethical" AI (we will discuss these later). But the fact that others do not want to keep them separate is evident in the *Next Generation of Artificial Intelligence Development Plan* of the PRC State Council released on July 8, 2017, two months before Putin's prediction.

First, the plan acknowledges the power of AI for domestic control, stating, "Artificial intelligence technology can accurately perceive, forecast [and] early warn [of threats to] infrastructure and social security operation. . . . It is indispensable for the effective maintenance of social stability." Next, the PRC State Council identifies its goals: "Promote the formation of multi-element, multi-field, highly efficient AI integration of military and civilian patterns. . . . Strengthen a new generation of AI technology in command-and-decision, military deduction, defense equipment, strong support, and guide AI in the field of defense technology to civilian applications."[6] The PRC plan obviously does not delineate between commercial and military AI. Instead of civilian AI developments being applied to military operations, military AI development will be the engine that drives commercial AI. This direction of development also facilitates societal control. The members of the PRC State Council—all required to be Chinese Communist Party members in good standing—were possibly contemplating the course of development of the Internet from its creation as a means of communication between defense science laboratories to its present status as an essential civilian utility. More likely, they are affirming that they are committed to the principle that power rules and that the first requirement is to apply AI to the means of power. It was Mao Zedong who famously said, "Political power comes out of the barrel of a gun." Perhaps afterward, there might be useful commercial applications.

THE MOST WORRISOME AND COMPELLING ASPECTS OF MILITARY AI

There are any number of reasons for the U.S. military to proactively leverage big data, artificial intelligence, and machine learning to make its weapons systems more effective. Perhaps the most compelling reason is that our potential adversaries—especially our peer competitors—are aggressively doing so. An old saw is the military adage, "The enemy gets a vote." In this case, Russia is voting with rubles, and China is voting with yuan.

These nations are investing heavily in AI technologies. Although the stock valuation of AI companies in the United States is over twice that of China, China pours more government money into AI than the United States and can decide which commercial companies succeed or fail. This is critical to channeling AI to the military sector and making the development of military AI predominant. Unlike in the United States, Chinese commercial AI developers cannot refuse to provide their programs to the People's Liberation Army (PLA).

Whereas AI was seen in the heady days of globalization as a commercial competition to develop profitable products, in the PRC there is no longer the pretense that AI systems market dominance is the primary goal. The Chinese would indeed like to dominate the civilian market and make money. But AI is primarily seen as a military tool, not solely a business endeavor.

Many analysts already accept that, through this method, China will soon surpass the United States as the AI superpower.[7] Yet Putin does not want to be far behind. The government-controlled Russian Direct Investment Fund raised $2 billion in 2019 alone from foreign investors. Clearly, the invasion of Ukraine and resulting sanctions have compelled most of these investors to bail out of their commitments. Nevertheless, Russia gained the seed money (which will undoubtedly be buttressed by oil money) and some commercial insights to add to the significant engineering capabilities that remain in their military-industrial complex.

Their military-industrial complex is hardly as large as it was in the days of the Soviet Union, when more than 15 percent of Soviet gross national product went to the military. However, Russia is still capable of producing world-class military technology—as reflected in submarines and air defense systems—albeit in small numbers. AI development is about software rather than hardware, and Russia still retains a core nucleus of expert technologists, including perhaps the best hackers in the world.

While Russia and China are making these investments for domestic as well as international reasons—especially to control their own citizens—they are deliberately and methodically inserting AI into their military systems as rapidly as possible to create an asymmetric advantage over the U.S. military. And in moves that may seem counterintuitive given Russia's and China's penchant for secrecy, neither nation has tried to keep these goals secret. Quite frankly, they see themselves in an "AI arms race" with the West.

There have been proposals in Western nations to try to use arms control agreements to stop this AI arms race. As we will discuss in a later chapter, we believe that, given the nature of AI, meaningful arms control arrangements are nearly impossible. One cannot count AI like one can count nuclear warheads or, as during disarmament efforts in the 1920s, battleships. AI isn't a "thing." In fact, some technologists describe AI as an "ideology."[8]

How does one write a treaty that controls ideology? Perhaps declared AI weapons systems can be counted. But how can one ever be certain which systems are controlled by AI? And how can the use of AI in intelligence analysis, command and control, operational decision-making, or war planning be accounted for?

It is unclear if U.S. decision-makers fully realize that, by no choice of our own, we are already thrust into an AI race with the authoritarian powers. Given what potential military adversaries are doing, perhaps the United States and its allies have no choice but to go all in with military AI. We will grapple with this dilemma throughout the book.

THE VOYAGE AHEAD

The book is structured as a rheostat; each chapter builds on the previous chapter, and the issues examined increase in intensity. By this method we hope to avoid plunging the reader directly into an examination of war using artificial intelligence without first explaining how and why the development of AI leads to this dangerous probability.

The first three chapters of the book are about the fundamentals of AI and the surrounding global environment. Chapter 1 is designed to simplify the continuing debate as to what constitutes big data, artificial intelligence, and machine learning. Chapter 2 describes why the convergence of AI with other technologies leads to the development of autonomous systems and explains how these systems will interact with humans. This requires a study of the history of AI development. Chapter 3 probes the motivations of both democratic and authoritarian countries to spur the development of AI and autonomy. This is followed by a deeper examination of how AI is being developed and utilized in Russia and China.

The next segment focuses on weaponization and control. Chapter 4 begins the discussion of how AI—combined with other technologies—becomes weaponized. Chapter 5 describes how such weapons are controlled by the method called human-machine teaming. Chapter 6 examines the extent to which autonomous weapons can remain under the control of humans while these systems carry out their missions, including the use of deadly force. Chapter 7 recounts the debate as to whether weaponized AI is a genie fully out of the bottle or whether the AI arms race that is already occurring can be contained by political or diplomatic efforts. A related examination of how AI and autonomy threaten to change the current laws of war constitutes chapter 8.

Chapter 9 begins the segment that examines how "World War III"—an AI-assisted or perhaps AI-directed war—would be fought. Given the fact that the nations leading large-scale development of AI see themselves as global powers, such a war is likely to be global in extent. How the war starts (chapter 9) and ends (chapter 10), as well as what happens in between, brings us into a world where humans might not have control over these events.

Can such a world and such a war be avoided? Will military AI lead to Armageddon? These are the quandaries examined in the final segment.

Chapter 11 presents the findings of the book in terms of facts concerning basic AI, military applications of AI, and dangers and critical issues that the people of the United States need to discuss in order to determine the role of AI in our national security. It encourages a national dialogue and provides recommendations that are necessary for the future security of the United States and its allies and partners. A conclusion brings the book to a close.

This book is not a protest against AI. Nor is it science fiction speculation about how AI will replace human control of the world—for good or for ill. Looking over the facts and possibilities, we do not see AI controlling humans. What we do see is humans using AI to control other humans.

We don't want our nation to be controlled by others armed with AI. That concern is the stimulus for this book.

1

WHAT IS AI, AND WHY IS IT IMPORTANT?

Just as electricity transformed almost everything 100 years ago, today I actually have a hard time thinking of an industry that I don't think AI will transform in the next several years.

ANDREW NG
former chief scientist at Baidu
(Chinese equivalent of Google)[1]

TO BEGIN TO UNDERSTAND AI and its evolving impact on our lives, we need to compare it to a much older technology and describe a man who transformed the world.

He was the epitome of our image of the "heroic" inventor: a man of humble origins, with a fanatical drive to succeed, a master of a difficult technical skill, who tirelessly applied pure genius in the face of multiple discouragements in trying to find an improvement in an emerging technology.

Yet his life also exhibited elements we associate with today's celebrity technology capitalists: the showmanship necessary to attract investors, disparagement of his rivals in the social media of his day, frequent patent lawsuits, and net worth estimated in the equivalent of billions—and, the ultimate irony, ouster by the board of directors from the public corporation he himself created.

He was Thomas Edison.

Given his role in its development, it is natural that Edison was asked in 1901 to predict electricity's impact on humanity. Two decades after the development of the light bulb, he foresaw a general purpose technology of unlimited possibilities. "Electricity is the field of fields," he said. "It holds the secrets which will reorganize the life of the world."[2]

Forecasts based on one's life work are often biased, particularly the life of an inventor-promoter. But Edison was right; in one generation, almost every American house, factory, government agency, and enterprise was electrified, and U.S. gross domestic product—considered a comprehensive scorecard of a nation's economic development—more than doubled. It is truly a general purpose technology. Today, the entire global economy is powered by electricity; no one would consider a world without it. Practically every activity of one's day—from opening the refrigerator for breakfast to turning on the lights at night—involves the use of electrical power. As with any technology, there can be downsides and negative second-order effects. In the case of electricity, the benefits have far outweighed the negatives.[3] Even survivalists have diesel generators.

AI AS GENERAL-PURPOSE TECHNOLOGY

Artificial intelligence is a different kind of general-purpose technology, but we are standing at a similar juncture and see a similarly wide-ranging impact. In the epigraph, Andrew Ng, former chief scientist at Baidu, points to the fact that AI has become the analytical power source for more and more of our everyday activities. Its use by Google to analyze our website clicks and sell the data for marketing purposes is obvious, if not in some sense quietly deceptive. After all, computers analyzing the output of other computers seems logical.

Yet the use of AI in "smart" appliances—and, for some people, entire "smart homes"—is less obvious because many of those functions had previously been completed by analog mechanical devices that aided human activity but required some sort of human intervention. We no longer have to light a gas stove using matches, but we do have to physically turn a knob to ignite the gas and control its temperature. However, AI-controlled devices are intended to "know" when to turn on and off and monitor themselves based on evaluating one's daily routine. Even if one avoids allowing AI to have considerable control over one's routine, the electrical devices now being sold—refrigerators, vacuums, televisions—are increasingly controlled by internal systems that mimic human decision-making.

What if other humans—the corporations that build the appliances, perhaps—exert their control over these decisions? To accept convenience, one might have to live with the potential vulnerability of others subtly controlling activities. If a power company arbitrarily decides to shut off the power at your home, your routine obviously will be disrupted, since the devices you depend on are no longer functioning. As AI becomes "like electricity," industries will be transformed—perhaps becoming more efficient—but everyday life will be as well. So it is with general purpose technologies. Convenience, efficiency, and control become entwined.

Baidu works in a nation that is utilizing AI to control its citizens, and AI advances at Baidu inevitably find their way to benefit the Chinese Communist Party. But Andrew Ng, a U.S. citizen who returned to Stanford University in 2017 to lead education-related AI start-ups, actually did not go far enough with his prediction. In addition to industry, it is hard to think of a government that AI will not transform to some degree in the upcoming years. This, of course, includes the military power that governments control.

GENERAL-PURPOSE CONFUSION

While many have compared the advent of AI to the invention and proliferation of electricity in an attempt to explain its impact on humanity and warfare, this association does create some confusion. While electricity is largely one "thing"—a physical motive force—AI is not.

The result is that mainstream media has used AI as a catch-all term that includes big data, artificial intelligence, and machine learning—as well as many other advances in the world of computers that have little to do with AI. Most technologists have also adopted this loose definition. As one analyst has noted, AI is often used to describe "anything we haven't done with computers already."[4] Meanwhile, the general public has been fed a steady diet of articles that describe AI in these vague but unduly complex terms.

More disconcerting has been the arbitrary use of the term AI by both proponents and opponents. Promoters use the term loosely and sometimes shamelessly in the hunt for venture capital. A report published in the *Financial Times* indicates that up to 40 percent of companies that claim to be "artificial intelligence start-ups" actually do not incorporate AI techniques into their software development. This deceptive practice is driven by the fact that "companies branded as AI businesses have historically raised higher funding," up to 15 percent higher than those that do not use the term "artificial intelligence."[5]

Meanwhile, opponents of what they describe as "killer robots" conflate artificial intelligence with autonomous weapons systems and "armed drones," despite the fact that autonomous weapons systems do not necessarily require AI and that armed drones used by the U.S. military have not been completely autonomous. Use of the term AI appears to introduce greater fear into discussions of future warfare, a goal of such regulation advocacy groups as Human Rights Watch.

SO, WHAT IS AI?

Despite its halo of hype and misinformation, AI is not a mystery. There are two practical definitions of artificial intelligence, one that is broad and one more specific.

Broadly, AI can be defined as "the capability of a machine to imitate human behavior." This was the objective of the scientists and engineers who initiated the quest for AI in the 1950s. Stanford professor John McCarthy—who coined the term "artificial intelligence" in 1955—described AI as a field of study, "the science and engineering of making intelligent machines."

However, there are a number of analog machines—those driven by mechanical processes rather than by digital computers—that *appear* to imitate humans for specific and generally repetitive tasks. For example, a bulldozer can be said to imitate humans in the sense that in replicates what humans do with shovels, albeit faster and more efficiently. A bulldozer does not look like a human and can perform but a single task: moving dirt. It also must be directly controlled by a human. But prior to its invention, humans dug large holes with hand shovels. Thus, a bulldozer can be said to imitate humans at the particular task of digging large holes.

To avoid conflating analog systems with digital, the description of *human imitation* was refined to focus on *computing capability*, with the consensus that the field of AI was the development of "a computer system able to perform tasks that normally require human intelligence, such as visual perception, speech recognition, decision-making, and translation between languages."[6] Under that definition, artificial intelligence capability is derived from computer software development. In fact, McCarthy created the world's second computer language, "list processor" or LISP, specifically to facilitate AI research.[7]

As a digital computer function, AI obviously differs greatly from an analog bulldozer. However, the question of what constitutes a computer system "able to perform tasks that normally require human intelligence" remains to some extent contentious. Current AI systems, often referred to as "narrow" or sometimes "weak" (the U.S. Navy has introduced the term "small AI"), are thus far designed to only perform as if human-like for one very specific function.

For example, AI systems that can perform visual perception–required tasks do not perform speech recognition. These functions can be combined by placing two different AI systems together so that both provide simultaneous output. But a single AI system cannot perform multiple functions for which it is not initially programmed, and programming requirements for visual perception and speech recognition are sufficiently different as to require different algorithms—the mathematical formulas that drive functions—and therefore different AI systems. In the case of the social control being carried out by the Chinese Communist Party in the PRC (for example, to track the actions of members of the Uyghur minority group), multiple AI systems are put together to provide analysis for use by the party security services.

Simply put, existing AI systems cannot independently multitask. The term narrow AI is used to denote that the system can only perform one human-like task. Critics can point to the fact that AI systems cannot multitask and change from doing one function to another unrelated function as meaning that they really do not imitate true human behavior. They are sophisticated bulldozers, although admittedly operating on autopilot.

The difference that defines AI, however, is that these systems can essentially self-program. This is done by "training" the system to build its own library of data. A visual perception system can categorize two different images so that when it detects a third image that it has not previously encountered, it knows the category to which it should be assigned. This does not always work; AI systems have mistaken turtles for guns. But having been trained for thousands of categories, a visual perception or recognition system is expected to assign the image of a poodle into the categories for dogs—or to categorize a Uyghur differently than a Han Chinese person.

This leads us to a more specific definition of AI, one that comes from Clive Swan, a vice president of the digital systems company Oracle. He defines AI as "the set of statistical techniques that teaches software to make decisions on past data."[8]

This definition refines the term AI to focus on systems that make "decisions" in a way that humans would when based on past experience. In this view, an AI system can perform a human-like task because it has been trained on *how* to make a decision based on the (big) data it will encounter in the future. The term for this is "machine learning." We will discuss the frequently used terms big data and machine learning shortly. Understanding them is crucial to understanding AI. At this point, it is important to remember that AI uses statistical methods (such as algorithms) to process and correlate amounts of data (big data) that are too vast for any one human to analyze.

WHAT ARE ALGORITHMS?

An algorithm, another term used almost as a religious incantation in discussions of AI, simply describes a process or set of rules to be followed in calculations or other problem-solving operations, especially by a computer.

Humans also use brain rule sets and processes that could be considered statistical analysis in order to make decisions. Much of this is purely instinctive, and we do not normally think in terms of performing statistical analysis when we recognize a creature that we mentally label as a turtle or an object that we label as a gun.

Algorithms are therefore formulas—methods by which to combine data in order to come up with a conclusion. From this, one can develop inferences or predictions. In the previous example, if one determines the object is a turtle, one can predict that the situation is not dangerous or life-threatening (at least if it is a small turtle). If one determines that the object is a gun, one might approach the situation with caution; it might be dangerous or even life-threatening.

Even simple math formulas are algorithms, although they are not usually referred to as such. But the function of multiplying two and two is a learned process with specific rules on how to do the calculation. It seems very easy because we memorize the multiplication tables in school—at least up to twelve times twelve. We don't have to envision the fact that twelve objects are being replicated twelve times.

Like humans, computers use algorithms. What AI provides is a method of processing immense amounts of data so the system can make a human-like decision in the narrow task for which it is designed. The result of AI algorithms is that the calculated conclusion can be used to predict what an outcome could be if a specific action is taken. If 12 objects are replicated 12 times, one ends up with a collection of 144 objects. Thinking about narrow AI in terms of statistical techniques makes it seem a lot less confusing—and also a lot less human.

STRIPPING AWAY THE MYSTERY

Thinking in terms of statistical techniques cries out for further amplification if we are to understand how these technologies are already changing the very foundation of our daily lives—and how they will change warfare tomorrow as profoundly as nuclear weapons did in the middle of the last century. As with any discipline, practitioners and insiders often attempt to cloak their field in some degree of mystery, which generates a unique appearance and eager curiosity in outsiders.

The first level of stripping away the unfortunate mystery that specialists induce in understanding these technologies is to return to the recognition that artificial intelligence is not some sort of magic trick created by computer coders. A sentient and motivated human (those same humans who write the computer code) can do the same things that artificial intelligence can do—that is, until that person bumps up against the limits of what his or her mental gymnastics can handle, or when the amount of data necessary to perform a task is so large that it just can't be remembered.

As noted, most humans can multiply two single-digit numbers in their heads. Some can do the same with two two-digit numbers. But even the most mathematically adept person stumbles when higher-digit numbers are involved. We can do that on paper, but not necessarily quickly. Computing machines can. Thus, all humans have done to "create" AI is to program machines (computer hardware) with software where algorithms manage data that has been collected, correlated, and curated in order to produce the answers humans desire. This is not magic, but it *appears* to be so when the machine beats a human at games as complex as Texas Hold'em poker.

On the other hand, AI appears much less magical when one recognizes that the whole purpose of computing is to retain and apply amounts of data too vast for any one human to remember. Just as a bulldozer can lift more than a human can, a computer can recall more data from storage and apply this data to complex formulas more quickly and presumably more accurately.

To strip away the mystery also requires eliminating the incredible hype surrounding AI. Ironically, this begins by questioning why a public gradually acclimated to having AI in their daily lives—with global positioning systems, smart phones, email response suggestions, Siri, Alexa, those smart appliances, and all the rest—would even recognize that AI is a powerful tool that they use every day. Most people do not recognize this as they go about what seems like an everyday routine.

The reasons for this lack of awareness are logical and clear. In highly publicized events, AI machines have beaten human masters of chess, Go, and Texas Hold'em because they can contain and recall more data in a shorter amount of time than the human brain can.[9] Thus, the general public tends to be desensitized to their daily use of AI and is instead focused on these "AI breakthroughs." In doing so, they place AI in the category of mystery and magic, a black box that coding experts have created and not something that has a routine impact on *their* daily lives.

What makes AI now possible as an everyday tool is the exponential growth in computing infrastructure combined with the dramatic reduction in the cost of obtaining, processing, storing, and transmitting data. This combination has revolutionized the way software is developed, as well as the way that automation is carried out. Put simply, we have moved from machine programming to machine learning. This transformation has created great opportunities but poses serious risks when we consider that it is the machine, not a human, that is programming itself.[10]

It is necessary at this point to unpack the terms big data, artificial intelligence, and machine learning and see what each one means and how they work together. We are walking a fine line, because, as Frank Sinatra once sang, "You can't have one without the other." And while all three of these aspects of AI operate together harmoniously (usually), unpacking them one by one does replace magic and mystery with a more concrete understanding of what AI can do and, importantly, what it cannot do.

BIG DATA ANALYTICS

Briefly, big data (or more correctly, big data analytics) attempts to curate huge amounts of digitally recorded data in order to make sense of it and derive value from what it contains. Artificial intelligence, as defined by its original developers, is simply the ability of a computer system to be able to perform tasks that normally require human intelligence. Machine learning is the ability of computers to modify their decision-making when exposed to increasing amounts of data.

Big data is the fuel of AI. AI is not especially useful without the data to fuel and train it. But that also means that data is the most critical component—proverbially, the cart that actually pulls the AI horse—in the equation.

Big data is a term that has come into vogue simply because it is so descriptive. Big data consists of hundreds of thousands of numbers used in the statistical analyses. Humans can typically manage a discrete amount of data with familiar tools: personal computers, calculators, spreadsheets, and the like. In these cases, there is no need for the extensive algorithms used by AI. Conversely, when the amount of information and effort to correlate the data is huge enough to require automated processes more advanced than any previously available, then big data exists, and there is a big enough cart to require a horse to pull it. That horse is artificial intelligence as originally defined by computer scientists.

When a sufficient amount of "clean" data (data that has been collected and sufficiently binned, correlated, and curated) is available, artificial intelligence can be applied to make sense of it, derive value, and come up with answers or conclusions faster and more effectively than humans can achieve in a discrete amount of time. AI—as in the Department of Defense's Project Maven—is simply demonstrating the capability of a machine to imitate human behavior. Said another way, it is the simulation of human intelligence processes by machines. But it would not happen if the AI could not be supplied with a steady flow of big data.

BIG DATA IN MILITARY ANALYTICS

The major U.S. military AI program publicly discussed most frequently by senior defense decision-makers is the controversial Project Maven. It was conducted by the Department of Defense from 2017 to 2020, under the direction of Deputy Secretary of Defense Bob Work. It was supposedly shut down (at least in part) by the protest of Google coders who claimed they wanted absolutely nothing to do with war, just or not. That certainly gave it publicity.

In April 2022 the National Geospatial-Intelligence Agency, which grew out of the former Defense Mapping Agency, announced it had taken over the analytical engine (algorithms and computing power) and associated unmanned aerial vehicles developed as part of Project Maven for use in mapping both physical and human terrain.[11]

Project Maven was (or still is) a visual recognition tool designed to sort through the countless hours of past video footage recorded by cameras in military drones as they performed their missions over Iraq, Afghanistan, or other regions that are directly menaced by terrorist groups. However one feels about U.S. involvement in these regions, the task is a logical one for an AI system to tackle. Rare is the human—even the most well-trained and dedicated servicemember—who can stare at months' worth of drone camera footage of the ground to determine that a terrorist might have once been lurking at a particular location.

Project Maven could compare the features of the people below to a computer database of known or suspected terrorists to establish where they might have been in the past—and where they might be in the future. Once the people and the areas they inhabit are identified, future drone operations could be focused on those particular areas, with missions not encumbered by having to monitor areas that terrorists are likely avoiding. Whether

Maven had the ability to recognize terrorists in real time so that the drones could take immediate tactical action has never been revealed. What was publicized is that Project Maven was sorting through past video footage captured by drones as a routine byproduct of their missions. The drones would be shooting the video anyway so that the drone operators would know (in real time) that they were not crashing into the ground.

Important for our purpose is the recognition that the algorithms developed for the project (by Google and others) would have no use if there were not a sufficient numbers of drones to obtain the video footage that the AI programming was designed to analyze.[12] Project Maven's value lay in the ability of a computer capable of complex visual recognition (an ability previously associated exclusively with human intelligence) to quickly sort through those thousands of hours of unmanned aircraft reconnaissance video and look for patterns that might help identify potential terrorists. Clearly, having no video footage would equate to zero effective AI analysis. Only in theory could the millions of pixels that make up the vast amount of drone footage ever be stored and sorted in human minds; hence, it certainly qualifies as big data.

MACHINE LEARNING

These processes include learning from constantly changing data, reasoning to make sense of data, and self-correcting to make decisions. As a reminder, the two human behaviors that had previously been outside the scope of computer software and that needed the addition of advanced algorithmic programming were visual recognition (such as in Project Maven) and natural language processing (such as in Siri).

Machine learning was originally defined as a field of study that gives computers the ability to learn without being explicitly programmed. Typically, when the "handoff" is made from the initial programming of artificial intelligence to machine learning, a certain amount of data is provided to the machine learning algorithm. Machine learning is then described as the ability of computers to modify their decision-making when exposed to increasing amounts of data. Although individual pieces of data might not be recognized, the overall pattern of data can be utilized in order to determine statistical trends, thereby allowing predictions concerning future data.

As we have noted, machine learning is achieved primarily through trial and error. The machine is provided with an initial package of data and algorithms that enable it to make a certain set of discrete predictions, decisions, or answers. Once the machine makes a decision, it "learns" that it is either right or wrong. If it is right, it continues on a programmed path. If it is wrong, it assesses that fact and then modifies its behavior to take a different action.

After it makes a decision or takes an action based on its initial knowledge (memory), the machine incorporates what it learned from the results. One way to explain this process is to default to one of the basic tenets of computer programming, the "if-then-else" statement.[13] What sets machine learning apart is that the process takes its original if-then information and combines that extant knowledge with the latest results of what it "experiences" to modify its actions. Said another way, machine learning simply (but elegantly) means that the machine learns from experience.

Machine learning becomes increasingly complex (and useful) when it is programmed to make decisions or take actions with progressively larger data sets. An easily understood example is facial recognition, where hundreds of thousands of if-then-else statements are used to manipulate enormous properly curated data sets. The programmed code that creates these statements is arranged in layers where an algorithm in one layer feeds results to an algorithm at the next highest layer, which, in turn, feeds the next highest layer, and so on.

One way to strip away the supposed magic of this progression is to think of the process of human learning delivered via computerized instruction. In this learning methodology, a lesson is presented, and then a test is given. If the student gets the answer right, he or she moves on to the next level of instruction. However, if the answer is incorrect, the person is taken on a path where additional, perhaps more detailed, instruction is provided. Then the test is administered again.

Each step in this process adds a corresponding layer of complexity by combining the multiple results of the previous layer into a new algorithm. This then evolves into what has become an increasingly useful and important part of machine learning known as deep learning.[14] First conceived in the late 1960s and subsequently introduced to the machine learning community in the late 1980s, deep learning is a descriptive term that refers to a sequencing of corresponding algorithms, some of which may be hidden from the operator. Deep learning can be thought of as machine learning on steroids.

We will not use the term deep learning in our narrative because we think the term itself adds to the confusion. In myths, characters of wisdom are often referred to as "deep minded."[15] Computer scientists define deep learning as occurring in systems that have more than two of the processing layers. Considering the number of calculation processes an AI system could do, more than two (like three) seems pretty shallow to us. Also, the current and near-future use of AI in military weapons systems does not necessarily require deep learning.

Deep learning systems with multiple layers are also referred to as deep neural networks. Although growing in popularity, this phrase adds confusion to any discussion of AI-related fields. Neural refers to how the human brain functions (biochemical processes), while computers performing the functions we have described in this chapter operate on electricity as they perform their if-then-else operations. Even with multiple layers, data is not quite processed in a fashion similar to the human brain, even if both machine and human get the same results.

SUPERVISED VERSUS UNSUPERVISED LEARNING

Two different methods are used to train machines to learn: supervised and unsupervised (deep) learning.

Under supervised learning, a human programmer or data scientist or engineer is continually involved in assisting the machine with the labeling of data. Following development of the underlying algorithms and providing the initial data, the human routinely evaluates the machine's assembly and association of data and corrects the labeling when it is wrong.[16] The human "cleans" the data and ensures the algorithm performs the desired function. Eventually the corrections cumulate so that the machine has a solid framework in which to calculate new data inputs. Supervised learning can also involve placing AI machines into simulations with known answers in order to evaluate their output.

In unsupervised learning, the machine itself is allowed to work its associations by trial and error, establishing its own guidelines. Algorithms and programming are developed and labeling methodologies are installed, but after initial trials, there are no continuing intrusive examinations of the computer processes. Rather, the integrity of the system is determined by evaluating the results. If the results are useful—they provide, for example, accurate self-driving for a vehicle—it is assumed that the system is "thinking correctly." If the results are not useful or fail to ensure the desired function, it is time to rebuild the algorithm and method of labeling data. To put it in a college setting, unsupervised learning is the equivalent of having the final exam be 100 percent of the student's grade.

Given the greater uncertainties involved in unsupervised learning by machine trial and error, why would anyone prefer it to the supervised learning method? The answer is cost. Supervised learning involves much greater costs (since it is more human labor–intensive) than allowing the AI machines to do their own trial-and-error learning and, afterward, have humans evaluate the output.[17] In the race between Tesla, Waymo, Uber, and other companies to develop fully autonomous self-driving cars, costs matter since they cut into potential profits. The company that can utilize the least costly sensors and fewest human engineers and still achieve results is perceived as the better investment. Unfortunately, unsupervised learning has also resulted in tragic accidents during testing.[18] Logically, the more that learning is supervised, the less likely such incidents would occur.

However, the debate is not only over costs. Those scientists favoring development of "strong" artificial intelligence that could do human-like thinking and multitasking—perhaps even better than humans—argue that supervised AI is not "actual AI," and AI machines should be free to map out "new paths to knowledge." We will discuss more about strong AI later. For now, it must be acknowledged that there are aspects of unsupervised learning that worry some scientists and enthrall others. Without supervision, it is difficult to determine exactly how AI machines "thought through" a particular problem, and, hence, difficult to duplicate the exact logic and process of the machine's decision-making.

With unsupervised learning, the actual AI process remains a mystery, evoking the image of potentially irrational (by human standards) results. This has been noted as "the dark secret at the heart of AI" and particularly observed through the artwork produced by unsupervised AI.[19] Scientists involved with utilizing AI to create a virtual model of the universe admit that they have no idea how the AI system actually processed the data to create the model.[20] Yet other scientists are intrigued that there might be modes of AI thought vastly different from that of humans, which might lead to unimagined discoveries.

For military applications, the use of unsupervised learning would seem to pose considerable additional risks. Since it involves some degree of learning from errors of initial perception, its application to combat systems could be fatal. For example, a combat system such as the forty-year-old Phalanx close-in weapons system, used as the last-ditch point defense system against antiship cruise missiles in U.S. and allied Navy warships, can be considered a "simple" AI system (or automated process) because it can detect, identify, track, and—if in full-auto mode—engage an incoming target without human intervention. (Since it is not designed with machine learning, others might question its depiction as AI.) But it cannot "learn from trial and error" without risking its destruction (along with that of the ship). The point is that there are limits to the application of unsupervised learning to military AI.

ARTIFICIAL GENERAL INTELLIGENCE: DOES AI "THINK"?

We now come to the terms used by ultra AI proponents, those who truly think AI will someday mimic human beings by being able to multitask and thereby move, act, think, and speak as if they were people. This is, of course, the staple of a hundred years of science fiction stories, novels, and movies.

While frequently overhyped, the advantage of artificial intelligence over the human mental processes that it imitates consists of its ability to perform calculations more rapidly and avoid the difficulties of actually being human. When people think of pitting a human against a machine—such as with chess, iGo, or Texas Hold'em poker and, perhaps, the strategy involved in competitive weightlifting some day—what they often fail to take into account is that humans are, well, human. People get tired, bored, irritated, and often emotional, all factors that make the human gladiator thrown into the coliseum to take on the machine less effective as time wears on. Add to this the fact that artificial intelligence can work around the clock and does not try to unionize, go on strike, demand a raise, or use vacation or sick days.

AI systems are not doing these things in 2023, though some speculate that eventually they might. Some AI advocates look to a day when artificial general intelligence will be as effective (or even better) at most tasks than humans, and this requires defining additional terms.

Systems capable of conducting such multitask operations are considered general AI, less frequently strong AI, and, in scientific terms, artificial general intelligence (AGI).

Since technology is emerging so rapidly, it is easy to become confused regarding these terms. As the U.S. military signals its intention to embrace AI to make its platforms, systems, sensors, and weapons more effective, it is important to understand that this refers to narrow AI used to do a specific task and *not* to AGI, or using a machine to perform multiple general intelligent actions.

Academic sources reserve the use of AGI to refer to machines capable of experiencing consciousness. Obviously, this is much different than AI designed to perform specific, discrete tasks, which is the level at which current technology resides. AI that can win at chess, iGo, or poker is still narrow AI; but these same AI systems cannot win at Monopoly, crosswords, or backgammon without being reprogrammed (by humans) and subsequently retraining themselves. Left to themselves, they just cannot perform any task other than the specific operation guided by the algorithms with which they are programmed. AGI does not yet exist. There is no consciousness involved.

Can AGI be created some day? That is a much more difficult question to answer than AI fans recognize. When they and other people refer to AI as "machines that think," this loose description obscures the fact that computer coders must program the AI to do what is desired by the end user. Thus, more appropriately, we can say that machines do not think, they only respond to instruction. This is a distinction with a difference because every "thinking machine" is really just hardware and software kludged together to perform the desired function.

At one level, a computer coder designs initial instructions for the machine. At the next level, the machine's internal programming function (its ability, designed by the computer coder, to "self-learn") takes over. In reality, it does not reprogram itself but adds more programming lines developed through trial-and-error learning. In simple terms, expected results are predicted by the original programming feature, and when the actual results differ from the expected, this difference is added to the program to ensure that the error is avoided in the future.

It is easy to see why people believe that AI enables machines to think for themselves and achieve results that make them "better" than even the smartest humans. Adding to this impression is the use of the term "neural networks" to describe programming layers, as if they acted similarly to layers in a human brain. An AI machine can quickly process incredible amounts of data at lightning speeds. And if AI has this apparent magical property, machine learning takes the perceived magic to the next level. Machine learning may seem like magic, but it is not "thinking."

The argument about thinking machines and whether AGI is possible has induced a sense of apprehension when AI is discussed, conjuring up fears of machines dominating humans. In subsequent chapters we will discuss how these (largely unreasonable) fears can serve as a brake on fully leveraging big data, artificial intelligence, and machine learning for military applications. The term "deep" adds to this apprehension, even though it still refers to just three or more layers of calculations.

SO, WHAT'S THE PROBLEM?

With this understanding of the component terms of AI, we can move beyond definitions and begin to understand the future path of these technologies, especially their impact on warfare. As the *Final Report* of the National Security Commission on Artificial Intelligence put it, "Americans have not yet grappled with just how profoundly the artificial intelligence (AI) revolution will impact our economy and national security. Much remains to be learned about the power and limits of AI technologies."

In focusing on the military uses of AI, it is worth quoting directly from the report regarding the profound national security implications of these technologies:

> AI systems will also be used in the pursuit of power. We fear AI tools will be weapons of first resort in future conflicts. AI will not stay in the domain of superpowers or the realm of science fiction. AI is dual-use, often open-source, and diffusing rapidly. State adversaries are already

using AI-enabled disinformation attacks to sow division in democracies and jar our sense of reality. States, criminals, and terrorists will conduct AI-powered cyber-attacks and pair AI software with commercially available drones to create "smart weapons." It is no secret that America's military rivals are integrating AI concepts and platforms to challenge the United States' decades-long technology advantage. We will not be able to defend against AI-enabled threats without ubiquitous AI capabilities and new war fighting paradigms.[21]

The report is notable in that it provides sufficient background behind the "what" of AI as well as a bit of the "why," especially the current momentum to leverage big data, artificial intelligence, and machine learning to make military platforms, systems, sensors, and weapons more capable than those that must have a human in the loop providing constant oversight and supervision. That is the first problem, because it is different than how war is fought today. This may be recognized by some in the Department of Defense but not necessarily by the general public.

The second problem is highlighted by the expression of fear that AI tools "will be weapons of first resort." If this is indeed the case, the United States and its allies will be forced to develop their own AI weapons in order to be able to defend themselves. There is little choice.

Third, the identification of AI systems as "dual-use" and "often open-source" is accurately ominous. As is openly stated in China's plan for AI, the same systems designed to defend the PRC will be used to control the population and ensure no one challenges the government by promoting democracy. At the same time, the equivalent AI developments that might turn a profit for Chinese companies will be entwined with military advances. The plan suggests that military development of AI could also be spun off into commercial development, although the developmental flow at the moment is the other way around—from commercial development to military. The reason for this is that many algorithms of AI are open-source, which makes them easier to derive from commercial usage.

Finally, the "diffusing rapidly" phrase points indirectly to the fact that much of China's AI prowess was derived from the commercial AI sold to it by U.S. and other Western corporations in the era of presumed globalization.

We sold China something more dangerous than bulldozers. We sold them a technology as transformational as electricity.

We will wrestle more with these three challenges. But it is important to spend a few moments trying to understand the "how" regarding the convergence of events and technologies that has brought us to the current state of AI technologies in 2023. That is our next chapter.

2

HOW DID WE GET HERE?

Human Minds and Converging Technologies

It's important to understand that artificial intelligence is not a technology, in much the same way that the Space Race is not a technology.

KATHLEEN WALCH
managing partner, Cognilytica[1]

If Carnegie Tech's computer program can beat Kasparov, that's about as interesting as the fact that a bulldozer can lift more than some weight lifter.

NOAM CHOMSKY
professor of linguistics,
on the then-forthcoming test of AI in chess[2]

ENTERING THE STANZE DI RAFFAELLO at the Apostolic Palace of the Vatican, one encounters the brilliant colors of sixteen of the most spectacular frescos of the High Renaissance. They are the work of the painter Raphael, and although their fame is often eclipsed by Michelangelo's frescos in the Sistine Chapel, they too are among the greatest artistic treasures of history.

Rather than the ceiling of a church, Raphael's huge frescos adorn walls of rooms used for the secular functions of the Pope as a world leader. Instead of depicting Biblical stories or the acts of Jesus, most depict the historical development of Christianity. But one that does not, "The School of Athens," painted sometime between 1509 and 1511, was intended to preside over the personal library of Pope Julius II. It is often considered Raphael's greatest masterpiece.

The painting is an imaginary scene of a gathering of students of philosophy in a courtyard of ancient Athens. Some of the students argue passionately, some lounge insolently. At the center are two of the greatest philosophers of their day, Plato and Aristotle, walking together while in profound discussion. To contrast their opposing ideas, the red-robed Plato points a finger to the sky, the realm of the lofty imaginations of the mind. The blue-robed Aristotle points downward to the earth, the abode of practical human experience.

As odd as it might seem, a number of AI scientists and engineers see that 500-year-old painting as representing both the quest to create artificial intelligence and the great division in the approaches to its development.

RATIONAL VERSUS EMPIRICAL

Interpreting the painting, Plato is pointing to the concept of *rationalism*, the belief that human knowledge is innate to every individual and is born of the logical thought natural to the human mind. Even if one has never experienced a particular object or event, its parameters can be determined by humans through what Plato called the knowledge of "forms" (or the recognition of emotions), such as kindness, beauty, and bravery, combined with physical observations to create the logical thinking expressed in an if-then statement. For example, if it is beautiful, then it must be some manner of "art."

Education in the basics—language and mathematics—helps with development of this process of logic. However, it is not the learned facts that determine what constitutes wisdom, but the workings of the mind itself. Our experiences are determined by our understanding. When someone chooses a successful course of action based on knowledge of forms and logic, we call them "rational." Rationalism "shifts the burden of explanation from the structure of the world to the structure of the mind."[3] Often this process of logic is referred to as deductive reasoning—such as that used in the fictional deductions of Sherlock Holmes—although that does not capture all of Plato's conception.

Aristotle, in contrast, is the patron of *empiricism*, the belief that all knowledge is grounded in experience. Our minds begin as a tabula rasa, a blank slate. They do not recognize a "form" called beauty until someone tells us that something is beautiful. Henceforth, we see similar objects as also being beautiful. Most of us see finely painted portraits as being beautiful because we were taught that they are. Most of us do not see guns as beautiful because we are taught that they are not. Some of us see turtles as beautiful, while some of us don't. It all depends on what one has been taught.

Individual experience is also the teacher. One does not really know what is truly "hot" until one stands close to the fire or burns a hand on a stove. Until then, the taught concept of "hot" is not personally understood. This form of learning is *empirical*: One experiences a burn, and therefore one learns that hot can be bad. The seventeenth-century philosopher and physician John Locke condensed an even earlier observation by Saint Thomas Aquinas (1225–74) that *nihil est in intellectu, quod non pruis fuerit in sensu*— nothing is in the intellect that was not previously in the senses.[4]

As in any intellectual debate, the rationalists had a reply. One of the developers of the mathematical branch of calculus, German mathematician Gottfried Leibniz, retorted, "Except the intellect itself."[5] Nevertheless, empiricism became the dominant technique of modern science. Empirical observation leads to inductive reasoning, determining a general principle by examining specific phenomena.

In terms of application to artificial intelligence, this idea of empiricism suggests that the development of AI should be focused on how best to manipulate experienced, "mined" data, rather than intuiting results based on what a human brain would conjure up independent of external data. However, in developing the concept of artificial intelligence in the 1950s, scientists involved started to divide into the two camps.

ADA LOVELACE AND THE DEBATE OVER AI DEVELOPMENT

Why discuss Renaissance art in a book about twenty-first-century technology? Because the divide between rationalism and empiricism explains why AI developed in the manner it has, why much of the popular hype about AI often has little practical basis, and why there have been "AI Winters" (such as in the 1970s)—periods in which there was little public interest and, more importantly, little corporate interest in funding AI research and development.

In the previous chapter, we identified the two principal ways of defining AI: as replication of human activity, or prediction based on statistical analysis by machines. These definitions represent the two alternate perspectives of the rationalist versus empiricist divide. We argue that it was not until the AI community began to deliberately combine both approaches that substantial progress in the practical application of AI was made. In military terms, this combination is referenced as "human-machine teaming," which we will later explore in depth.

The initial approach to developing artificial intelligence was rationalist. The goal was to create a thinking machine. What exactly it would "think" about was not a primary concern.

Development of the computer is the sine qua non of the journey to achieve artificial intelligence, a necessary—but not sufficient—implement.[6] So perhaps we need to start with Augusta Ada King, Countess of Lovelace, commonly referred to as Ada Lovelace. The only child of Lord and Lady Byron, she was born in 1815. She had an unhappy childhood and a tumultuous and relatively short life.[7] But she was a genius at math.

Lord Byron, one of the most famous English poets of the eighteenth and nineteenth centuries, abandoned the family when Ada was five weeks old and never again saw his daughter. Essentially abandoned by her mother as well, Ada was raised by a loving grandmother who ensured that she was well tutored in arts and sciences. Suffering a number of incapacitating illnesses, including temporary paralysis that confined her to bed for a year, Ada focused her mind on mathematics.

Through a tutor, she met Charles Babbage (1791–1871), a nineteenth-century scientific celebrity and inventor—but one who rarely completed his designs due to financial concerns or disputes with assistants. To say that

Babbage was mercurial is an understatement; his activities ranged wildly and included performing astronomical calculations for navigation (he helped found the Royal Astronomical Society), being an indifferent lecturer at Cambridge University, proposing new methods of data collection, recommending a single postal rate, and leading a political campaign against "public nuisances" such as organ grinders. Amidst this activity, Babbage designed two calculating machines, one of which could be "programmed" using punch cards, a procedure that had been developed for changing the designs of fabric looms. Many credit him as being the "father of the computer," although in reality his partially built design—meticulously reconstructed as a history project from prototype parts and his full notes—was never fully operational until 1991.

Lovelace's contribution was what could be called the first computer algorithm, a mathematical formula for calculating a string of Bernoulli numbers (sums of a series of positive numbers and their squared and cubed powers) using Babbage's analytical engine design. For this, she has been credited with being the first "computer programmer," although, as with all such designations, historians continue to dispute which ideas were Lovelace's and which were Babbage's.

Nevertheless, Lovelace's algorithm provided a start for modern computing and has also been identified as an inspiration for the development of AI. The connection to the rationalist approach is that Babbage's attempt was to create a machine that could "think" (calculate) regardless of the data or purpose of the calculation. In other words, it was the internal working of the machine (its "mind") that was the focus of development rather than the task ("practical experience") it would perform. Lovelace's contribution was to identify a task and invent a method of programming the machine to complete it. It could be said that she was "training" a computer, a task necessary for AI.

Ironically, Lovelace herself did not accept the notion that a machine could be said to think and wrote, "The Babbage Analytical Engine has no pretensions whatsoever to originate anything. . . . It can do whatever we know how to order it to perform. It can follow analysis; but it has no power of anticipating any analytical relations or truths."[8] To her, calculation did not mean intelligence.

THE TURING TRICK

While the idea of training computers to do an increasing number of useful things advanced in fits and starts for the ensuing century, the majority of experts in the fields of big data, artificial intelligence, and machine learning attribute the inflection point that accelerated these disciplines to where they have arrived to one man, Alan Turing.

Born two years before the start of World War I, Turing was an English mathematician universally credited with the development of theoretical computer science. A British graduate of Cambridge, Turing earned his PhD at Princeton, giving him a cross-Atlantic view of scientific research.

During World War II Turing was instrumental to the success of Britain's code-breaking organization credited with producing the Ultra machine that was able to crack intercepted German coded messages.[9] He was awarded the Order of the British Empire and made a fellow of the Royal Society of scientists. However, due to the Official Secrets Act, the Ultra effort was not fully revealed until the 1970s. Turing's papers on statistical methods of cryptanalysis were not declassified until 2012. Turing himself committed suicide in 1954 at the age of forty-two after having been prosecuted for homosexual acts and forced to submit to hormone treatment. In 2009 British prime minister Gordon Brown publicly apologized for the treatment of Turing, and Queen Elizabeth II granted a posthumous pardon.

In 1936 Turing had developed his "Turing machine." This invention was the first model for what we now call a general purpose computer, a feat that earned Turing recognition as the father of theoretical computer science and artificial intelligence. The machine itself was a basic device that was not capable of doing advanced computation. But while the machine did not represent a momentous breakthrough, it was Turing's hypothesis as to what constituted artificial intelligence that would lead to the criterion that is now famously known as the Turing test.

After the war, Turing worked at Britain's National Physical Laboratory where he designed an automatic computing engine, which was one the first designs for a stored-program computer. Later, he joined the Computing Machine Laboratory where he helped design a series of computers.

In 1950 Turing asked what was then an unheard-of question: "Can machines think?" This singular—and profound—query instigated an avalanche of inquiry and interest in Britain and elsewhere. Turing proposed his answer as to whether a machine had "intelligence" in a unique fashion that is remembered to this day: "If a machine can trick a human into thinking it is a human, then the machine has intelligence."[10] This is the essence of the Turing test.[11] This is also where the perception of AI as magic is formed.

Although providing a criterion for evaluation—and celebrated by scientists as indeed profound—the Turing test does not actually answer the question of whether machines can be created to "think" in a fashion similar to humans. Turing's answer would certainly not satisfy either those who welcome artificial general intelligence as a creative force or those who fear a future "Terminator." Instead, Turing's answer can be interpreted in a very Machiavellian manner. In *The Prince*, his famous discourse on effective government, Renaissance strategist Niccolo Machiavelli (1459–1527) observed that it does not matter if a prince is sincere in his relations with his subjects and other nations. It only matters that he *appears* sincere.

Turing essentially argues that it does not matter what the machine does; it only matters that people believe that it thinks and accept the results as valid. Somewhat wryly, he dismissed Lovelace's insistence that a programmed machine could not—by definition—"originate anything" by referring to it as "Lady Lovelace's objection." It is possible that Turing's conclusion stems from a debate he had during a lecture by the Austrian philosopher of science Ludwig Wittgenstein at Cambridge in 1939.[12]

Wittgenstein argued that mathematics does not discover truth but rather invents it. Therefore, science does not reveal truth; it creates that which humans believe to be true. Regardless of whether Turing was convinced by the argument, the question of whether an AI system actually simulates human reasoning or is simply a more advanced mathematical formula to which we attribute human-like features haunts discussions of artificial general intelligence to this day.

POWER OF COLLABORATION:
MCCARTHY AND THE SUMMER STUDY

In the aftermath of Turing asking his provocative question in 1950, the next breakthrough in the journey to create artificial intelligence occurred on the other side of the Atlantic. In 1955 John McCarthy, then an assistant professor of mathematics at Dartmouth College, gathered a group of like-minded colleagues to try to clarify and develop ideas about thinking machines. He picked the name "artificial intelligence" for the new field.

Proceeding cautiously, and mindful of the potential difficulties of trying to jam such an effort into Dartmouth's challenging academic curriculum, McCarthy and his colleagues (who included such future luminaries in computer science and related fields as Marvin Minsky, Julian Bigelow, and Ray Solomonoff) floated a proposal in September 1955 for a summer study to determine whether learning (or any other feature of intelligence) could be so precisely described that a machine could be made to simulate it.

It is now recognized that McCarthy and his colleagues were asking the right question at the right time and in the right way. They were modest in their request, asking not for a huge amount of funding to support scores of researchers for several years, but rather to support a discrete number of scientists (less than one dozen) who would do their work over the course of one summer between semesters. Given its iconic place in the history of artificial intelligence, it is worth presenting the beginning of this proposal here:

> We propose that a 2-month, 10-man study of artificial intelligence be carried out during the summer of 1956 at Dartmouth College in Hanover, New Hampshire. The study is to proceed on the basis of the conjecture that every aspect of learning or any other feature of intelligence can in principle be so precisely described that a machine can be made to simulate it. An attempt will be made to find how to make machines use language, form abstractions and concepts, solve kinds of problems now reserved for humans, and improve themselves. We think that a significant advance can be made in one or more of these problems if a carefully selected group of scientists work on it together for a summer.[13]

The McCarthy-led proposal was accepted, and in the summer of 1956 the Dartmouth Summer Research Project on Artificial Intelligence got under way. However, while the Summer Study is widely recognized as the founding event of the discipline of artificial intelligence, it was primarily a brainstorming session of like-minded men. Although no report was published, what did emerge was the definition of artificial intelligence as "the science and engineering of making intelligent machines."[14]

To be fair, the project did advance several areas of computer science such as early expert systems, deductive systems, and symbolic methods. But what was most significant was the fact that people had met and seriously attempted to address Turing's profoundly challenging question. McCarthy's team had not only completed their assigned project, but also had, perhaps unwittingly, thrown down the gantlet: If Dartmouth College could do this, so could others.

FROM SUMMER TO SPRING

The Dartmouth College Summer Research Project on Artificial Intelligence ignited a cottage industry of like-minded efforts to establish artificial intelligence seedling laboratories at academic institutions, government and private laboratories, and nascent individual efforts (the proverbial Silicon Valley garage). In conjunction with the explosion in commercial computer development, this stirring of interest—and passion—ushered in what is widely known as the "AI Spring."[15]

The history of the computer industry is rich and well told. During the first AI Spring, the distinction between developments in computing and efforts at achieving AI was naturally blurred. AI was largely—and naturally—seen as a research field within computing sciences and proceeding simultaneously with other computer developments.

In 1960 General Motors introduced its first industrial robot, Unimate. The machine—which could be said to be AI-powered—was the first to replace workers on the assembly line and was a portent of things to come over the ensuing decades. In 1964 Joseph Weizenbaum of the Massachusetts Institute of Technology introduced Eliza, a pioneering chatbot designed to hold conversations with humans. The "brains" in Eliza's head consisted of an early natural language processing computer program. Ironically, part of the science behind Eliza can be traced to professor Noam Chomsky's formal theory of natural language, which was hailed as a milestone in the cognitive revolution of the 1950s. (Chomsky remains critical of the hype surrounding AI and unimpressed with its public feats.)

Eliza was an early attempt to create a machine that could pass the Turing test. While Eliza was not mature enough to do so, it was an important inflection point due to the law of unintended consequences. Weizenbaum invented Eliza with the intent of showing the superficial—that is, basic and uninteresting—nature of communication between man and machine. What Weizenbaum did not anticipate was the number of people who attributed human-like feelings to the computer program. Eliza was eerily prescient of machines taking on human-like qualities (witness the popular 2013 movie *Her*, where a man develops a relationship with his smart phone's artificially intelligent virtual assistant personified through a female voice).[16]

As one can discern from today's proponents and opponents of AI, the public attribution of human-like feelings to a machine has been both a blessing and a bane in obtaining funding for AI development. But in the late 1960s, the U.S. military—and the Soviet military as well—became interested in the possible effects of AI in war as well as peace.

In 1966, using funds provided by the Defense Advanced Research Projects Agency (DARPA), scientists and engineers at the Artificial Intelligence Center of Stanford University (today's SRI International) introduced a general-purpose mobile robot dubbed "Shakey." This "first electronic person" was able to reason about simple actions. While basic and generally uninspiring to many, Shakey was a breakthrough invention that heralded what is known today as the robotics revolution.[17]

FROM SPRING TO WINTER

Unimate, Eliza, and Shakey were good as far as they went but were largely unknown outside of a small circle of scientists and engineers and a few pioneering companies. Still, as with the Summer Study at Dartmouth College, these inventions inspired a wide range of institutions, armed with substantial funding (much of it provided by federal government organizations such as DARPA's predecessor ARPA and others) to jump on the bandwagon and start their own projects. If someone could create Unimate, Eliza, and Shakey, *they* could create a better version.

But as this wave of enthusiasm gained momentum, so did the hype, and visions of artificial intelligence–powered robots doing increasingly fabulous things reached levels that were clearly unattainable. As the 1960s gave way to the 1970s, interest in AI did not just wane; it collapsed. A host of factors coalesced to put the brakes on work in the field:

- AI developers overpromising and underdelivering
- media drastically overhyping what AI could actually do for consumers
- disappointing results from artificial intelligence experimentation
- criticism from outsiders who resented the sums being spent on AI research
- wildly inflated expectations from government and private AI buyers
- funding cuts.

The result was a period—from about 1970 until almost 2001—colloquially known as the AI Winter. So many people and organizations had been burned by the collapse of AI funding that the result was a cataclysmic halt to work on artificial intelligence.[18] Certainly, a small number of well-funded and determined pioneers, such as Marvin Minsky and Roger Schank, soldiered on, but the AI wave had broken on the shore and would not form again until just before the turn of the century, when Deep Blue emerged from IBM labs and began its tenure as a chess champion.

DEEP BLUE, DEEPMIND, AND DEEP PUBLICITY

Two widely publicized events brought artificial intelligence to the attention of the general public. The first was Deep Blue, an IBM computer capable of playing chess, that defeated the reigning chess grandmaster Garry Kasparov in 1997.

Once programmed with the rules and previous grandmaster games, Deep Blue "taught" itself by playing hundreds of thousands of simulated chess matches within its circuitry and modifying its software. By the time the match was scheduled with Kasparov, Deep Blue had examined every possible chess move and with the speed and accuracy of a computer could counter Kasparov's attacks.

IBM turned the actual match into a spectacle to publicize its AI research and engineering, later building an AI machine named Watson that beat champions and won the television game show *Jeopardy!* IBM chief executive officer (CEO) Ginni Rometty boasted that "I think it awakened the entire artificial intelligence community."[19]

However, other scientists remained less than impressed. Perhaps the most colorful dismissal came from Noam Chomsky (see the epigraph to this chapter). His view is significant because many AI scientists credit his theories of human linguistics as fundamental to their efforts to create the AI systems that could do natural language processing (such as Siri). Chomsky's reference to a bulldozer points to the inherent ability of all computers to be programmed with more data than any human mind could hold—specifically, 700,000 past grandmaster games at a speed of 2 million possible moves in seconds. Just as a bulldozer with a hydraulically powered blade or bucket can lift more weight than any human ever could, a computer should beat a human in rules-based games that require logic as a matter of course.

Defeated grandmaster Kasparov—who later helped to develop the chess-playing programs that appear even as smart phone apps—ruefully remarked, "Deep Blue was only intelligent the way your programmable alarm clock is intelligent . . . not that losing to a $10 million alarm clock made me feel any better."[20]

The public perception that Deep Blue and Watson represented "intelligence" clashed with the views of even those scientists who built these machines. Some argued that instead of demonstrating human-like ability, they actually demonstrated how far AI science was from being able to build systems that emulate the human ability to both multitask and operate beyond the rule set—that is, to change the rules in order to play a different game instead of simply labeling and compiling knowledge to complete a simple task.

Piling on to this sentiment, Professor John Searle of the University of California at Berkeley argues, "Watson did not understand the questions, nor its answers, nor that some of its answers were right and some wrong, nor that it was playing a game, nor that it won—because it doesn't understand anything. IBM's computer was not and could not have been designed to understand. Rather, it was designed to simulate understanding, to act as if it understood."[21]

Inadvertently, Searle suggests that Watson (along with Deep Blue) actually passed the Turing test. Therefore, under the initial definition of AI as "the capability of a machine to imitate human behavior," Watson did indeed qualify as artificial *intelligence* regardless of whether its circuitry and software perceived it was playing a game.

More importantly, the American public—many of whom had never heard of the Turing test—now came to believe that Deep Blue represented a form of intelligence, a belief fanned by media searching for attention-grabbing topics, researchers searching for funding, and technology companies trying to attract venture capital.

This was reinforced by the next highly publicized intellectual sport challenge, the victory of AlphaGo from DeepMind Technologies—a subsidiary of Google/Alphabet—over professional iGo (also known as Go) master Lee Sedol in 2016. iGo, an ancient Japanese-Chinese strategy game (called *weiqi* in Mandarin Chinese) is considered a more complex game than chess since it has many more possible moves. The goal is to use playing pieces to surround and capture an opponent's pieces and to occupy the most territory of a board having up to 361 positions. Theoretically, there are 2×10^{170} possible game configurations. Subsequently, DeepMind built AI programs that could beat its earlier programs, and other companies developed programs that beat Texas Hold'em poker champions.

Inspired by these AI results, authors Ray Kurzweil and Vernor Vinge publicized the term singularity, meaning the point at which AI machines are not only smarter than humans but can design themselves to increase their intelligence, therefore no longer needing humans. Media treatment of this concept produced even more public awareness—and greater fear of AI. Even though scientists currently cannot conceive how singularity could be possibly achieved, Vinge absurdly predicted singularity would occur by 2030. This, in turn, prompted scientific luminaries such as Stephen Hawking to give public warnings about the future dangers of AI.

Whether AI programs represent intelligence, pass the Turing test, or can potentially achieve singularity, since the 1990s AI has been put to use for practical applications, including being used to conduct predictive maintenance, enable precision agriculture, monitor livestock, allow cities to optimize transportation routing, and, more recently, to enhance and accelerate COVID-19 research.

GETTING STUFF DONE

Scientists and engineers want to work on difficult problems. As Palmer Luckey, founder of drone manufacturer Anduril, put it, "Most engineers want to engineer. They want to get stuff done."[22] This was no different in the early 1950s. Few then could think of a harder question than the one Turing asked, and this attracted large numbers of men (and just a few women). Not until a decade later when President John F. Kennedy declared that America would put a man on the moon were scientists and engineers so energized to take on such a hard problem.

A detailed history of the development of the computer industry and associated disciplines on which AI depends is beyond the scope of this book. However, the bottom line is that by the 2000s, AI research caught fire again and the winter turned to spring, but this time on steroids. Other AI-enabled developments followed in rapid succession.

Spurred by high-flying stock valuations (if not profitability) of the companies that mastered the algorithms that produced commercially successful AI-enabled breakthroughs, new products and services emerged and delighted consumers: the Massachusetts Institute of Technology's Kismet in 1998, Sony's Aibo in 1999, iRobot's Roomba in 2002, Apple's Siri in 2011, Chatbot Eugene in 2014 (with one-third of participants who interacted with the chatbot opining that Eugene passed the Turing test), DeepMind's AlphaGo in 2016. AI research once again flourished.

There were missteps and hiccups in this generally ascending success story, perhaps none more notable than Microsoft Corporation's colossal and embarrassing failure that occurred with the 2016 release of its Tay (Thinking About You) artificial intelligence chatter bot on Twitter. Tay was designed to respond to human tweets as if it were a person, but it soon learned (through interaction with users) obscene, lewd, insulting, offensive, and inflammatory rhetoric, which it interpreted as normal conversation and applied indiscriminately. Tay was shut down within sixteen hours of being launched. However, the relentless optimism of Silicon Valley finds a way to brush off missteps like Tay by returning to the familiar mantra: "Fail fast, fail often." The Tay fiasco was quickly forgotten.

The Tay misstep was the exception to the rule, and now consumers have come to expect better and better AI-enabled tools to make life easier.

And as just one indication that the companies that build the algorithms will likely keep doing so (only faster), in 2022 the biggest U.S. technology companies, the so-called FAANG Five (Facebook, Apple, Amazon, Netflix, and Alphabet [Google's parent company]), had a market capitalization of over $8 trillion. Importantly, this dizzying growth of the FAANG Five occurred during the worst economic downturn in generations.[23]

GETTING WAR DONE

War is shaped by technology. From stone knives to swords to guns to missiles, armed forces have sought increasingly advanced technological weaponry to defeat their enemies. The convergence of AI-enabled technologies can be seen as a continuation of this evolution.

In his best-selling book, *War Made New*, military historian Max Boot notes, "My view is that technology sets the parameters of the possible; it creates the potential for a military revolution."[24] He supports his thesis with historical examples to show how technology-driven "revolutions in military affairs" have transformed warfare and altered the course of history. Importantly, Boot points out the importance of technology in giving the nation that innovates and fields new military technology quickly a war-winning advantage.

Boot is not alone, and the concept of revolutions in military affairs is a constant staple in the American defense dialogue. And, in truth, the U.S. military has embraced a wave of technological change that can be considered a true revolution in the way that war is waged. As the pace of global technological change has accelerated, the United States has been especially adept at inserting new technology to pace the threat. As Bruce Berkowitz points out in *The New Face of War*,

> Wartime experience suggests that the right technology, used intelligently, makes sheer numbers irrelevant. The tipping point was the Gulf War in 1991. When the war was over, the United States and its coalition partners had lost just 240 people. Iraq suffered about 10,000 battle deaths, although no one will ever really be sure. The difference was that the Americans could see at night, drive through the featureless desert without getting lost, and put a single smart bomb on target with a 90 percent probability.[25]

Both Boot's and Berkowitz's books are now more than a decade old, but what they and many subsequent volumes say about technology remains on point regarding the ways that the U.S. military has embraced new tools. In the decades of the Cold War, these tools included nuclear weapons and successive versions of better (and more lethal) ships, aircraft, tanks, and other hardware-dominant weapons of war. This all worked until it didn't, as U.S. peer competitors (often using stolen technology) caught up and leveled the playing field.

THE SHIFT IN RESEARCH AND DEVELOPMENT

In response, in the middle of the last decade, the Department of Defense (DoD) initiated the third offset strategy to ensure that the United States retained the military edge against potential adversaries. We will address the specific elements of this strategy in later chapters. What is important to say now is this: the national industrial base has, of compelling necessity, now morphed into the national innovation base.

The U.S. DoD still depends on the traditional major defense contractors but increasingly looks to the FAANG Five companies and their smaller cousins to enable a new strategy, one whose technology pillar is powered far more by software than by hardware. The computer industry has hastened a sea change regarding the source of funding for these kinds of breakthroughs and other emerging technologies. The innovation base has shifted from being government-directed to commercially driven.

From the 1950s into much of the 1970s, the U.S. government funded the majority of research and development (R&D) for advanced technology conducted in the United States. Increasingly, this funding found its way to academic and research institutions in Silicon Valley and its surroundings. Many of the companies and their spinoffs spawned by this funding are now the ones that write the algorithms that DoD finds so valuable today. And the equation has flipped 180 degrees, with so-called high-tech companies providing the lion's share of R&D funding in America and the federal government–provided share now quite modest by comparison.[26]

As anyone who has bought a product or used a service knows, technological refresh happens with accelerating speed, and what was cutting-edge as little as a year ago is now at best dated and at worst useless. The

Department of Defense recognizes this and has created ways to accelerate working with Silicon Valley to buy these AI-enabled technologies.[27] Part of this initiative has grown organically with forward-thinking defense officials (such as former Deputy Secretary of Defense Robert Work) coming to understand the value of AI-enabled military platforms, systems, sensors, and weapons.

But for others, this impetus originated outside the Pentagon—in fact, outside of the United States. It has come from the moves the authoritarian regimes of America's peer competitors—China and Russia—are making in this arena. As former Google CEO Eric Schmidt stated, "We believe this is a national emergency and a threat to our nation unless we get our act together with respect to focusing on AI in the federal government and international security."[28] The concerns expressed by Schmidt as well as many others have ushered in an AI arms race as dynamic—and in many ways as terrifying—as the nuclear arms race that began three-quarters of a century ago.[29]

With that impetus, this effort of many contributors over quite a number of years with alternative paths of AI development has much in common with America's race to the moon in the 1950s and 1960s. From that perspective, AI is more than a technology.

3

WHAT IS AT STAKE?

China, Russia, and the Race for AI

It cannot be excluded that Russia will develop novel weapons systems and supporting infrastructure independent of the trajectory of weapons development in the West.

SAMUEL BENDETT ET AL.[1]

We have no competing fighting chance against China in 15 to 20 years. Right now, it's already a done deal; it is already over in my opinion. . . . Whether it takes a war or not is kind of anecdotal.

NICOLAS M. CHAILLAN
first chief software officer of U.S. Air Force
and Space Force, speaking about military AI
following his resignation in protest from his
position, October 2021[2]

PICTURE YOURSELF IN TWO different scenarios. In the first, you are about to leave your apartment for work. You double-check to ensure you have your cell phone, not only to communicate to family members, friends, and associates, but also because you are legally required to carry it so your movements can be tracked. Upon leaving the apartment, you encounter your first official video camera at the end of the hallway; you will pass a second one upon leaving the building.

Walking to the end of the block, you encounter the first checkpoint. A police officer checks your identification and travel pass, and then you line up for the obligatory facial scan. Once scanned, the police monitor displays AI system–provided personal information—not just your identity, home address, and employer, but all the places you have visited, the public events you have attended, whether you go to a church, the identity of your friends, the events your friends have attended, all the people to whom you have talked, the Internet websites you have viewed, the websites your family members and friends have visited, and any remarks you have made that indicate a lack of support for the ruling party.

Once the information is assembled (in seconds), an algorithm calculates your "social credit" score. Your score determines if you may proceed beyond your block, whether you get tickets for the next public event, whether you get a loan—or, if you are an ethnic Uyghur in the Xinjiang province of China, whether you need a visit to a reeducation camp.

In the second scenario, you are a military leader of a country involved in a "special military operation." You are not personally involved in the operation; your particular task is to recommend how the military is organized for future contingencies. The question is how to spend your remaining resources. Training for troops could be significantly improved and greater professionalism fostered. But there is the opportunity for greater investments in developing autonomous weapons systems: drones, tanks, perhaps even robots (albeit rather primitive ones) that could make their own decisions on the battlefield—or perhaps within villages.

How do you choose to invest military resources? You have tested semi-autonomous tanks in a limited intervention in a far country, but the results were reported as poor.[3] On the other hand, your country has a shrinking manpower base, and the determination—and perhaps loyalty—of the soldiers cannot be assured. The bulk of these troops are not performing well in the special military operation. Your civilian engineers have promised significant system improvements, the science of artificial intelligence seems to be publicly advancing everywhere, and your commander thinks AI might rule the world.

In this scenario, it is easy for you to conclude that whatever resources can be obtained should be put toward AI-driven military systems rather than personnel. The logical assumption is that, given sufficient amounts of resources, glitchy semiautonomous systems that require some cumbersome human decision-making can eventually be transformed into autonomous systems that can make decisions in less than a second. From this perspective, success seems to be only a matter of time, unlike with human-dependent special military operations.

AI REALITY IN CHINA

Neither scenario is a fantasy. The first is the day-to-day reality for Uyghurs in Xinjiang. Indeed, Paul Scharre has termed what is happening in Xinjiang as "a new techno-dystopian state." Government cameras and other devices register information on faces, fingerprints, eyes, voices, blood, DNA, and license plates. Electronic police "sniffers" track Wi-Fi and cell phone usage. The border police have been known to install spyware on phones that automatically detects banned material, such as Muslim religious literature or photographs of the Dalai Lama.[4] In one month alone, Chinese Communist Party (CCP)–led authorities conducted 500,000 biometric facial scans in order to build a database that can be correlated by AI to other big data captured by over 1.5 million video cameras, along with the electronic logs of all Chinese Internet and social media providers (including TikTok), as well as routine financial transactions.[5] In Xinjiang, this monitoring system is known as the integrated joint operations platform.[6]

This intrusive surveillance is now being expanded to other places in the People's Republic of China. More than two thousand miles away, in Chongqing, a city almost in the center of China, the journalist Liu Hu, an ethnic Han Chinese, was monitored similarly and effectively confined to his home for an extended period. He had made the mistake of accusing a local official of corruption—during a campaign against corruption sponsored by the CCP itself.

Having destroyed his official reputation in the AI-driven social credit system (in addition to paying a fine), Liu found that his status was too low to merit the purchase of train tickets, handle financial transactions, conduct his profession, or (after being allowed to leave his home) go beyond the limits of his city. All of these decisions were enforced by a surveillance network enhanced by AI. As Liu describes,

> Once you leave home and step into the lift, you're captured by a camera. There are cameras everywhere. For instance, when I leave home to go somewhere, I call a taxi. The taxi company uploads the data to the Government. The Government knows my whereabouts. I may then go to a café to meet a few friends. The authorities know my location through the camera in the café. There have been occasions where I have met some friends and soon after, someone from the Government contacted me to say, "you have met so and so." They warned me, "don't see that person, don't do this or that." With artificial intelligence we have nowhere to hide. Don't you think it's horrifying?[7]

Obviously, the Chinese Communist Party does not view it as horrifying. It is its ultimate tool for maintaining perpetual political control.

In fact, in 2022 an AI institute in the eastern Chinese city of Hefei announced that it had developed "mind-reading" software that can gauge the loyalty of party members that would be used to "further solidify their determination to be grateful to the party, listen to the party, and follow the party."[8]

AI REALITY IN RUSSIA

The second scenario illustrates Russia's motivation to focus directly on military applications of AI. Despite its crackdown on dissent, Putin's Russia has yet to develop a comparable AI surveillance network. Russian AI systems may provide assistance in intelligence analysis—and in determining counterintelligence actions—but the necessary spider web of omnipresent cameras does not exist. An authoritarian state different from the PRC, Russia is controlled by an individual and a small coterie of oligarchs, not by a powerful, hierarchical political party. Therefore, there is less of an impetus to spend the necessary resources—money and personnel—to develop an AI social control–type network; there is no collective organization to perpetuate.

Rather, the intent of the Russian government—as suggested by the second scenario—is to focus government-sponsored AI development toward a force of unmanned/uncrewed weapons systems that would substitute for (rather than simply augment) current military capabilities. Although it might be expected that Russia's potential opponents (North Atlantic Treaty Organization [NATO] and the PRC) would look for some degree of similar capabilities, the current Russian development program goes beyond what other nations might contemplate.

As an example, in 2014 the Russian government announced the development of the highly mobile "ground robot" Taifun-M to protect its strategic nuclear missile launch sites (Yars and Topol-M strategic nuclear-armed missiles, primarily targeted at the United States). Taifun-M takes the form of a tank-like tracked vehicle armed with laser and cannon, painted in woodland camouflage.[9] It is assumed that the initial version was operated by humans via remote control, but it has been suggested that AI intelligence systems have been developed to provide a degree of autonomy for these "robots."

Guarding nuclear weapons launch sites using autonomous systems is not something that U.S. decision-makers are likely to consider. An autonomous system at nuclear weapons sites reintroduces the Cold War fears of computer-driven nuclear wars that cannot be prevented by humans. While such "robots" might currently be confined to providing a guard force, scenarios can be envisioned in which the autonomous guards could attack human guards, thereby leaving the site unprotected against control by terrorists or other hostile groups. Additionally, a growing degree of comfort by Russian forces in allowing AI-driven systems to play significant roles in the operations of strategic nuclear weapons appears to hold other considerable risks.

The first epigraph to this chapter rings ominously. If Russia develops "novel weapons systems and supporting infrastructure independent of the trajectory of weapons development in the West," what form will they eventually take?

There are three causes of apparent Russian willingness to utilize AI in a tactical mode: a relative lack of military manpower, a lack of faith in the ability of military personnel to effectively carry out their missions, or even a distrust of military personnel to obey the orders of their leadership.

The first reason, a lack of military personnel, is obvious—the Russian population is approximately one-half that of the United States and one-sixth that of the PRC, resulting in a smaller military-age cohort. A future war fought to a bitter conclusion would require a significant number of personnel as well as smart combat systems.

Can AI-driven autonomous systems make up for the disparity in available military personnel? Since commercial AI is generally used to reduce the number of required employees (and thus increase corporate profits), it would seem that there is a military analogy: More tasks that can be performed by robots means fewer military personnel are required. As noted in other chapters, current U.S. policy requires that humans remain in the loop in any decision to use deadly force. If the need to use reservists and criminals in the front lines in Ukraine is an indicator, it is likely that Russia will opt for building AI augmentation for its professional military rather than improving the training of conscripts.

However, the war in Ukraine has also reduced the Russian leadership's confidence in the capabilities and competence of their professional military. The use of poorly trained reservists and mercenaries in the attrition battle in eastern Ukraine has overshadowed the fact that the initial assault toward Kyiv was led by highly trained special operations forces—who were defeated by Ukrainian forces presumed by the Russians (and other analysts) to be less capable and less motivated. Elite special operations forces were the pride of the Soviet Union and were considered a significant threat to NATO nations during the early stage of any Cold War conflict. To have the best Russian forces suffer a severe defeat at the hands of a nation that Vladimir Putin claims does not exist would naturally shake the confidence of the highest decision-makers. Would autonomous robots have done better?

Third, chaotic retreats and the subsequent behavior of Russian military personnel in Ukraine may be an indicator that the conscripts and reservists that make up the bulk of the forces in Ukraine are unwilling to endanger themselves for the Putin regime. If the loyalty of Russian military personnel is suspect, would it not be better for the regime to put its money into building AI-driven autonomous systems, the loyalty of which presumably would not be questioned?

These are questions that the Russian military leadership is asking. U.S. analysts believe that, as of the moment, "outside of experimental prototypes"—which may include the Taifun-M and the Uran-9, a small tank tested in Syria—"Russia's current UAVs [unmanned aerial vehicles] and unmanned ground vehicles are remotely operated."[10] However, the same analysts concede that Russian strategists anticipate that "AI will play an increasingly larger role," particularly in air combat platforms (such as UAVs). Russian defense minister Sergey Shoigu has stated that "it is necessary to ensure the introduction of artificial intelligence technologies in weapons that determine the future appearance of the Armed Forces."[11]

DIFFERENT INCENTIVES FOR DEVELOPING AND INTEGRATING AI

To understand the comparative trajectories of AI in the United States, China, and Russia, one has to start by recognizing each country's differing incentives for AI development.

United States

Business competition is something we all take for granted. Businesses vie for consumers in order to maximize their profit. Most business executives view their natural environment as a "win or lose" competition for customers. In an effort to increase productivity while keeping an even playing field, the U.S. government encourages and directly or indirectly funds basic research in AI. However, most (perhaps as much as 80 percent) AI R&D is funded by the corporations involved in this capitalist business competition.[12]

Thus, the primary incentive for AI development in the United States is commercial—to turn a profit. This can be done in a direct fashion, such as Google selling personalized Internet ad time to retailers, or an indirect fashion, such as automating assembly lines so as to reduce the costs of employees. By law, the U.S. government can neither determine winners or losers nor force corporations to share their intellectual capital or research results with government agencies. The U.S. government has largely treated AI development as an aspect of business competition.

The U.S. government has also become interested in utilizing AI within DoD for both administrative and operational objectives. However, this remains a secondary priority for the United States. From a corporate per-spective, product development for DoD is never going to turn a profit at the scale of commercial sales. As described by an experienced defense acquisition official, to do business with DoD requires producing "high-cost, complex, specialized, even unique products in low volumes to one principal customer in a highly regulated business environment."[13] This is not the same situation as the potential to sell a million cell phone apps.

As a result, several U.S. secretaries of defense have made multiple vis-its to major Silicon Valley firms to cajole more cooperation and convince them that entering the "highly regulated business environment" is in their best interests and could be profitable in the long term. The appeal is also one of patriotism and preventing Chinese dominance and the creation of an authoritarian world order. However, many of these firms view themselves as "global corporations" and are sensitive to their employees potentially protesting "involvement in the military-industrial complex," as occurred during Project Maven. Although some corporate leaders, such as former Google CEO Eric Schmidt, have urged greater collaboration between Silicon Valley and DoD, the United States—unlike China—has no legal mechanisms to compel it.

China

The primary objective of the CCP is to retain political power at all costs. It is not simply a question of the personal desire of the leadership. Their core ideology maintains that any alternative form of governance is "unsci-entific" and—from their Leninist perspective—fundamentally flawed. They will utilize social credit systems, advanced AI-controlled surveillance sys-tems, and, if necessary, military weapons controlled by AI in order to pre-serve societal control.

It should be noted in the last regard that the PLA is pledged to the party, not the state government of China. Western policymakers often treat that as mere nuance. It is not. The PLA is the CCP's military, and its foremost purpose is party control of China. If party control is threatened, military AI applications will be used internally in the PRC against Chinese citizens as necessary. There is no greater incentive for such a government to fur-ther the development of military AI. It will utilize all available resources to maintain AI leadership. The strategy of prioritizing military AI ahead of commercial development is a consequence of responding to this incentive.

The CCP's incentive to put large resources toward AI development in general and military application in particular is therefore immense. Total spending on AI by the Chinese government is kept secret, but at least two provincial governments have publicly pledged to invest more than $14 billion in AI development.[14] We can only speculate on the national government's level of investment. Recent estimates that China plans on doubling current AI investments to a total of $27 billion by 2026 are undoubtedly too low since they appear only to count commercial—not military—spending.[15]

Admittedly, China also has incentives to be the leader in commercial AI. Statements by CCP leaders, particular Xi Jinping, indicate that commercial AI leadership is a firm economic goal. At the nineteenth congress of the CCP in 2017, Xi stressed the need to "promote the deepened integration of Internet, big data, and artificial intelligence with the real economy."[16]

In October 2018 Xi Jinping led an AI "study session" with outside experts for the CCP Politburo, the party's top decision-making body. At the session, Xi firmly asserted (using military metaphors) that the party must "ensure that our country marches in the front ranks . . . and occupies the high ground in critical and AI core technologies."[17]

According to the 2017 *Next Generation Artificial Intelligence Development Plan*, the CCP's objective is that "by 2030, China will become the world's 'primary' AI innovation center, with a core AI industry gross output exceeding $150.8 billion (RMB 1 trillion) and AI-related industry gross output exceeding $1.38 trillion (RMB 10 trillion)."[18] The CCP definitely wants to make money. Nevertheless, commercial incentives remain secondary, even if strongly felt by Chinese businesses and often alluded to by Xi.

The American public has not yet recognized that the Chinese incentive to develop military AI dwarfs that of its own government. While the United States desires to be the leader in commercial AI and will develop military applications at a pace that follows commercial development, it does not view the survival of democracy and fate of its current political leaders under constant threat.

In fact, it is evident that many Americans view AI and its development as *a threat*. Nor do American AI developers see themselves as extensions of the government and dependent on the U.S. government for their financial success. Instead, they primarily seek to avoid government control and official coercion to cooperate, and they largely have the financial resources to influence government policy. A number of the largest AI developers view themselves as "global corporations" with national loyalties that are somewhat fungible.

Russia

Russia also has an incentive to develop commercial AI. However, Western analysts point to the fact that Russia's "private-sector AI ecosystem is relatively small, and there are real problems with talent development and retention."[19] Some analysts have also been skeptical of Russia's potential to fully develop emerging technologies. They point to the fact that "Russia spends much less on R&D than either the United States or China, in terms of both overall value and share of [gross domestic product]."[20]

Meanwhile, significant Russian computer programming talent has immigrated to the United States and Western Europe over the past decades. This flow appears to have increased as the result of the war against Ukraine. Certain analysts claim that Russia's AI industry has already experienced a "disaster" due to the economic sanctions.[21] Nevertheless, Russia maintains a continuing network of research organizations centered on universities that could provide commercial AI expertise when economic sanctions are lifted.

A "Putinized" Russia also seeks to utilize AI to preserve government control over Russian society by identifying, tracking, and jailing or eliminating dissidents. To do so provides an incentive to develop police and military applications of AI. However, the Russian government simply does not have the resources in money and personnel to create a system on the scale of the CCP. The incentive to utilize AI mainly for social control exists, but it is likely judged impracticable. Hence, the primary incentive for developing military AI is to automate weapons systems to make up for a deficit in military manpower.

The Russian war against Ukraine into which the Russian military had no qualms about throwing poorly trained "reservists" and criminals recruited by the Wagner mercenary company might initially seem to belie this deficit. But as previously noted, Russia's population is half that of the United States and one-sixth that of the PRC. Autonomous systems would provide compensatory power.

This assessment is shared by the U.S. Department of Defense. In 2021 Lt. Gen. Michael Groen, USMC, then-director of the Pentagon's Joint Artificial Intelligence Center, observed that "the Russian military seeks to be a leader in weaponizing AI technology."[22] This is facilitated by a small but innovative military-industrial complex that has survived since the days of the Soviet Union. Additionally, Groen reportedly advised that "while Russia is not a leader in commercial and academic AI research—as the United States and China are—it would be a grave mistake for the Pentagon to take its eyes off the threat."[23]

Groen's warning is underpinned by the fact that "Russia was not a major leader in the development of the Internet or computer networking, but Russia has become a leader in weaponizing those technologies for advanced cyber-attacks and cybercrime capabilities."[24]

WESTERN APOLOGISTS FOR SOCIAL CONTROL AI

Individuals involved in Chinese AI development excuse the use of AI for social credit and identification of anyone who could be seen as a threat to CCP control. Seeing immense potential profits, Kai-Fu Lee, a Chinese tech investor well known in Western financial circles, points to the fact that "China has an advantage in developing A.I. because its leaders are less fussed by 'legal intricacies' or 'moral consensus.'"[25] Supporting this view have been AI-developing corporations that conduct some of their research in the People's Republic, including IBM and Google (Alphabet), and individuals and funds that have been investing in Chinese AI companies, such as Fidelity International and Qualcomm Ventures.

Only relatively recently have several of these U.S.-based firms expressed some concern over the purposes for which AI is used in China. Whether these concerns will withstand the lure of future profits is uncertain. For example, Google pulled its AI-driven search engine from China in 2010 due to increasing government censorship. However, in 2017 it started planning to build a censored search service acceptable to the Chinese Communist

Party until protests from employees made it back down.[26] (Google/Alphabet still builds cell phone hardware in China.)

Apple, another long-term AI developer, started asking its component suppliers to diversify to other countries, but in December 2022 apparently pulled AirDrop, an app used by Chinese protestors to avoid government censorship, from all its cell phones in China.[27]

IBM willingly shares facial recognition databases with Chinese universities (and those of other countries) under the justification that it will train AI systems to be "less biased"—despite the fact that those universities feed their research directly to China's PLA and security services such as in Xinjiang.[28]

Meanwhile, there are those who contend that the social credit system is not as nefarious as portrayed by Western media. A newsletter published by *MIT Technology Review* maintains that there have been only "some contentious local experiments" by city governments (Rongcheng is the only city identified) in which "people are now able to opt out."[29] Echoing the newsletter editor, a Chinese "colleague" writes that "the reality is, that terrifying [AI-powered social credit] systems doesn't [sic] exist, and the central government doesn't seem to have much appetite to build it, either."[30] Nevertheless, she concedes that a system that *does* exist—described by her as "mostly pretty low-tech"—is designed in part to "promote state-sanctioned moral values."

The obvious problem for the apologists is that the official CCP/Chinese government AI planning documents specifically state that AI identification and surveillance systems are necessary for the purpose of social control. Their predominant *Next Generation of Artificial Intelligence Development Plan* declares that AI "is indispensable for the effective maintenance of social stability" since it "can accurately perceive, forecast [and] warn" security agencies of those who don't comply with "moral values" such as those espoused in "Xi Jinping thought," the official philosophy that is now referenced in the same manner as was Mao Zedong's "Little Red Book" under his regime.

When confronted with this evidence, most apologists—who might have financial or personal interests in China that could be threatened by government seizure—fall back on thin moral relativistic arguments such as that

Western (nongovernmental) credit bureaus also use AI systems in personal credit reports, that Americans do not have sufficient federal privacy laws, and that Westerners "would do better to look closer to home" and ignore activities in China.[31]

Apologists close their eyes to the underlying political incentives for the development of AI and the fact that social control can be used as a military application, particularly in conquered territory.

SOCIAL CONTROL AS A MILITARY APPLICATION

Beyond any doubt, the primary use of AI by the government of the People's Republic of China—permanently under the control of the Chinese Communist Party—is for government control over the activities (and perhaps the thoughts) of the Chinese population.

However, social control AI can function as a military application, and it can be modified to feed into further military use. For example, the existing system utilized in Xinjiang needs but little adaptation to be used against a population in areas captured by PLA forces during a conflict. These same methods apply in identifying those who might potentially form a resistance movement. The utilization of the system might thereby reduce the number of occupying troops needed to maintain local control, thereby freeing other troops for frontline combat.

The *Next Generation of Artificial Intelligence Development Plan* states that for the purpose of future AI development, military applications of AI will be prioritized and that commercial uses would be further developed under this priority. Civil-military fusion is a term applied to a symbiotic relationship between military and commercial applications. This is possible because AI is—in the vernacular of defense analysts—a dual-use technology, one in which products can be used for either civilian or military purposes without the need for fundamental modification. As previously noted, systems designed for assembling the big data needed for social control can also be used to support military operations.

Since the start of the Russian invasion of Ukraine, Western apologists for the use of AI by the Russian government to track dissidents have largely evaporated. In any event, Russia simply does not have the resources to create a social credit system on the scale of China and has not attempted such. The government focus on AI has centered directly on military applications that—in Putin's depiction—could help "rule the world."

The Putin regime's willingness to kidnap Ukrainian children to be raised by families in Russia is a warning of its potential for eventually applying social control over populations. Utilizing some amount of AI to facilitate this activity is but a small step. The United Nations has declared this activity "genocide," and the International Criminal Court has issued arrest warrants for Vladimir Putin and Maria Lvova-Belova, the so-called Russian children's rights commissioner. AI algorithms would be a very efficient aid in assigning children removed from conquered territory, ensuring their indoctrination and monitoring their activities.

HOW WOULD OPPONENTS USE MILITARY AI?

Exactly how potential opponents would use AI in military operations cannot be determined by mirror-imaging U.S. capabilities and policy debates. Mirror-imaging is the term for viewing an opponent as if it would operate as oneself. It is indeed likely that the PRC and Russia—and eventually Iraq and North Korea—will develop military capabilities similar to those of the United States and its allies, including human–machine teaming that might keep "humans in the loop" to a certain extent.

Nevertheless, the political regimes of those countries will shape AI usages to match their systems of control, which will inevitably impact their military development. It is reasonable to assume that a government less interested in individual human rights would be less concerned with a high degree of autonomy in weapons systems and allowing these systems to make decisions that democratic states attempt to reserve for humans. Allowing machines to make decisions as to the use of deadly force is faster and more efficient. As previously suggested, properly programmed machines—with the right AI algorithms—might be more loyal to the state and ruling party than humans who might question orders.

Assuming that military capabilities will be quite similar also discounts cultural and political effects on technological development as well as the incentives behind developing AI. As the first epigraph to the chapter notes, these opponents may indeed "develop novel weapons systems and supporting infrastructure independent of the trajectory of weapons development in the West."

To examine that possibility requires us to take a deeper look at the systems that we know are now under development.

CHINESE MILITARY PROGRAMS

The Center for Security and Emerging Technology at Georgetown University has identified 343 contracts by the People's Liberation Army for the acquisition or development of AI-related equipment.[32] They refine the estimate of PLA spending on AI and autonomous systems at the equivalent of $2.7 billion in 2018 in comparison to $3 billion for the United States.[33] However, most analysts believe that actual military spending by the PRC is underreported.

The first fact to recognize is that the PLA is modeling itself on the U.S. military to the point that it buys the equivalent of whatever the U.S. military buys. This is especially noticeable regarding the PLA Navy (PLAN). Not only is the PLAN duplicating U.S. aircraft carrier technology (such as electromagnetic catapult systems), it is also building equivalent ships that do not necessarily fit its own strategy. Once the U.S. Navy developed a maritime logistics platform (MLP) ship to assist with the offload of equipment from its civilian-crewed maritime prepositioning ships (that are stationed in Guam and Diego Garcia in case of major war), the PLAN built an MLP equivalent. However, the PLAN has no maritime prepositioning squadrons. Watching as the United States prototyped an electromagnetic rail gun, the PLAN rushed to install its own version on one of its ships—despite the fact that it likely does not function. (As far as it is known, it has never actually been operated at sea.)

Unfortunately for the United States, the PLA is able to buy more of everything (ships, aircraft, and missiles) because its costs are lower due to the comparatively low wages of its manufacturing work force. A Chinese weakness is that it is dependent to some extent on sophisticated Western-manufactured computer chips, but it is seeking to develop its own.

This quest for equivalency (and eventually superiority) applies to AI as well. The PLA appears poised to add AI capabilities to its unmanned aerial vehicles—and might already have—as well as ground combat vehicles and surface ships. However, China perceives AI as a way to catch up to the United States in particular warfighting domains.

The PLA is focusing AI efforts in two warfare areas in which it assesses that its capabilities are significantly behind those of the United States: eroding the U.S. advantage in undersea warfare, and jamming and blinding a U.S. combat information network that is global and larger than its own.

Until recently, the PLA was assessed as being unable to detect and track U.S. submarines operating in the Taiwan Strait.[34] This is an area of weakness the PLA intends to rectify. Undersea warfare involves submarines, surface and air platforms versus submarines, and mine warfare—all backed by underwater sound analysis, both onboard those platforms and from long-range analysis.

In 2017 the PLAN began significant investment in an "Underwater Great Wall" of acoustic sensors that would include autonomous unmanned undersea vehicles (UUVs) to detect and track U.S. submarines. Acoustic analysis is a difficult art that has long been enhanced by computer analysis with the same type of algorithms that constitute artificial intelligence. New AI methods could presumably substitute for the level of experience that has supported American superiority in the underwater domain.

Chinese autonomous UUVs are reported "to be proliferating in number and growing in capability."[35] The Haidou 1 autonomous UUV demonstrated its ability to dive below 33,000 feet in 2020 (in the Marianas Trench, just east of the American commonwealth of the North Mariana Islands). Sea-Whale, an autonomous UUV, navigated 1,250 nautical miles over 37 days, also in 2020. Neither of the autonomous UUVs has demonstrated military capabilities, but they appear to be prototypes for future naval UUVs. For them to operate autonomously requires extensive AI.

Jamming or blinding U.S. command, control, communications, computers, intelligence, surveillance, and reconnaissance (C4ISR) networks is considered "systems confrontation" or "systems destruction" warfare, described by the PLA as "won by the belligerent that can disrupt, paralyze or destroy the operational capability of the enemy's operational system."[36] The United States maintains a global C4ISR network much larger and more comprehensive than that of the PRC, whose comparable network is centered on the Western Pacific—the nearby region. Due to the vast oceanic distances that U.S. forces need to cross both physically and electronically to transit from the continental United States to the Western Pacific, they are more dependent on long-haul wireless communications (primarily via satellite) than Chinese forces.

The PLA considers this an American dependency and a weak spot that it could exploit. But to manage the various exploitation techniques (including cyber warfare) effectively requires a high degree of AI capability in various forms. Using only open-source material, the Center for Security and Emerging Technology has identified twenty-nine PLA projects that relate AI to "systems confrontation" and "systems destruction" warfare."[37] Many more secret projects are suspected.

Western militaries usually use the term electromagnetic warfare, a capability Russia also intends to exploit in any warfare against NATO.

RUSSIAN MILITARY PROGRAMS

A federally funded research and development institute, the CNA Corporation, has identified at least forty potential Russian AI-enabled military systems in various stages of development.[38] A particular focus is unmanned/uncrewed ground combat vehicles.

In its ongoing intervention in Syria, Russia has tested a variety of unmanned/uncrewed systems that appear ripe to be converted to AI control and that may already have embedded elements of AI. In 2019 the Russian defense ministry announced that it was developing "intelligent decision-making systems" to reduce the "conditions of ambiguity" that create the fog of war.[39]

In ways similar to current military applications by the United States, unmanned ground platforms have been used for demining and intelligence, surveillance, and reconnaissance (ISR). The primary vehicle for mine clearing is Uran-6. Two of the ISR unmanned vehicles are referred to as Scarab and Sphera.

As previously noted, Russia has also tested a fighting vehicle in actual combat. In May 2018 it sent an Uran-9—the same "small tank" assigned to defend nuclear missile launch sites—into a "near-urban combat" mission. The Uran-9 was primarily controlled by a remote human operator and reportedly failed to complete its missions. However, according to the

Russian defense ministry, numerous improvements have been made. AI applications may have been installed in order to assist remote-controlled operation—an example of human-machine teaming. Meanwhile, a Russian project named Shturm (Storm) is designing a larger unmanned tank (based on the manned T-72 main battle tank) specifically designed for street combat in cities. A smaller combat vehicle named Nerehta has been reported as "a test-bed for military AI applications," presumably with a similar mission.[40]

Electronic warfare is the jamming, spoofing, and deception of enemy sensors, such as radar. The Soviet military prided itself on its electronic warfare capabilities directed against NATO systems. Post-Soviet Russia has maintained this focus. As in intelligence analysis, here is where AI can be an enabler in controlling an automated process at machine speed—detecting the enemy's transmission frequency, attacking the signal, and instantly matching any change of frequency. Part of this network involves the use of UAVs for local jamming. The Russian Leer-3 UAV is reportedly capable of jamming cell towers and transmitting false signals to almost six thousand cell phones.[41] To perform this mission requires some degree of AI.

Russia has certainly used UAVs in its invasion of Ukraine. Thus far, however, there is little evidence that any have been flown autonomously using AI. Most of the UAVs have been under the remote control of human operators, particularly those used for ISR, such as Orlan-10, an artillery spotting drone. "Kamikaze drones," such as the Iranian-produced Shahed-136, act as loitering munitions that can remain aloft for extended periods (like the Israeli Harpy system), unlike ballistic or cruise missiles. In fact, sources suggest that the extensive use of Shahed-136—particularly to attack civilian infrastructure—is the result of Russia depleting much of its cruise missile inventory. Since Shahed-136 attacks based on remote orders, it is less AI-driven than a U.S. Tomahawk cruise missile, rarely identified as an AI weapon despite its ability to steer by terrain mapping.

However, Russian interest in a fully autonomous UAVs remains, particularly those capable of attacking in swarms that could overwhelm air defenses. In the Ukraine war, Russia has created swarms of kamikaze drones by launching them in sequence rather than by means of AI direction. This is a limitation it is striving to correct.

On a comparative basis, Russia has taken the lead on incorporating AI into ground combat vehicles and utilizes it in their electronic warfare systems. In terms of AI incorporated into UAVs, however, it would appear to be behind developments in the United States and possibly China.

The United States appears to maintain an advantage over China in UUVs due to its greater long-term experience in operating undersea warfare systems. The Russian defense industry remains on par with the United States as concerns undersea warfare, having inherited world-class submarine design bureaus from the days of the Soviet Union. But it cannot compete with the United States (or China) in terms of scale. In the area of unmanned surface (naval) vessels, the technology is still immature, and it is hard to determine a leader.

IS THE UNITED STATES REALLY FAR BEHIND?

On the surface of the issue, the United States would seem to be an AI leader in many categories, not behind its potential opponents. But even now, it appears that it will not remain so in the future.

This chapter's second epigraph by Nicolas Chaillan expresses despair at the U.S. Department of Defense's lack of urgency in developing military applications of AI. Despite the rhetoric of defense leaders—all of whom publicly extol the virtues of AI and encourage public-private partnerships—Chaillan and other critics view military AI development as woefully underfunded and stifled by DoD bureaucracy.

At the same time, many high-tech corporations are reluctant to identify themselves as a military supplier for ideological reasons or—primarily—due to the complexity of DoD procurement regulations. In its effort to prevent waste, fraud, and abuse, Congress has passed numerous laws concerning defense acquisition that the federal bureaucracy has turned into volumes of regulations with mind-numbing required application formats. Smaller tech startups have found the process daunting, while larger corporations with more experience with the process and larger business development and administrative staffs maintain an advantage.

Yet the United States does not appear to be behind—today. It appears to be leading in the number of commercial AI firms, in incorporating tech startups, filing patents, publishing academic papers on AI, and other measurements devised for comparing AI progress between nations. But because 80 percent of AI R&D is funded by commercial firms rather than the U.S. government, there is no guarantee of access to algorithms that could potentially provide a military advantage.

In contrast, the advantages of the CCP include the ability to tap into every commercial Chinese AI development and divert the product to military uses. There is no escape from this in the PRC. Every large PRC tech company is required to have a communist party cell. Small tech firms are now receiving party representatives.[42]

In March 2022 a PRC regulation came in effect that requires all "recommendation algorithms"—algorithms that suggest choices, such as Siri or Amazon's "customers who bought this product also bought"—to be registered and deposited with the government. Particularly sought is any algorithm that has any effect on disseminating information to the public. China's largest Internet platforms such as Tencent, Alibaba, and ByteDance—the owner of the globally popular site TikTok—have submitted algorithms to this registry.[43] Chinese scholars euphemistically refer to this situation as representing the fact that "China has strong AI promoting policies and weak privacy regulations"[44]—quite an understatement.

An increasing number of analysts maintain that the United States is losing its previous edge in emerging technology applicable to national security. The PRC is poised to file more patents and publish more academic papers on AI than any other nation. (Some analysts say it surpassed the United States in 2017.)

This has alarmed significant leaders in the tech industry, including Eric Schmidt, former CEO of Google (Alphabet) and still a principal shareholder in that company. In 2020 Schmidt stated that "we're a year or two ahead of China. We're not a decade ahead."[45] From 2020 to 2021 Schmidt and former Deputy Secretary of Defense Robert O. Work co-chaired the congressionally mandated National Security Commission on Artificial Intelligence, the final report of which   completed after exhaustive research—concluded with an alarming note: "As a bipartisan commission of 15 technologists, national security professionals, business executives, and academic leaders, the National Security Commission on Artificial Intelligence (NSCAI) is delivering an uncomfortable message: America is not prepared to defend or compete in the AI era. This is the tough reality we must face. And it is this reality that demands comprehensive, whole-of-nation action."[46]

The recommended whole-of-nation action includes greater cooperation between the U.S. government and the commercial AI developers—with these efforts directed toward national defense—as well as extensive government funding for AI research and development and greater science, technology, engineering, and mathematics education at all public and private educational levels. However, such an effort has not yet been organized or substantially funded. And it certainly has not matched the level of resources applied to the "space race."

WHO WILL BE THE FUTURE AI LEADER?

The reality is that if current trends continue, the future AI leader—and specifically the leader in military applications—will not be the United States. It might have the most creative scientists and engineers, but that does not appear to be enough. Despite the creativity and inventiveness of entrepreneurs and technologists in the American tech sector and the research conducted in major universities, the disadvantages that the United States—and other democracies—face in competing with technology development in authoritarian states have been identified.

As Schmidt and Work maintain, unless the U.S. government intends to pour resources (money) into AI development, perhaps akin to the 1960s space race to reach the moon, the People's Republic of China, led by the Chinese Communist Party, will be the global AI leader, both in commercial and military applications.

This will primarily be due to the relative incentives. According to the Gordian Knot Center for National Security at Stanford University, China appears poised to infuse $1 trillion into its tech industries—some portion of which will fund AI development. One of the center's founders proffered that "China is organized like Silicon Valley," while the Pentagon is organized like a Detroit auto maker—implying outdated, slow, and stodgy business practices.[47] However, many of the small Silicon Valley enterprises exist only because of routine infusions of cash by venture capitalists—who can easily shift their money to other commercial sectors. The 2023 collapse of the Silicon Valley Bank revealed considerable weaknesses in commercial tech funding, requiring federal government intervention.

Nevertheless, there is great validity in the impression that—despite efforts such as DoD's Defense Innovation Unit located in Silicon Valley— the Pentagon remains a difficult customer due to federal regulations. This is a severe detriment to the United States maintaining any technological advantage over the PRC.

Given the relative incentives and current Chinese and Russian development of military AI, how is the United States responding? We will examine that question in later chapters, but first we must describe the specifics of military AI.

4
___

WEAPONIZING AI

Why AI Is Important for Military Weapons

My view is that technology sets the parameters of the possible;
it creates the potential for a military revolution.

MAX BOOT[1]

Technology makes possible the revolution, but the revolution
itself takes place only when new concepts of operation develop
and, in many cases, new military organizations are created.

ANDREW MARSHALL[2]

THE ODDS WERE FOUR hundred to one. Outside the city, almost eighty thousand battle-hardened warriors were encamped. Many were veterans fresh from a bloody victory over a rival army that also numbered in the thousands. Inside the city were 168 soldiers. They had brought with them sixty-two horses.

   With the confidence of a conqueror, the emperor of the richest, largest, and most powerful empire on the continent entered the city gates with but a portion of his massive force, a retinue of about seven thousand guards.

Though more lightly armed than those outside, the guards retained suitable weapons for close combat. The emperor did not expect an ambush, but he knew that with a word from him, his entire army could swarm the city. In addition, the enemy soldiers facing him had been lured deep into his empire. Even if they escaped, they would face miles of hostile territory.

Though ready to fight, most of the 168 soldiers were concealed in houses and behind walls. Admittedly, they were tense and scared. It was later recalled that many "urinated out of pure terror." However, at the direction of their leader, the company's chaplain and an interpreter strode forward—not to surrender, but to demand the emperor's surrender to them and to God. The conversation ended with the emperor stating he would kill them all, at which time the soldiers emerged from hiding with twelve harquebus (early rifles), four small cannon, and mounted cavalry.

The seven thousand warriors had never faced men on horseback or the strange weapons that belched fire and hurled deadly metal at them. As many as two thousand may have been killed in the melee, and the tiny Spanish army of the conquistador Francisco Pizarro seized the emperor of the Incas as a hostage and would eventually take control of the Incan empire. Leaderless and terrified of a technology they could not understand, the Inca army melted away. Armed with weapons made of stone and wood, they had no answer to the advanced military technology of steel weapons, guns, and cannon (and horses).[3]

REVOLUTIONS IN MILITARY AFFAIRS

For millennia, beginning when our cave-dwelling ancestors sought to fashion new tools to gain an advantage over opposing groups, humankind has sought to use technology in innovative ways to prevail in warfare. From the first bows and arrows, the use of horses to carry mounted warriors, gunpowder, the longbow, muskets, the Gatling gun, ironclad warships, tanks, and eventually nuclear weapons—technological advances have given the side that uses them in innovative ways the upper hand.

Historians and strategists have come to call these advances revolutions in military affairs (RMAs). These technological innovations have transformed warfare and altered the course of history. The side that fields these technologies first often does not know their true impact until they are actually used in a conflict.

Today, emerging technologies offer the same promise as they offered to Pizarro. Leveraging AI for military applications can transform warfare and usher in the next revolution in military affairs.

ENTER ROBOTS AND UNMANNED SYSTEMS

During the last half of the past millennium, humans began to imagine new technologies that could be used in combat. Three hundred and fifty years after Pizarro's conquest of the Incas, a number of writers speculated on what would happen if nonhuman entities made war on humans. Perhaps most famously, English author H. G. Wells serialized his story, *War of the Worlds*, in the late 1890s.

War of the Worlds was one of the earliest stories to detail a conflict between mankind and an extraterrestrial race, Martians, invading Earth. The Martians use fighting machines armed with heat rays and chemical weapons that emit poisonous black smoke. The Earth dwellers are destroyed by these "robotic weapons." The book's plot was similar to numerous works of invasion literature published around the same period, but what made this book memorable was its dramatization in a 1938 radio program starring Orson Welles. The dramatic reading caused public panic among listeners who did not know the book's events were fictional.

Throughout the twentieth century, more writers began to speculate what would happen if robots (the common term then for what we call unmanned systems today) were used in conflict.[4] Many of these ideas posited apocalyptic scenarios where the machines dominated humans who were completely outmatched.

Inspired by these stories, as well as by their own imaginations, scientists and engineers began to create systems that operated without a human aboard, albeit with an operator exercising control. A primary reason for creating unmanned systems was to keep one's own warfighters out of harm's way, letting the (expendable) machines sortie into dangerous situations instead of their manned counterparts.

The earliest recorded use of unmanned systems for warfighting occurred in August 1849 when the Austrians attacked the Italian city of Venice with unmanned balloons loaded with explosives. The first pilotless aircraft were built shortly after World War I. The U.S. Army led the way, commissioning a project to build an "aerial torpedo"—comparable to a cruise missile—resulting in the "Kettering Bug," which was developed for wartime use but not deployed in time to be used in World War I. The gyroscope-controlled unmanned aircraft was designed by Charles Kettering with the assistance of Orville Wright and Elmer Sperry and was built by the Dayton-Wright Company. Foreshadowing modern concerns about autonomous unmanned aircraft, officials were reluctant to authorize the unmanned flying of explosives over friendly troops.

In the United States, the military services continued to develop various types of unmanned systems during the interwar years. Much of the experimentation focused on unmanned aerial systems such as Reginald Denny's RP-1 target drone, adapted directly from his radio-controlled model aircraft.

Denny, whose actual name was Reginald Leigh Dugmore, was a British actor and silent film star who served in the Royal Air Force in World War I and continued his involvement in aviation. Becoming interested in "free-flight" model airplanes (as model drones were originally called), he opened a model airplane shop and, later, a chain of hobby stores. In 1935 he began to modify his remote-controlled "Radioplane" for military use as a target drone. Winning a contract with the U.S. Army for the Radioplane OQ-2 flying target, his company went on to build 15,000 drones during World War II. The company was purchased by the aircraft corporation Northrop in 1952, and Denny returned to acting.

In 1919 the U.S. Navy converted the decommissioned battleship *Iowa* (BB 4), a veteran of the Spanish-American War (1898), into a remote-controlled target ship to test aerial bombing. *Iowa* operated from 1920 to 1923, under the control of accompanying ships, to test the ability of aviators to detect and target a moving vessel before it could be positioned for attack against shore. Historians credit it for helping to develop the Navy's air doctrine used in World War II.[5] It was sunk (as planned) in 1923 by surface fire from an active battleship during a fleet exercise. The Navy resurrected the remote-controlled target vessel concept using a series of decommissioned destroyers starting in 1930. Then in 1932 another decommissioned battleship, *Utah* (BB 31), was configured to operate occasionally as a remote-controlled target ship. However, she still retained a reduced crew for more complex exercises and maintenance. *Utah* was sunk at Pearl Harbor in the December 7, 1941, attack by the Japanese.

Development of unmanned aerial systems and unmanned ground systems continued through World War II and into the second half of the last century. Remote-controlled unmanned warships were not seriously pursued during and immediately after World War II due to the complexity of operating large warships in combat. The aspirations for what these new gadgets could do, as well as the hype generated by proponents of these unmanned systems, resulted in as many failures as successes. Compared to today's technologies used to control unmanned systems, the technology of the 1950s, '60s, and even the '70s was primitive at best. In many cases, what was being attempted with drones was, literally, a bridge too far.

One of the most prominent examples of this technological overreach was the U.S. Navy's QH-50 DASH (drone antisubmarine helicopter) program. In 1958 the Navy awarded a contract to modify a small RON-1 Rotorcycle helicopter to explore its use as a remote-controlled drone. In 1965 the Navy began to use the QH-50 as a reconnaissance vehicle in Vietnam. Equipped with a TV camera and a telemetry feedback link to inform the remote-control operator of drone responses to his commands, the QH-50 began to fly Landing Zone Snoopy missions from destroyers off the Vietnamese coast to provide over-the-horizon target data to the destroyer's five-inch batteries.

But by 1970 DASH operations ceased fleet-wide. Although DASH was a sound concept, the Achilles' heel of the system was the electronic remote-control system. The lack of feedback loop from the drone to the controller, and its low radar signature and lack of transponder, accounted for 80 percent of all drone losses. While apocryphal to the point of being an urban legend, it was often said the most common call on the Navy Fleet's 1MC general announcing systems during the DASH era was, "DASH Officer, Bridge," when the unfortunate officer controlling the DASH was called to account for why "his" system had failed to return to the ship and crashed into the sea.[6]

THE GULF WAR AND BEYOND

As new technologies made remote control of unmanned systems more effective, scientists and engineers—sensing that unmanned systems could change the character of war—continued to experiment with ways to usher in a revolution in military affairs and use these systems in combat to achieve a war-winning advantage. These efforts were given new impetus during the wars in Kuwait, Iraq, and Afghanistan where U.S. and Allied forces used air and ground unmanned systems in innovative ways to meet urgent operational needs as well as to keep soldiers, sailors, airmen, and Marines out of harm's way.

These conflicts ushered in explosive growth in the use of unmanned systems. For the U.S. military alone, at the height of these conflicts, more than 10,000 UAVs and 12,000 unmanned ground vehicles (UGVs) were in use in these theaters of conflict. A primary use for the UGVs was the detection and detonation of roadside bombs—the improvised explosive devices. This task is very dangerous for humans, and UGVs substituted for military explosive ordnance disposal (EOD) personnel in that specific supporting task. Reportedly, the U.S. Army purchased 7,000 EOD UGVs, 750 of which were destroyed in action.[7] Many other military UGVs are still in the experimental or prototype stage. However, analysts agree that the expanding use of military unmanned systems (UxSs) spurred by these conflicts is already creating strategic, operational, and tactical possibilities that did not exist a decade ago.[8]

Perhaps most famously, on February 27, 1991, forty Iraqi soldiers on Faylaka Island surrendered to an RQ-2 Pioneer drone launched from the battleship USS *Wisconsin*. Previous Pioneer overflights had led to precisely targeted air attacks on Iraqi patrol boats and island trenches, causing them to believe that detection by the drone would result in similar attacks.[9] For the Iraqis—in much the same way as for the Incas—these new weapons not only caused injury or death, but also had the psychological effect of sowing alarm and confusion in the minds of adversaries. More contemporaneously, UAVs such as the Predator and the Reaper have been used extensively to find, target, and kill terrorists in several theaters.

Spurred by the promise of unmanned systems due to their success in these conflicts, many nations are investing in them in all domains. That said, the

United States is, arguably, leading this effort. From the highest level policy documents such as the *National Security Strategy*, the *National Defense Strategy*, and DoD's *Unmanned Systems Integrated Roadmap*, the United States is indicating that it is "all in" regarding the use of unmanned and autonomous systems in future conflicts. As the *Unmanned Systems Integrated Roadmap* puts it: "Advances in autonomy and robotics have the potential to revolutionize warfighting concepts as a significant force multiplier. Autonomy will greatly increase the efficiency and effectiveness of both manned and unmanned systems, providing a strategic advantage for DoD."[10] But therein is the rub. Like other publications, testimonies, and speeches, leaders at the highest level often conflate "unmanned" with "autonomous." It is clear to most that for a military system to be autonomous, it must be unmanned. However, an unmanned system being controlled by a remote operator is not autonomous. The term of art for these systems is semiautonomous.

THE REALITY OF AUTONOMY

Military weapons systems can perform tasks in three degrees of autonomy: semiautonomous, supervised autonomous, or fully autonomous mode. These are distinctions with enormous differences, and they are important to unpack in any discussion regarding military weapons systems autonomy. Said another way, these are differences in degree, not kind. Importantly, it is not how much "intelligence" the system has but the degree of freedom that it is given that defines it:

- In semiautonomous systems, the machine performs a task and then waits for a human user to take action before continuing. A human is "in the loop" and directing next steps. The semiautonomous system goes through its own sense, decide, and act loop and can even recommend actions, but the human exercises control along the way.
- In supervised autonomous systems, the human sits "on the loop" The machine can sense, decide, and act on its own, but the human can observe the autonomous system's behavior and intervene when it appears that the machine is not carrying out the desired orders or procedures.

- Fully autonomous systems sense, decide, and act entirely without human intervention. Once the human activates the machine, it conducts the task without communicating with the human. In this case, the human is "out of the loop."[11]

With these definitions in hand, we are better able to understand how artificial intelligence is used in military operations, and the different methods (and results) of inserting AI into military weapons systems. The extensive use of unmanned systems in recent conflicts—most recently in Russia's 2022 invasion of Ukraine—all involved humans in or at least on the loop controlling the UxS. Against an unsophisticated adversary, this is a successful tactic. In a future fight with a peer adversary, this would be a recipe for failure. The *Unmanned Systems Integrated Roadmap* describes the issue this way: "Unmanned systems operations ordinarily rely on networked connections and efficient spectrum access. Network vulnerabilities must be addressed to prevent disruption or manipulation."[12]

The answer to operating unmanned systems when network connections are compromised by adversaries—something that has repeatedly occurred in a wide array of conflicts—is to insert artificial intelligence into these systems so that once launched, they can accomplish their mission without constant human control.

AI AS A MILITARY NECESSITY

"When everything is important, nothing is important" is an old saying that laments a lack of priorities. In a budget-constrained environment, what priority should military leaders give to outfitting unmanned systems with artificial intelligence (as well as machine learning) to gain an edge in combat?

America's peer adversaries are making enormous investments in artificial intelligence and machine learning to make their unmanned systems truly autonomous. We assert that the United States is losing the AI arms race and must make an extraordinary effort to catch up. This is not just our opinion but is the consensus view of experts in the field.

The National Security Commission on Artificial Intelligence *Final Report* provides a clear call to action. A key finding of the report noted, "We can still defend America and our allies without widespread AI adoption today, but in the future, we will almost certainly lose without it." The 756-page report presents a detailed analysis of how the United States must "up its AI game" to compete with peer competitors, going on to say,

> America is not prepared to defend or compete in the AI era. This is the tough reality we must face. And it is this reality that demands comprehensive, whole-of-nation action. AI systems will also be used in the pursuit of power. We fear AI tools will be weapons of first resort in future conflicts. AI will not stay in the domain of superpowers or the realm of science fiction. AI is dual-use, often open-source, and diffusing rapidly.
>
> State adversaries are already using AI-enabled disinformation attacks to sow division in democracies and jar our sense of reality. States, criminals, and terrorists will conduct AI-powered cyber-attacks and pair AI software with commercially available drones to create "smart weapons." It is no secret that America's military rivals are integrating AI concepts and platforms to challenge the United States' decades-long technology advantage. We will not be able to defend against AI-enabled threats without ubiquitous AI capabilities and new warfighting paradigms.[13]

SPEED OF WARFARE AND AUTONOMOUS DECISIONS

One of the primary reasons that artificial intelligence and machine learning are so important for military weapons systems is that the speed of warfare, where having a human (even in a benign electronic environment) control the unmanned system, slows down reaction time sufficiently that an adversary's system that is truly autonomous will dominate on the battlefield.

This is not a new concept, but one that Air Force Col. John Boyd originated during the Korean War: the OODA (observe, orient, decide, and act) loop. Boyd's theory was that the key to victory was to create situations where one can make appropriate decisions more quickly than one's opponent can. It is clear to us that an autonomous weapon is capable of getting inside a human's OODA loop in the overwhelming number of cases.[14] Here is how one analyst described what would happen in such a confrontation:

> If artificial intelligence was aggressively applied to every element of the OODA loop, in essence, the OODA loop could collapse on itself.

Artificially intelligent systems would enable massive concurrent coordination of forces and enable the application of force in optimized ways. As a result, a small, highly mobile force (e.g., drones) under the control of AI could always outmaneuver and outmass a much larger conventional force at critical points. Consequently, the effect of platforms under AI control would be multiplied many fold, ultimately making it impossible for an enemy executing a much slower OODA loop to contend or respond.[15]

This is not all new science for the United States. A number of U.S. *defensive* weapons systems—while not autonomous, but rather automated—are capable of operating without human control. These include the Aegis combat system (originally designed during the 1970s as a means to defend ships against aircraft and antiship cruise missiles), the Phalanx gun-based close-in weapons system, and the Patriot air defense system. And the United States is not alone. As of this writing, more than thirty nations have defensive supervised autonomous weapons for those OODA loop engagements where the speed of what is occurring is too fast for humans to respond effectively.

Inserting artificial intelligence and machine learning into *offensive* weapons is the new emerging frontier that will change the character of war by enhancing weapons accuracy, effectiveness, and lethality, all while keeping friendly attacking forces out of harm's way. And while the United States has fielded offensive weapons systems such as the Tomahawk missile and precision-guided munitions (kits that turn "dumb bombs" into "smart bombs" capable of hitting a target with vastly more accuracy), these are automated, not autonomous, weapons. Once launched, the weapon makes no decisions on its own; it simply goes to the spot where it was programmed to arrive.

The use of AI-enabled autonomous weapons in war is not just aspirational or on a distant horizon; they are in use today. A prime example is the Israeli Harpy drone. Unlike its U.S. cousins like the Predator and Reaper, which are continuously under the control of an operator, the Harpy can search a wide area for specified targets (for example, a group of enemy radars in reasonably close proximity to one another) and, once it finds one, can attack that target on its own without looping back with the controller.[16]

Harpy may be the first AI-enabled autonomous weapon in general use today, and it certainly will not be the last.

One factor rarely discussed in the dialogue regarding AI-enabled military weapons is the issue of cost. The military phrase "Quantity has a quality of its own" raises cost as a factor that is critical to decisions on which weapons to develop and field (a few expensive, "exquisite" platforms, or a larger number of less capable ones).

While there are many examples that demonstrate the dramatic difference in cost between conventional platforms and AI-enabled weapons, one example stands out and helps emphasize this point. U.S. attack helicopters are generally recognized as the most potent in the world. But recent export orders show that they now cost between $100 million and $125 million per aircraft. While capabilities vary based on platform, in general, these helicopters carry anywhere between eight and sixteen antitank guided missiles (ATGMs), enjoy a loiter time of about 2.5 hours, and carry two pilots. In contrast, the Bayraktar TB2 armed drone manufactured by the Turkish firm Baykar Makina (currently being used in Libya and Nagorno-Karabakh) has a loiter time of twenty-four hours, carries two ATGMs, requires zero on-board pilots, and costs about $2 million.[17]

Circling back to systems such as Harpy, these weapons take the giant step from semiautonomous weapons to those that are fully autonomous. In the case of a semiautonomous weapon, the operator launches the weapon at a specific target. The human selects the target, and the weapon carries out the attack. Conversely, an operator can launch a fully autonomous weapon into a general area without the human having full knowledge of the exact position of any of the targets. The weapon searches for and locates targets on its own, and then chooses which target to attack.

Israel exports Harpy to a number of nations, and there is evidence that China is attempting to reverse-engineer this system for its own use. The technology to build such systems has existed for decades (witness the U.S. Navy's tactical antiship missile [TASM] system, in service from 1982 to 1994 but never used in combat). Therefore, given the fact that most militaries recognize that always having a human in the loop can be a recipe for defeat, it is fair to ask: Why haven't fully autonomous weapons already proliferated more widely?

CONCERNS ABOUT AUTONOMY

The TASM, a Tomahawk missile variant for use against targets at sea and designated RGM/UGM-109B, offers a compelling case study regarding a lingering reluctance to develop and deploy fully autonomous weapons. First, naval units—ships, aircraft, and spacecraft—constantly move, and if a TASM was launched toward a discrete area of uncertainty, the original target might no longer be in that area. While the TASM could conduct a search for the adversary ship, as the area of uncertainty widened (a ship travelling at thirty knots generates a wide area of uncertainty), there would be concerns that the TASM could not discriminate between naval and commercial vessels and might strike an innocent target. Finally, missiles such as TASM are costly, and launching one (or more) without having some level of certainty that there is a valid target downrange risks wasting an expensive asset.

Some of these concerns that caused TASM to have a brief and uneventful career have carried forward to today. Unlike tanks, aircraft, and ships, AI is not something operators can really see or touch. Telling operators that a weapon is now AI-enabled and can essentially think for itself and shunt the operator to the sideline clearly induces, at best, a healthy dose of skepticism, and at worst, a reluctance to use the weapon in the first place.

This is not a new phenomenon. Threatening the prevailing top-of-the-line weapon with something "newfangled" and unproven can slow down or impede adoption of even the most promising military technology. Whether it was the longbow threatening the bow and arrow, or motor-driven ironclad ships positioning to replace sailing men-of-war, or aircraft carriers replacing battleships as navies' most valuable capital ship, the "old guard" rarely surrenders gracefully. And beyond the weapon-to-weapon tradeoff, there are other factors that can impede the adoption of a paradigm-shifting weapon.

The most telling example of an AI-enabled weapons system that could have ushered in a true revolution in military affairs was the joint unmanned combat air system (J-UCAS), a U.S. Navy/U.S. Air Force unmanned combat air vehicle procurement project. J-UCAS was managed by the Defense Advanced Research Projects Agency. The program was envisioned to have stealth technologies that allowed unmanned combat air vehicles to be armed with precision-guided weapons and used to conduct attacks in high anti-access/area denial environments where the risk to manned air-craft was unacceptably high. However, in 2006 the J-UCAS program was terminated.

While there were a number of reasons that the J-UCAS program was cancelled, one is the fact that at the time it was cancelled, DoD was making a commitment to the F-35 Lightning II Joint Strike Fighter (JSF) program (which remains DoD's most expensive weapons system program, with costs for the life of the program now at $1.7 trillion) to replace legacy fighter air-craft for the Air Force, Navy, and Marine Corps. It is easy to see how field-ing an AI-enabled autonomous aircraft like the J-UCAS could pose a direct threat to the JSF program. While there is no cause-and-effect smoking gun that proves this connection, strong anecdotal evidence makes a compelling case that the J-UCAS had to die so that the JSF could live.

ARE ROBOTS A NECESSARY EVIL?

Be that as it may, concerns regarding what happens when machines are made too powerful are vastly more ubiquitous than just military service infighting. *War of the Worlds* was not a one-off. For over a century, the pub-lic has been fed a diet of dystopian stories involving robots turning on their human creators. The 1921 play *R.U.R.* (*Rossum's Universal Robots*) showed how machines could enslave humans.[18] The 1968 film *2001: A Space Odys-sey* had as its central theme the issue of autonomy of robots, where HAL, a supposedly "good" robot, turns on its human masters. More recently, in the 2014 film *Ex Machina*, a man selected to give the Turing test to a strikingly attractive humanoid robot is seduced by the robot, which ultimately escapes while the man meets his death.

Just these few examples demonstrate how the public might conclude that robots are inherently evil. Add to this the fact that DoD has indicated a plan to arm autonomous systems, and a healthy skepticism can quickly turn into resistance. Indeed, there is a cottage industry—not only in the United States, but also internationally—of organizations such as Human Rights Watch and the Campaign to Stop Killer Robots calling for a ban on lethal autonomous weapons systems.[19]

To be fair, DoD has issued strict guidance regarding the fielding and employment of autonomous weapons systems, stipulating the need for high-level approval even during their development phase. The directive notes,

> Persons who authorize the use of, direct the use of, or operate autonomous and semiautonomous weapon systems will do so with appropriate care and in accordance with the law of war, applicable treaties, weapon system safety rules, and applicable rules of engagement. The use of AI capabilities in autonomous or semi-autonomous weapons systems will be consistent with the DoD AI Ethical Principles.
>
> Autonomous and semi-autonomous capabilities will be expected to complete engagements within a timeframe and geographic area, as well as other relevant environmental and operational constraints, consistent with commander and operator intentions. If unable to do so, the systems will terminate the engagement or obtain additional operator input before continuing the engagement.[20]

Another issue gives the public pause when it comes to inserting artificial intelligence and machine learning into military weapons systems. Unlike the weapons that militaries field today such as ships, planes, tanks, and other platforms that were designed, developed, fielded, and used strictly for military purposes, artificial intelligence and machine learning are dual-use technologies that have already proliferated widely in everyday life.

People seem comfortable with a "black box" that does everything from suggesting a response to an email to recommending purchases on various websites to providing driving directions. However, while the consequences of artificial intelligence and machine learning making an error in civilian technology are typically benign (except, perhaps, in the case of self-driving cars having numerous fatal crashes), having a black box in a military platform, system, sensor, or weapon fail completely (or even hiccup) raises serious concerns that must be addressed if the United States is to fully leverage artificial intelligence and machine learning to stay steps ahead of our potential adversaries.

We are cautiously optimistic that DoD will find the sweet spot to do just this. However, we are mindful of the three-decade-long AI Winter (1966 to 1997) when AI overpromised and underdelivered. DoD would be well served to not overhype the benefits of artificial intelligence and machine learning.

These technologies may help usher in a revolution in military affairs, but the jury is still out, and much R&D remains to be done. We are loath to declare that an RMA is upon us—that term is thrown around far too loosely, and to be clear, a true RMA comes about not just with the arrival of a breakthrough technology, but also with new concepts of operation that leverage that technology in innovative ways.

Said another way, for a new technology to *help* usher in an RMA, intellectual impediments must be swept away. This is precisely what Germany was able to do in World War II with its Blitzkrieg concept of operations. The British and French also had tanks, aircraft, and radios but were stuck in old paradigms regarding how to use them. Germany combined and leveraged these technologies in a way that revolutionized mechanized warfare in the twentieth century.

Therefore, in spite of the emergence of brilliant algorithms, the transformative military potential of AI is exciting, even motivating, but is not yet assured. As writer and commentator Ralph Peters cautions, "When the first early man discovered that he could bind a sharp stone to a stick with a leather thong, you can be certain that he turned immediately to his pals across the campfire and shouted, 'I've just achieved the ultimate revolution in military affairs!'"[21]

This brings us to the sine qua non of the quest to develop and field AI-enabled weapons, the concept known as man-unmanned teaming. The next chapter will explore how this evolving idea can help make the leap from autonomous systems being interesting technologies of limited use to being "loyal wingmen" to their human companions.

5

ROBOTS AT WAR

The Untested Theory of
Human-Machine Teaming

Humans versus machines is a false choice. The best systems
will combine human and machine intelligence to create hybrid
cognitive architectures that leverage the advantages of each.

PAUL SCHARRE[1]

The naval future is not just one of humans or machines; it will
feature the blending of humans and machines. The only viable
path is one in which humans and machines work together,
combining the speed of machines with the wisdom of humans.

JOHN ARQUILLA AND PETER DENNING[2]

IN GREEK MYTHOLOGY, hidden places in the world were inhabited by
strange creatures, some of which were half-human and half-beast. The most
famous were the half-human/half-horse centaurs—not always friendly to
full humans, but admired because they were archers who could attack or
retreat at speeds no human could match. Chiron, one of the centaurs,

taught the great heroes of legend—such as Achilles and Jason—the abilities and tactics they would need to defeat their enemies. These tactics included the use of special skills only the heroes possessed to defeat opponents much larger and much stronger than themselves. Today we would call these exclusive skills asymmetric advantages.

COLLABORATION BETWEEN WARRIOR AND WEAPON

Since the day when a human first reacted in anger to an enemy or animal by hurling a rock to scare the intruder away, the interdependent relationship between man and weapon helped define warfare. (We will use the term man throughout this chapter for simplicity's sake, but acknowledge that a woman is just as capable of hurling a rock or other weapon.) How big of a rock could the man heft? How far could he throw that projectile? Was it thrown right-handed or left-handed? Was he holding a number of rocks and hurling them rapidly to frighten the adversary, or was he throwing them with care so he might actually hit and injure him? It is clear from even this straightforward example that the man and the (simple) machine have a collaborative arrangement.

Unmanned systems, coupled with exponential advances in big data, artificial intelligence, and machine learning, are proliferating in all domains. In the previous chapter we introduced various degrees of autonomy in weapons systems: semiautonomous, supervised autonomous, or fully autonomous mode (even finer gradations can be made, but these suffice for our purposes). A considerable number of weapons systems have some degree of autonomy today, and the trend lines point to more platforms, systems, sensors, and weapons having autonomous capability. One might assume that when it comes to autonomy, the focus is exclusively on the capabilities that reside in the machine. However, as the epigraphs suggest, this is only part of the equation.

Much of the debate regarding autonomous military systems focuses on the choice between humans and machines in making decisions as to what targets to engage with deadly force. However, seeking to weigh what a human can accomplish alone versus what a machine can achieve on its own is actually not a particularly useful exercise. Rather, more useful is to assess what can be done when human and machine work together—which is called man-machine teaming.

It is important to not only unpack what we mean by man–machine teaming (more precisely, manned-unmanned teaming [MUMT]), but also to examine how a military organization might harness the best qualities of both the man and the machine. Throughout this chapter we will emphasize that when examining how man and machine operate together, it is not about the intelligence of the machine, but rather its relationship to a human controller.

This concept of manned-unmanned teaming is perhaps best articulated by Paul Scharre in his book *Army of None*: "Hybrid human-machine cognitive systems, often called 'centaur warfighters' after the classic Greek myth of the half-human, half-horse creature, can leverage the precision and reliability of automation without sacrificing the robustness and flexibility of human intelligence."[3]

Manned-unmanned teaming presents a solution to complex problems, as it combines the critical social intelligence of a human with the processing speed of a machine. Some psychologists utilize the Theory of Mind (ToM) to define the critical thinking of human beings. In their view, ToM allows an individual to process information, interpret it, and respond to the behavior accordingly. Without some form of ToM, an AI system may not respond correctly to a situation. Combining human and machine into a team—with the human providing the ToM and the machine providing speed in dealing with complexity—allows solutions to be reached faster and more efficiently than before.[4]

Before diving into military cases, it is worth looking at a familiar example of man-machine teaming in the civilian world. Many people recall that in 1997 an IBM supercomputer called Deep Blue defeated the then-world chess champion, Garry Kasparov, in a widely publicized chess match. This was the first defeat of a reigning world chess champion by a computer under tournament conditions and was the subject of a documentary film, *Game Over: Kasparov and the Machine.* The outcome marked the end of the AI Winter.

Less well known, however, is that the following year, Kasparov founded an organization in which humans and AI cooperated in playing chess. In this mash-up, the AI analyzed the opportunities or weaknesses of possible moves and fed this information to the human, exposing things that the human player might have missed. In this teaming arrangement, the human player directs the AI to focus its searches in the most promising areas and then uses this information to make the optimal moves. The results, in match after match, were that the human-AI team defeated both human players and individual machines such as Deep Blue.[5]

It is important to note that the concept of man-machine teaming is not as new as some of its proponents allege.[6] The idea of manned-unmanned teaming has been discussed in academic, scientific, and military circles for more than thirty years.[7] It was ultimately formalized in DoD in 2014 as a key component of the third offset strategy.

THE FIRST TWO OFFSETS

The Department of Defense inaugurated the third offset strategy as part of the Defense Innovation Initiative in 2014 to ensure that the United States retained its military edge against potential adversaries. An offset strategy is defined as an approach to military competition that uses asymmetric advantages to compensate for a disadvantaged position.

Rather than competing head-to-head in an area where a potential adversary may also possess significant—perhaps superior—strength, an offset strategy seeks to shift the axis of competition through the introduction of new operational concepts and technologies. The objective is a shift toward a competition in which the United States has a significant and sustainable advantage.

During the Cold War, the United States was successful in pursuing two distinct offset strategies. Both enabled the United States and NATO to "offset" the Soviet Union's numerical advantage in conventional forces in Europe—soldiers, artillery, tanks, bombers—without absorbing the enormous financial costs would have been required to match the Soviets soldier for soldier and tank for tank. Instead, these offset strategies relied on fundamental innovations in technology, operational techniques, and organizational structure to compensate for the Soviet advantage in time, space, and force size.

The first offset strategy centered on the development of new forms of nuclear weapons. In the 1950s, President Dwight Eisenhower sought to overcome the Warsaw Pact's numerical advantage by leveraging U.S. nuclear superiority to introduce battlefield nuclear weapons. Instead of threatening massive retaliation against Russian cities in the event of a Soviet invasion of Western Europe—which no longer seemed a credible deterrent—the American nuclear arsenal was modified in part to focus on destroying the larger Soviet armies. This shifted the axis of competition from conventional force numbers to an arena where the United States possessed an asymmetrical advantage—in technological development. This approach provided stability and reestablished the foundation for deterrence from the 1950s to the 1970s.

The second offset strategy arose in the late 1970s and early 1980s with the U.S. recognition that the Soviet Union had achieved nuclear parity in both strategic and tactical (battlefield) nuclear weapons. The second offset strategy sought to create an enduring advantage by leveraging the combined effects of conventional precision weapons and the real-time, long-range ISR sensor and communications networks that supported real-time precision targeting. With these networks synchronized and executed over the full breadth of the battlespace, the new "smart weapons" were expected to provide almost a "one-shot, one-hit" capability.

Fortunately, the military technologies that comprised the second offset strategy were never actually tested against the Soviet Union in a head-to-head battle. However, they were deployed against Iraq's Soviet-trained and -equipped army during Operation Desert Storm. The Iraqi defeat was total and represented one of the most lopsided campaigns in modern warfare.[8] America's potential foes noticed the crucial part that technology played in this victory.

TOWARD A THIRD OFFSET: HUMAN-MACHINE TEAMING AND AI

At the time of the introduction of the second offset strategy in the early 1980s, the United States was the only nation with the knowledge and capacity to develop, deploy, and successfully execute the ISR capabilities, the space-based systems, and the precision weapons that supported this approach.

Today, competitors such as Russia and China (and countries to which these nations proliferate advanced capabilities) are pursuing and deploying advanced weapons and capabilities that demonstrate many of the same technological strengths that have traditionally provided the high-tech basis for U.S. advantage. This emergence of increasing parity in the international security environment made it imperative that the United States consider a mix of technologies, system concepts, military organizations, and operational concepts that might shift the nature of the competition and give it an edge over potential adversaries. This set of capabilities provides the basis for a third offset strategy.

As was true of previous offset strategies, a third offset strategy seeks, in a budget-constrained environment, to maintain and extend the nation's competitive technological and operational superiority by identifying asymmetric advantages that are enabled by unique U.S. strengths and capabilities.

In explaining the technological elements of the third offset strategy, then–Deputy Secretary of Defense Robert Work emphasized the importance of emerging capabilities in unmanned systems, artificial intelligence, machine learning, and autonomy. He pointed out that these technologies offer significant advantages, enabling the future force to develop and operate collaborative human–machine "battle" networks that could synchronize simultaneous operations in all domains: space, air, sea, undersea, ground, and cyberspace. Artificial intelligence could allow new levels of autonomy—and some delegation of decision-making authority—within these battle networks. This ingredient is leading to entirely new opportunities for human–machine collaboration and combat teaming.[9]

Within DoD, the formal name for the third offset strategy was the Long-Range Research and Development Plan.[10] The term has fallen out of favor, but a strong component of the strategy has been retained—an emphasis on human–machine teaming to keep decisions to use deadly force in the hands of humans, not machines alone. This requires human–machine teaming be an imperative.

ELEMENTS OF HUMAN-MACHINE TEAMING

There are five basic building blocks in the concept of human–machine collaboration and combat teaming:

- autonomous deep learning systems, which will leverage machine learning to operate "at the speed of light" in areas where human reaction time is too slow, such as during cyberattacks, electronic warfare attacks, or large missile raid attacks

- human-machine collaboration, which will allow machines to help humans make better decisions faster. The F-35 Joint Strike Fighter and the Naval Integrated Fire Control Counter-Air ISR and battle management system have been cited as examples of these concepts.
- assisted human operations, which will focus on the ways in which man and machines can operate together, through tools such as wearable electronics, exoskeletons, and combat applications to assist warfighters in every possible contingency
- advanced human-machine combat teaming, which will focus on humans working with unmanned systems in cooperative operations; one example is the operation of the Navy's P-8A Poseidon with an MQ-4C Triton. Going forward, the next level of teaming will examine swarming tactics and cooperative autonomy.
- network-enabled, cyber-hardened autonomous weapons, which will be resilient to operate in an electronic warfare and cyber environment. A current example is the Navy's tactical Tomahawk Block IX, whose targets can be updated in flight.[11]

The list provides considerable examples of how to develop human-machine teaming. In truth, we are only at the nascent stages of implementing any of these building blocks. Part of the challenge is that many U.S. weapons systems are conceived, designed, built, and fielded without input from operators, and how the human interacts with the machine is only considered when that entity arrives in the field or at sea.

Given this background, it is certainly fair to ask whether the technological components of the third offset strategy are being implemented today or whether they remain "aspirational." This is a question without an answer that offers a point solution. However, the available evidence suggests that while the DoD leadership has a lofty vision of an AI-enabled U.S. military on a distant horizon, it may be missing significant opportunities to jumpstart that journey.

Instead of focusing on a future vision with ambitious outcomes, a viable approach would be to go after easier initial demonstrations—what could be termed "low-hanging fruit." Success is said to breed success, and positive

outcomes from applying human-machine teaming to the less difficult challenges can encourage further development and demonstrate its value in
deterrence and war.

A RECOMMENDED OPPORTUNITY:
THE U.S. NAVY'S MQ-4C TRITON UAV

While there are many examples that we could propose, one target of opportunity that seems evident in the fourth of the building blocks described
above is advanced human-machine combat teaming. This consists of cooperative operations between humans and unmanned systems. Two potential
examples are the operation of the Navy's P-8A Poseidon with an MQ-4C
Triton and the MH-60S Knighthawk aircraft with an MQ-8C Fire Scout.

The fact that these systems are identified as leading candidates for
manned-unmanned teaming in the DoD strategy would lead one to assume
that significant effort has been made to apply MUMT. However, these
air assets currently operate in a manner that does not begin to approach
manned-unmanned teaming. The MQ-4C Triton and MQ-8C Fire Scout
are unmanned aerial vehicles that are currently in operation and forward-
deployed in key areas around the globe but are not yet "loyal wingmen" to
their manned counterparts. So it is fair to ask how far MUMT has advanced
with these systems in the years following the unveiling of the third offset
strategy in 2014.

The P-8A Poseidon is a long-range manned maritime patrol and reconnaissance aircraft optimized for antisubmarine warfare. Based on Boeing's
737 airliner, it carries a crew of seven. The MQ-4C Triton is a long-range
unmanned maritime patrol and reconnaissance air vehicle based on the
RQ-4 Global Hawk high-altitude reconnaissance UAV used by the U.S.
Air Force in Iraq and Afghanistan and during other antiterrorist missions.
The MH-60S Knighthawk is the Navy's latest shipborne helicopter with
a crew of four. The MQ-8C Fire Scout is an unmanned shipborne reconnaissance and targeting helicopter that operates as an extension of the ship's
sensors. Currently, it does not carry weapons.

The Poseidon operates from bases on the East or West Coast of the
United States or is forward-deployed to overseas airfields. The Triton is typically forward-deployed to Guam and is flown by operators in a windowless

room in Jacksonville, Florida. Rarely are these two air platforms even in the same airspace.

In a similar fashion, while both are deployed together on the two variants of the littoral combat ship, the MH-60S Knighthawk aircraft and the MQ-8C Fire Scout are not yet used in a symbiotic relationship. The MH-60S Knighthawk flies its missions independently, while operators (pilots or other designated personnel) launch, operate, and recover the MQ-8C Fire Scout. Manned-unmanned teaming does not yet occur.

We believe that the technology exists to enable both these unmanned aerial systems (UAS) platforms to become more autonomous and become loyal wingmen to the P-8A Poseidon and MH-60S Knighthawk.

The idea of making our unmanned aerial systems smarter has gained currency not only within DoD but also in the open media. As an article in the *National Interest*, "The Strategic Problem of Persistent Surveillance," describes: "Newer kinds of data analysis and transmission, enabled by advanced command and control and advanced artificial-intelligence-empowered algorithms, might make platforms like the MQ-4C Triton as capable in some respects as the much larger, less stealthy and more vulnerable manned P-8A Poseidon."[12]

Focusing on the current—and potential future—capabilities of the MQ-4C Triton, its primary concept of operations is to serve as an ISR asset. That said, the Triton is not yet equipped with AI-enabled capabilities and is being operated as a remotely piloted vehicle (RPV). Today, a Triton operator receives streaming video of what the MQ-4C sees. But this requires the operator to stare at this video for hours on end (the endurance of the Triton is thirty hours), seeing mainly empty ocean space.

The U.S. Navy has made a commitment to procuring the Triton as currently configured and used as an RPV. Given the fact that a carrier strike group represents the "unit of measure" for the U.S. Navy, the best way to assess what a Triton does—and more importantly has the potential to do—is how it would support a carrier strike group. A strike group commander has many assets that can look ahead of the force to assess the tactical situation. A Triton could be used to perform this scouting mission.[13]

Using big data, artificial intelligence, and machine learning, the MQ-4C can be trained to send only video of each ship it encounters, thereby greatly compressing the human workload. Taken to the next level, the Triton could do onboard analysis of each contact to flag it for possible interest. For example, if a vessel is operating in a shipping lane, has filed a journey plan with maritime authorities, and is providing an automatic identification system (AIS) signal, it is likely worthy of only passing attention by the operator, and the Triton will flag it accordingly. If, however, it does not meet these criteria (for example, the vessel makes an abrupt course change that takes it outside shipping channels or has no AIS signal), the operator would be alerted. As this technology continues to evolve, a Triton could ultimately be equipped with classification algorithms that have the potential to lead to automatic target recognition.

Once the Triton has processed this information, big data, artificial intelligence, and machine learning can help determine how to communicate with the flagship. In today's contested electronic warfare environment, different communications paths have varying levels of vulnerability. Prior to Triton's launch, the commander can determine the acceptable level of risk of communications intercept, as well as the danger of giving away the presence of the strike group.

Armed with this commander's intent, and using big data, artificial intelligence, and machine learning, the Triton can assess the electronic environment, select from multiple communications paths, and determine which path offers the least vulnerability to intercept. If the Triton determines that this vulnerability is too high, it can fly back toward the flagship and communicate via line-of-sight ultra-high frequency. Given the size and growth potential of the Triton, it could even carry a smaller UAS and launch it back toward the force to deliver this surveillance information.

Aboard the flagship, the commander must make sense of the data his sensors have collected and then make a number of time-critical decisions. Should he continue forward, wait, or retreat? Should he scout directly ahead or in a different direction? Should he call on other forces, or are his organic assets sufficient to successfully complete the mission without undue risk to his forces? This is where big data, artificial intelligence, and machine learning can contribute to helping the commander make critical decisions by processing the data it collects onboard the Triton rather than sending unprocessed terabytes of raw data down the link.

HUMAN-MACHINE TEAMING: TRITON AS LOYAL WINGMAN

Once the MQ-4C Triton has been upgraded in the manner suggested above, it is worth going back to the original concept of operations for this UAS—to be the unmanned teammate of the P-8A Poseidon. Many scenarios could be used to examine how these two capable platforms could operate in tandem, but an ISR mission in the Western Pacific is one example that will likely resonate in an era of great power competition.

Imagine that both platforms are based at Naval Air Facility Atsugi, Japan, that their operators have trained together extensively, and that they are given a mission to surveil an area in the Sea of Japan and look for suspicious vessels. The P-8A mission commander has overall control of the operation, and the Triton is operating with some degree of autonomy rather than as an RPV. Once it is launched, it responds to direction from the P-8A in much the same way as your smart phone responds to your voice questions or commands. Here is what the dialogue might sound like:

P-8: "We're heading west; stay on my wing for now."

Triton: "Roger that. Fuel state 17+15, Angels [altitude] 2.5."

P-8 (45 minutes later): "Vector WNW and search for ships."

Triton: "Roger. Any vessels at all, or just larger ships?"

P-8: "Just larger ships."

Triton (Just over one hour later): "I see a ship; it's a large one."

P-8: "Send me the video."

Triton: "WILCO."

P-8: "Got it. Is it in a normal shipping channel?"

Triton: "Wait. . . . No."

P-8: "Query its AIS."

Triton: "It is not sending an AIS signal."

P-8: "That's worrisome. Anchor over its position."

Triton: "WILCO. Elevating to Angels 8.0."

Triton (10 minutes later): "There is another ship; it appears to be closing our guy."

P-8: "Query its AIS."

Triton: "It's not sending an AIS signal either."

P-8: "Stay anchored. Keep me posted. I'm 300 miles away, but closing your posit."

Triton (20 minutes later): "The ships are together with hoses strung between them. I'm sending you video."

The dialogue continues, and it might seem apparent that the Triton has located a Chinese ship flouting an international embargo and illegally transferring oil to a North Korean vessel. This has been—and will likely continue to be—an important ISR mission for manned and unmanned aircraft and one that can be enhanced when the Triton operates as a loyal wingman to the Poseidon.

It is worth pointing out what a loyal—and smart—wingman the Triton can be. Note that when the P-8A mission commander directs the Triton to stay in his wing, the Triton volunteers its fuel state and altitude, figuring, correctly, that this information is of value to the mission commander. Later, when the Triton is told to anchor over the suspicious ship, it decides to elevate to a higher altitude to decrease the chances that it will be seen. Finally, when it detects activity it has been programmed to identify as highly suspicious—two ships with refueling hoses extended between them—it tells the P-8A crew about it.

ADDING AI TO CURRENT SYSTEMS

This vision for the Triton would involve some basic coding—not an exquisite and expensive solution, but rather plucking a low-hanging fruit. Development becomes a question of will.

This is the essence of manned-unmanned teaming as envisioned in the third offset strategy and something that can, in this Navy example, be extrapolated to a naval air force predicted to be approximately 40 percent unmanned in less than fifteen years.[14] The other services have equally ambitious plans for unmanned aerial systems.

Thus far, we have used aviation examples of manned-unmanned teaming because military unmanned aerial systems have proliferated most widely and are already in use in all the U.S. military services. The U.S. Navy operates the MQ-25 Stingray carrier-based unmanned aircraft in addition to the Triton and Fire Scout.

This is not to imply that this is the only area where AI-enabled weapons systems can be developed and leveraged in a manned-unmanned teaming taxonomy. The undersea domain also represents an area where MUMT can provide tremendous benefit by enabling U.S. Navy submarines to operate with unmanned underwater vehicles.

In their *New York Times* bestselling book, *Blind Man's Bluff*, Sherry Sontag, Christopher Drew, and Annette Lawrence Drew chronicled U.S. Navy submarine operations during the Cold War, especially the use of USS *Parche*, USS *Halibut*, and USS *Jimmy Carter* to tap Soviet undersea communications cables inside the Soviet Union's territorial waters.[15]

These missions—deemed essential at the height of the Cold War—were extremely hazardous; witness the medals for bravery awarded to the commanders of these submarines and their crews. When these missions were conducted decades ago, UUV technology was nascent at best. Today, the U.S. Navy is investing heavily in these unmanned underwater vehicles.

It is easy to see how AI-enabled UUVs could be teamed with today's U.S. Navy submarines to conduct these—and other—ISR missions. The use of AI to enable the UUV to operate in fully autonomous mode is key, because the physics of the underwater medium does not support constant communications between the submarine and the UUV if they are not in reasonably close proximity.

Our backgrounds commanding U.S. Navy surface combatants make us well aware of the potential for manned-unmanned teaming between surface ships and unmanned surface vehicles, and the U.S. Navy is leaning into a substantial investment in unmanned surface vehicles. In 2022 then-Chief of Naval Operations Adm. Michael Gilday emphasized the Navy's goal to reach 500 ships by adding approximately 150 unmanned surface vehicles to the Navy's inventory. This represents a strong commitment to developing large, medium, and small unmanned surface vessels.[16]

Previous speeches and interviews alluding to the number of unmanned surface vehicles the Navy intends to field culminated in the issuance of *NAVPLAN 2022* and *Force Design 2045*, which both call for a "hybrid fleet" comprised of 373 manned ships and 150 large unmanned surface and subsurface platforms.[17] These official U.S. Navy documents provide the clearest indication yet of the Navy's plans for a future fleet populated by large numbers of unmanned surface vehicles. Specially regarding unmanned surface vehicles, *Force Design 2045* notes the plans: "Unmanned surface and subsurface platforms to increase the fleet's capacity for distribution; expand our intelligence, surveillance, and reconnaissance advantage; add depth to our missile magazines; supplement logistics; and enhance fleet survivability. This transition will rebalance the fleet away from exquisite, manpower intensive platforms toward smaller, less-expensive, yet lethal ones."[18]

While the Navy has signaled a commitment to procure large, medium, and small unmanned surface vehicles (USVs), the current state of development, while fielding them in a number of exercises, experiments, and demonstrations, has not yet explored their integration with surface ships and even nascent forms of manned-unmanned teaming. This is likely due to the fact that USV development has lagged behind unmanned air and ground systems and is now catching up.

THE QUESTION OF TRUST

As the services move forward on increasing the autonomy of their unmanned air, surface, underwater, and ground unmanned vehicles and begin efforts to leverage what each asset brings to the fight and how they can be used together as a synergistic team, one issue that must be addressed is the degree of trust operators will put in unmanned systems.

We have addressed this in the context of concerns operators might have when a black box, whose workings are opaque to the operator, is inserted into military platforms, systems, sensors, or weapons. These concerns are valid, and they are beginning to be addressed by military research organizations such as the Naval Postgraduate School (NPS). This research seeks ways to engender the degree of trust in unmanned systems that will give the operators of their manned counterparts enough confidence to employ these systems at their full potential. As one defense analyst put it, "The key to building that trust might be allowing operators to help train the AI-powered machines that serve beside them, as opposed to just handing a Soldier, Sailor, Marine, or Airman a robot and sending the pair off to war together. Teaching and developing AI agents within a simulated environment by the end user indicate there is the potential for better trust in the AI agent by the end-user when placed as a teammate within a human-machine team."[19]

NPS researchers are also exploring many fundamentals of autonomous systems, especially in the trust and confidence arena. The NPS team created a virtual environment that enabled Marines to train their robots to help build trust in these unmanned teammates. The results were dramatic. Marines who were involved in the development and integration process from the start trusted the unmanned capability to a greater extent when using them during simulated operations. Conversely, those Marines who were merely given a robot to take into the operational environment tended to be risk-adverse and not use the unmanned asset.[20]

That the importance of this trust-building as an essential building block of advancing manned-unmanned teaming goes beyond what some might call "academic exercises" is not lost on DoD senior leaders. Then-Commandant of the Marine Corps General David Berger put the issue of trust this way:

> In the same way that a squad leader has to trust his or her Marines, the squad leader is going to have to learn to trust the machine. In some instances today, I would offer we don't trust the machine. We have programs right now, capabilities right now that allow for fully automatic processing of sensor-to-shooter targeting, but we don't trust the data.
>
> And we still ensure that there's human intervention at every step in the process. And, of course, with each intervention by humans we're adding more time, more opportunities for mistakes to happen, time we're not going to have when an adversary's targeting our network.[21]

Fielding autonomous systems that the human in the MUMT equation can themselves program appears the best method to generate trust that the machine will operate autonomously in precisely the way that is desired. This does not remove the human from "control" of the fully autonomous weapon; rather, this control must be baked in carefully with full operator oversight.

Trust between humans is normally binary; most people view others as either trustworthy or not trustworthy, with no middle ground. With machines, trust is more nuanced. As the National Security Commission on Artificial Intelligence *Final Report* puts it, "Ultimately, those charged with using AI tools need to formulate an educated answer to this question: In the given circumstances, how much confidence in the machine is enough confidence?"[22]

Work is ongoing to help operators develop trust in AI-enabled unmanned systems in whatever mode they operate, but no degree of trust can absolve human operators from their ultimate responsibility—to borrow a medical term, "first do no harm." Said another way, whether in, on, or even off the loop, human operators are always the primary member of the team, responsible for the actions that their unmanned vehicle takes. Machines—even intelligent autonomous ones—cannot be held accountable; only humans can. In the words of Secretary Work, "The human is the ultimate circuit breaker."[23]

The human operator has three distinct roles when working with machines: essential operator, moral agent, and failsafe.[24] In our discussion of manned-unmanned teaming, we focused primarily on the relationship between a human (or humans, in the case of an aircrew in an aircraft such as the P-8A Poseidon) and the unmanned AI-enabled machine. But there is one area in which big data, artificial intelligence, and machine learning might make an even more important contribution to the warfighter. Available evidence suggests that helping operators make better decisions, faster, with fewer people and fewer mistakes, especially under stress in high-tempo operations, offers the potential to change the character of war and afford the side that employs these technologies in this fashion a profound warfighting advantage. That is the subject of the next chapter.

6

DECISION-MAKING

Can AI Do It Better and Faster?

The most valuable contribution of AI to U.S. defense will be how it helps human beings to make better, faster, and more precise decisions, especially during high-consequence operations.

LT. GEN. JOHN "JACK" SHANAHAN
founding director, Joint Artificial Intelligence Center[1]

[The Defense Department has set] forth a pathway to enable our leaders and warfighters to orient, decide, and act faster than our competitors. Doing so requires providing operational commanders with data-driven technologies, including artificial intelligence, machine learning, and automation. . . . We must adopt interoperable AI-enabled sensor fusion, asset tasking, mission autonomy, and real-time decision advantage planning tools.

DEPUTY SECRETARY OF DEFENSE MEMO[2]

IN AN AIR COMBAT TRAINING scene from the original *Top Gun* movie, Lt. Pete "Maverick" Mitchell has put Top Gun's leader, Cdr. Mike "Viper" Metcalf, in his gun sights and has a decision to make.

Maverick had previously lost his radar intercept officer in a tragic accident, and although he has been cleared to fly again, he is plagued by an uncertainty that he has not felt before. Maverick's new radar intercept officer tells him, "Take the shot, take the shot." But nothing happens. Top Gun's senior instructor pilot is flying in trail and also tries to coax Maverick through his hesitation, saying, "Take the shot, kid, take the shot." But Maverick is frozen for too long, and his target escapes. What has happened?

In chapter four we introduced you to the OODA loop—observe, orient, decide, act—developed by U.S. Air Force fighter pilot Col. John Boyd. During the Korean War, warfare changed in ways that dramatically compressed the decision cycle. Russian MiG-15s and American F-86 Sabres fought heated battles for mastery of the air. Seeking a way to mitigate U.S. combat losses, Boyd conceptualized the OODA loop.[3] The construct was originally a theory of achieving success developed out of Boyd's energy-maneuverability theory and his observations on air-to-air combat. Later it was applied to other decision-making in crises. It also directly influenced the design of the Air Force F-16 Fighting Falcon aircraft. Harry Hillaker, chief designer of the F-16, said of the OODA theory, "Time is the dominant parameter. The pilot who goes through the OODA cycle in the shortest time prevails because his opponent is caught responding to situations that have already changed."[4]

The scene from *Top Gun* can help us understand how, under conditions of stress, operators might find it daunting to complete the OODA loop. Flying his analog F-14 Tomcat, Maverick is stuck in the orient and decide steps of the loop. He has observed the tactical situation and has all the data he needs to collect. He must act, but he can't. He needs help to orient himself to the tactical situation and then quickly decide what actions to take in the stress of simulated combat so that he can take the shot and win the tactical engagement.

THE OODA LOOP GETS FASTER

Military history is replete with examples of naval commanders who made the better decisions and were victorious, even when their opponent had a geographic or material advantage. In the early years of the U.S. Navy, the service struggled in multiple conflicts.[5] Dwarfed by the immense British

Royal Navy, the survival of the Navy—and the nation—was tenuous in the years between 1775 and 1815. Deployed to the Mediterranean, small U.S. Navy task forces—wooden ships under sail—faced the Barbary states while over 5,000 nautical miles from their homeports. In recalling this history, it is essential not to miss the importance of decision-making in the Navy's victories as well as in its defeats. Choices made ranging from where to build these ships to choosing the areas where they would operate to which battles they would fight and which they would avoid and a host of others were—in the main—the right decisions that enabled the nation to survive those perilous decades.[6]

While the U.S. Navy's platforms and weapons today bear no resemblance to those of the Navy of 1812, today's captains must still make the kind of life-or-death decisions their forebearers made. What is vastly different is the speed of modern decision-making. While the captains of ships such as USS *Constitution*, USS *Constellation*, and other early frigates often had hours or even days to make critical choices, today's captains must make decisions in minutes or even seconds.[7] Better decisions have won naval battles and changed history, but the OODA loop of the past went at a snail's pace compared to the speed of warfare today.

The U.S. military has a long history of preparing commanders to make effective decisions. These include a lengthy apprenticeship before assuming command, intensive training, and many other means that have stood the test of time. However, the speed of warfare today strongly suggests that the tactics, techniques, and procedures honed over the past quarter-century will no longer enable commanders to make effective decisions. Here is where pressure to adopt AI as a decision aid that speeds the OODA loop is prevalent.

INSUFFICIENT INFORMATION AND THE SPEED OF DECISION

Air-to-air combat is arguably a highly stressful military operation. But increasingly, military leaders have become more aware that stress—and especially the inability to process information—has caused military operators across a wide spectrum to have their own OODA loops unravel and thus to make suboptimal decisions.

The challenge of making crucial military decisions under stress had found its way into popular culture long before *Top Gun* in the 1965 movie

The Bedford Incident. Loosely based on a number of Cold War incidents between U.S. Navy ships and Soviet submarines, the plot revolves around the cat-and-mouse game between a U.S. destroyer, USS *Bedford* (DLG 113), and a Soviet submarine.

The *Bedford*'s crew becomes increasingly fatigued by the days-long search for the submarine. As the urgency to find the Soviet adversary intensifies, *Bedford*'s captain ignores warnings that his crew is wilting under the pressure and ratchets up his demands, even running over the diesel submarine's snorkel. When someone asks the captain if he will take the first shot against his adversary, he replies that he will not, but "if he fires one, I'll fire one." A tired ensign mistakes his captain's remarks as a command to "fire one" and fires an antisubmarine rocket that destroys the submarine, but not before it launches a nuclear-armed torpedo that annihilates the ship.[8]

Although fictional, *The Bedford Incident* was eerily prescient of a real-world event fifty-five years later—the January 2020 Iran Revolutionary Guard Corps shootdown of a Ukrainian jetliner. An investigation of the event will take years, but what is known today is that in the stress of combat, where Iran had just fired a barrage of ballistic missiles at U.S. military forces, the country was on high alert for an American counterattack.

Somewhere in the Iranian intelligence or military chain of command, a warning of incoming cruise missiles was issued. The officer in charge of an antiair missile battery tried to reach his higher echelon command center for authorization to shoot. Tragically, he could not get through, and armed with incomplete information, he fired two antiaircraft missiles; 176 people died.[9]

These incidents—one fictional and one real—had one thing in common: Humans were forced to make crucial decisions with insufficient or erroneous information. In the case of *The Bedford Incident*, the issue was the air gap between humans a few feet apart. In the case of the Ukrainian aircraft shootdown, it was the inability to communicate, as well as the incorrectly perceived threat.

It would be easy to dismiss incidents such as these as either implausible fiction or poor decision-making by a military inferior to that of the United States, but doing so would be a tragic mistake. There are compelling examples of U.S. military personnel making bad decisions that resulted in loss of life. This breakdown in decision-making has dogged the American military for more than four decades:

- In May 1987 USS *Stark* (FFG 31) was on patrol near the Iran-Iraq war exclusion boundary. Incorrectly believing that neither of the belligerents would target a U.S. warship, the captain was not initially alarmed when *Stark* attempted to communicate with an incoming aircraft. The Iraqi Mirage jet fired two Exocet missiles, killing thirty-seven Americans and wounding almost two dozen others.

- In July 1988, with memories of the captain of USS *Stark* failing to take action to protect his ship, with the Iran-Iraq war still raging, and while his ship was being hounded by Iranian gunboats, the captain of USS *Vincennes* (CG 49) mistakenly believed that an approaching aircraft was closing and descending on an attack profile. He fired an SM-2ER missile and shot down Iran Air Flight 655, killing all 290 people on board.

- In April 1994 two U.S. Air Force F-15 Strike Eagles shot down two U.S. Army UH-60 Blackhawk helicopters over Iraq, believing that they were Iraqi Mi-24 Hind helicopters, killing all twenty-six military and civilians aboard. Miscommunication between the Air Force airborne warning and control systems control aircraft and the Strike Eagles, as well as failures of automated identification friend or foe systems, were the proximate causes of this tragedy.

- In February 2001, ten miles south of the island of Oahu, in a demonstration for VIP civilian visitors, the nuclear submarine USS *Greenville* (SSN 772) performed an emergency ballast-blow maneuver and surfaced under the Japanese fishing vessel *Ehime Maru*. Nine of the thirty-five people on board were killed.

- In 2003 U.S. Army Patriot batteries mistakenly shot down a Royal Air Force Tornado GR4 and a U.S. Navy F/A-18C Hornet within a week and a half, killing three aviators. While the batteries were being operated in automated mode, investigators determined that there should have been oversight by a human on the loop.

- In June 2017 USS *Fitzgerald* (DDG 62) collided with the container ship MV *ACX Crystal*. Seven of her crew were killed, and several others were injured. Just three months later, USS *John S. McCain* (DDG 56) collided with the Liberian-flagged tanker *Alnic MC*. Ten of her crew died as a result of the crash.

While there were multiple reasons behind all of these tragic accidents, most notably the fatal collisions involving USS *Fitzgerald* and USS *John S. McCain*, in every case, data clearly was available that—properly used—might have broken what safety experts call the "accident chain" and prevented tragedy.[10]

What is striking in all these accidents across several decades is that in every case, tragedy ensued because data was not properly curated, analyzed, and displayed to the decision-maker in a sufficiently timely fashion to make the right decision. This is not to say that better technology could have averted disaster in each case but simply that the technology exists today to provide decision-makers with better tools to make the right decision. Furthermore, in today's shadowy warfare against terrorists, the U.S. military is investigating incidents where drone strikes unintentionally killed civilians, such as the strike that killed ten civilians in Kabul, Afghanistan, in 2021.[11]

THE CHALLENGE IN APPLYING AI TO MILITARY DECISION-MAKING

It is important to note that the military people who made these suboptimal decisions were doing the best job they could with the tools at hand. What occurred was that the speed of warfare exceeded the ability of the human brain to make the right decision.[12] As one scientist put it, "The principal feature of information age warfare—the ability to gather and store communication data—has begun to exceed human processing capabilities."[13]

As Dr. Alexander Kott, chief scientist at the U.S. Army Research Laboratory, explained at a command and control conference, "The human cognitive bandwidth will emerge as the most severe constraint on the battlefield."[14] Another scientist, Dr. Eric Haseltine, made this point in another way, noting, "AI is exploding, but humans have leveled off. The highest promise of AI is bridging this gap."[15] A U.S. Air Force report stated the challenge this way: "Although humans today remain more capable than machines for many tasks, natural human capacities are becoming increasingly mismatched to the enormous data volumes, processing capabilities, and decision speeds that technologies offer or demand. Closer human-machine coupling and augmentation of human performance will become possible and essential."[16] For these reasons and others, the U.S. military needs big data, artificial intelligence, and machine learning to give its warfighters the edge in combat when making decisions, especially under stress.[17]

While commanders in centuries past suffered from too little data, in the last several decades, the quantity of data available to those in the midst of battle has increased dramatically. Indeed, the U.S. military has demonstrated that it can collect a sea of data, but this deluge has not enhanced warfighting effectiveness. This challenge should come as no surprise to anyone using technology today. Any smart phone user knows that having access to sufficient data is rarely an issue. What is sometimes overwhelming is sorting through vast amounts of data and trying to tease out only what is essential at the moment.

From a warfighting perspective, this means having systems that present a decision-maker with only that well-curated information that helps him or her make better decisions, often in the stress of combat.[18] In the case of the U.S. Navy, leaders have recognized that much work needs to be done to assist humans by turning data into useful information that can inform effective decision-making.

THE NAVAL APPROACH TO THE CHALLENGE

At the 2017 Current Strategy Forum, the U.S. Navy's annual conference to discuss and assess the service's contributions to national and international security, Chief of Naval Operations (CNO) Adm. John Richardson, a nuclear submariner—not a fighter pilot—took the audience back to an aviation tactic invented more than seven decades ago.[19]

The CNO turned the clock back to the 1950s to Col. John Boyd and the OODA loop, using it as a way of discussing the kinds of new technologies the U.S. Navy is fielding.[20] He noted that the Navy had already invested heavily in the observe and act parts of Boyd's taxonomy. He pointed out that until the advent of emerging technologies such as big data, machine learning, and artificial intelligence, the Navy could not do much about the orient and decide aspects of the OODA loop but that today, the service can.[21]

This is precisely why the CNO used Boyd's OODA loop in his remarks. He explained that today's naval warfighters have an enormous—even over-whelming—amount of data to deal with. They need big data, artificial intelligence, and machine learning to curate this data to present only that information that helps decision-makers and those pulling the trigger make better decisions faster. It is easy to see that this effort to turn data into tac-tically useful information is important to all aspects of warfighting, not just fighter tactics.

The U.S. Navy has conducted decades-long efforts to leverage tech-nology to help warfighters make better decisions faster with fewer people and fewer mistakes in stressful situations. In the 1980s the Office of Naval Research initiated a program to study how warfighters could make bet-ter decisions in high-stress situations.[22] Dubbed tactical decision-making under stress (TADMUS), this initiative used cognitive science to break new ground in understanding how decision-makers work through their options.[23] The goal of this years-long effort was to develop a prototype decision support system to enhance Navy tactical decision-making. This led to several prototypes: Multi-Modal Watch Station (a display system that integrated multiple sensors on a single screen and provided operators with a superior tactical picture than extant systems), Knowledge Wall (a large vertical display to be used in command centers to enable decision-makers to evaluate multiple operational events in real time), and others designed by scientists and engineers at Naval Information Warfare Center Pacific that were beta-tested and that showed promising results in helping decision-makers achieve improved decisions.[24]

TADMUS—along with similar Navy programs—was good as far as it went. But as Admiral Richardson pointed out, until recently, the technol-ogy to take enhanced decision-making to the next level did not exist. Today, it does, and leveraging what big data, artificial intelligence, and machine learning can provide to warfighters can lead to the next breakthrough in naval warfare, especially in the area of decision-making.[25] Organizations such as Naval Information Warfare Center Pacific, along with partners through the Navy R&D community, industry, and academia, are leading efforts to ensure that U.S. warfighters are equipped to make better decisions, faster, with fewer people and fewer mistakes.

The Navy's budget director, Rear Adm. Dietrich Kuhlmann, put the question of how the Navy can best use big data, artificial intelligence, and machine learning this way: "How do we leverage AI, not to produce autonomous platforms that kill people, but to give commanders the edge in combat?"[26] Indeed, the essence of what the U.S. Navy—and by extension, the U.S. military—wants to do with big data, machine learning, and artificial intelligence is not to launch Terminator-like unmanned systems downrange against our adversaries with no human oversight, but rather to help operators make faster, more informed decisions.

Military operators will always be in the loop and will be assisted by big data, machine learning, and artificial intelligence. What the military wants to achieve with these cutting-edge technologies—whether applied to unmanned systems or to other aspects of warfighting—is to get inside the adversary's OODA loop. James Geurts, then-assistant secretary of the Navy for research, development, and acquisition, put it this way: "If a force can harness AI to allow decision-makers to make decisions faster than the adversary, it will win every time."[27] A few years later, then-CNO Adm. Michael Gilday emphasized the importance of leveraging new technologies to enhanced decision-making when he noted, "The real power of this AI is to put us in a position where we can actually decide and act as a fleet faster than the opponent."[28]

Other naval leaders have reinforced these themes. Deputy CNO for information warfare and intelligence Vice Adm. Jeffrey Trussler put the importance of better decision-making this way: "It's not about accumulating a lot of great information. If you don't act on it in an appropriate amount of time, that decision advantage you have may just go away. It requires the speed of decision."[29] The deputy CNO for plans and strategy, Vice Adm. Phillip Sawyer, built on this theme, saying, "We know how to dynamically maneuver our forces. What we [are] working on now is how to do this with speed, such that we have decision superiority."[30]

As one indication of how rapidly the Navy intends to move forward with enhanced decision-making, the CNO's annual planning guidance added "decision advantage" to its list of "Force Design Imperatives" and described the goal of this new focus: "Naval forces will out-sense, out-decide, and out-fight any adversary by accelerating our decision cycles with secure, survivable, and cyber-resilient networks, accurate data, and artificial intelligence. Connecting sensors, weapons, and decision-makers across all domains enables naval forces to mass firepower and influence without massing forces."[31]

Lt. Gen. Michael Groen, then-director of DoD's Joint Artificial Intelligence Center, put the emphasis on how big data, artificial intelligence, and machine learning can enhance decision-making this way: "When I think about artificial intelligence applications, I'm thinking beyond just the use case of near-instantaneous fires upon the detection of a target. There is a broad range of decision-making that has to occur across the joint force that can be enabled by AI."[32]

DEVELOPING DECISION SUPPORT SYSTEMS

These statements make clear that if U.S. civilian and military leaders at the highest echelons have learned anything over the past years, it is that, unaided, humans drowning in a sea of data cannot make the most effective decisions, especially in the stress of combat.[33] Indeed, with the widespread DoD adoption of smart devices interconnected within the Internet of Battlefield Things, DoD has exponentially increased its data collection capabilities. The resulting large volumes of unsorted and unfiltered data are too time-consuming and expensive for humans to process.[34]

To this end, the U.S. military has signaled a desire to move forward to embrace big data, artificial intelligence, and machine learning to help curate massive amounts of data and present only information that is useful in the heat of battle to enable commanders to out-think their adversaries.[35] At the time of this writing, the Office of Naval Research is moving forward with a command decision-making program designed to advance cognitive theory and computational modeling to create decision support tools for warfighters that are mission- and task-sensitive and therefore proactive in providing relevant information at appropriate times.[36]

Outside experts have echoed what DoD officials have stressed regarding the importance of leveraging these technologies to enhance decision-making. The Center for Strategic and Budgetary Assessments monograph, *Mosaic Warfare: Exploiting Artificial Intelligence and Autonomous Systems to Implement Decision-Centric Warfare*, notes,

> The design of U.S. military units reflects an attrition-centric view of warfare in which the goal is achieving victory by destroying enough of the enemy that it can no longer fight. To better address the operational challenges presented by great power competitors, this study proposes that DoD embrace a new theory of victory and operational concepts that focus on making faster and better decisions than adversaries, rather than attrition.
>
> Instead of destroying an adversary's forces until it can no longer fight or succeed, a decision-centric approach to warfare would impose multiple dilemmas on an enemy to prevent it from achieving its objectives. Decision-centric warfare is intended to enable faster and more effective decisions by U.S. commanders while also degrading the quality and speed of adversary decision-making.[37]

This brings us full circle to the idea of manned-unmanned teaming and how to leverage the best qualities of the human and the machine when making decisions in high-stress situations. Tom Dieterrich, president of the Association for the Advancement of Artificial Intelligence, described the balance: "The humans should be taking the actions and the AI's job should be to give the human the right information that they need to make the right decisions. The human is in the loop or very intimately involved. The whole goal is to get inside your opponent's OODA loop. You want to make your decisions faster than they can."[38]

Said another way, the U.S. military can use big data, artificial intelligence, and machine learning to speed up decision-making so that its forces can operate at a tempo that overwhelms opponents. This speed of decision-making can lead to adversaries not knowing what U.S. and allied forces will do next, inducing a "fog of war" that causes them to make suboptimal decisions.

The U.S. military has had tactical decision aids for decades. These have helped the operator determine where to place sonobuoys in an antisubmarine warfare prosecution, where to deploy tanks against an adversary armored force, and where to vector combat air patrol aircraft to intercept enemy aircraft. These models are useful as far as they go, but they are deterministic and do not begin to leverage what artificial intelligence and machine learning can bring to the table.

To be clear, decision-makers are loath to have machines dictate a point solution ("do this and you will be victorious"). Rather, they want several courses of action (COAs) to choose from. This is not new. U.S. military officers have been schooled for decades to do just this. However, development of these COAs has been done manually with paper and pencil up until the present, and this is not a viable way ahead in twenty-first-century warfare.

SPEEDING UP THE RAPID RESPONSE PLANNING PROCESS

Our experiences as former commanding officers of amphibious warfare ships provided us with a window on one of these COA development processes. The U.S. Marine Corps used the Rapid Response Planning Process (R2P2) taxonomy to develop COAs. We participated in many of these processes. R2P2 is a time-constrained, six-step process that mirrors the Marine Corps planning process: Upon receipt of a warning, alert, or execute order, a crisis action team is assembled to commence initial staff orientation, frame the problem, determine information requirements, and identify the commander's guidance for COA development.[39]

In twentieth-century warfare, the R2P2 taxonomy (and similar ones used by all the U.S. military services) was adequate for the task at hand. Today, they are not, and that is why big data, artificial intelligence, and machine learning must be employed. The need for intelligent systems to assist in COA development was demonstrated in one U.S. Navy laboratory decades ago in a video entitled "Eye of the Storm."

Produced to provide a window on how the same scientists and engineers who had worked with the former commanding officer of USS *Vincennes* in the wake of the Iranian Airbus shootdown, this video centered on U.S. and allied forces preparing to invade an unnamed Middle Eastern nation. The commander consulted a decision support machine and was provided with three courses of action. While the machine recommended one COA and gave the reasons behind the recommendation, it did so "gently," not intimating that the recommended action amounted to a point solution.

Hundreds of senior DoD and Navy officials viewed this movie and declared that what it depicted was precisely the kind of technology breakthrough that they wanted. A quarter-century ago, the technology to build a real decision support machine envisioned in that futuristic movie simply did not exist. Today, it does.

Subsequent iterations of videos made by this same Navy laboratory had decision support entities that provided even more well-nuanced suggestions to the commander (specifically, a carrier strike group commander and her staff), even listening in to staff conversations to make unsolicited suggestions regarding various COAs to select and providing pros and cons for each one.

These videos were made not in some wild-eyed aspirational context but rather with the confidence that scientists and engineers at this laboratory (and others) could write the code to field such systems in the near term. That said, even in the most recent videos where the decision support entity is treated not as a machine, but as a member of the staff, this is "narrow AI" used to perform a specific task of aiding decision-making in discrete situations and not artificial general intelligence. This latter term is also referred to as strong or full AI, or as the ability of a machine to perform general intelligent action. Academic sources reserve strong AI to refer to machines capable of experiencing consciousness.

Thus far, we have focused on leveraging what big data, artificial intelligence, and machine learning can do to make the machine a better partner in decision-making. However, in the case of a human operator using an unmanned system, the relationship between the operator and the machine is the most important attribute that can enhance effective decision-making.

Focusing solely on making the machine more brilliant in support of enhanced decision-making is only one side of the equation. The humans must, to use a sports metaphor, "bring their A-game." There is emergent work in this area that we believe has the potential to help humans become better decision-makers.

BUILDING BETTER HUMAN BRAINS

An article in the *Wall Street Journal* entitled "To Keep Up with AI, We'll Need High-Tech Brains" described the need to enhance the processing and learning capabilities of the human brain in order to keep up with today's technologies. The article described how neuroscientists implanted an array of electrodes in the region of a volunteer's left motor cortex and used a technique called transcranial direct current stimulation to jolt the subject's brain in an attempt to enhance cognitive capabilities.[40]

While it is unlikely that today's (or tomorrow's) military personnel will line up to volunteer for transcranial direct current stimulation, the U.S. military is leaning forward to explore how to enhance the human side of decision support. One such effort sponsored by the joint staff through the Strategic Multilayer Assessment, a series of analytical projects funded by the special activities and operations directorate, explored this idea via conferences such as "The Mind-Tech Nexus: How Will Minds Plus Technology Win Future Wars?"[41] The conference panel noted that China has launched the "China Brain Project," which is focused on the dynamic interaction of human cognitive capabilities and state-of-the-art technology. China's focus was on exploring ways and means to augment human performance, citing a DARPA project that is using applied neuroscience to examine ways to improve human cognition and enhance brain-computer interfaces.

Similar work is being done under the auspices of monitoring the physiology of the human at war to understand what technologies such as big data, artificial intelligence, and machine learning mean for a warfighter who increasingly perceives, acts, communicates, works with, and is monitored by increasingly sophisticated digitized systems, all with an eye to gaining a decision advantage.

This focus on understanding and, where possible, improving the human side of achieving a decision advantage is a new frontier, and there will be much more to be said on this subject. For now, it is enough to understand that key questions are being asked, among them: In a conflict, what is the warfighter looking at, and for how long? Which sounds do their brainwaves tell us that they are paying attention to? Artificial intelligence can monitor a warrior's physiology to sense when they are losing the ability to make effective decisions.[42] This work is still emerging, and as the U.S. military races ahead to field better technology to enhance decision-making, there is a general recognition that enhancing the warfighter's ability to fully leverage it is an area worthy of further study and investment.

Recent analysis suggests that while prediction and presentation of various COAs are being enhanced by advances in AI, human judgment will become even more critical.[43] This assessment echoes what two computer scientists at the Naval Postgraduate School noted several years ago: "The naval future is not just one of humans or machines; it will feature the blending of humans and machines. The only viable path is one in which humans and machines work together, combining the speed of machines with the wisdom of humans."[44]

CREATING COUP D'OEIL

Thus far we have focused on the "display" level of a warfighting scenario when the decision-maker, aided by an AI-enabled machine, is making a time-critical decision in the stress of combat. For the U.S. Navy, this could occur aboard an individual ship, in the tactical flag coordination center aboard an aircraft carrier (the command center where the carrier strike group commander coordinates the efforts of the entire strike group), in a maritime operations center at a numbered fleet headquarters (where the three-star fleet commander oversees the actions of the naval ships, submarines, and aircraft in his or her geographic area of operations), or at other levels of command.

Clearly, there are other actions that can be taken at various stages of the OODA loop to enhance decision-making. That said, we believe that this display level is the area where the nexus of technology—both AI-enabled decision support systems and humans with enhanced cognitive assistance—can achieve the greatest improvement.

In eighteenth- and nineteenth-century warfare, writers used the French term coup d'oeil to describe the ability of great military commanders to perceive at a glance the overall tactical situation in a battle and make an instant decision. Coup d'oeil literally means the "stroke of the eye." We could also call it a "single glimpse." It was a quality of the most successful tacticians of that era, such as Napoleon Bonaparte and Frederick the Great of Prussia. The great nineteenth-century Prussian philosopher of war Carl von Clausewitz noted, "When all is said and done, it really is the commander's coup d'oeil, his ability to see things simply, to identify the whole business of war completely with himself, that is the essence of good generalship. Only if the mind works in this comprehensive fashion can it achieve the freedom it needs to dominate events and not be dominated by them."[45] In essence, this is a premodern argument that the commander whose brain passes most rapidly through the OODA loop wins the engagement.

In twentieth-century warfare, the unit of measure for military superiority was tanks, ships, or aircraft and the ability to "out-gun and out-stick" an opponent. Rapidity through the OODA loop was relatively devalued. In twenty-first-century warfare, where military leaders have minutes or even seconds to make crucial decisions, the ability to out-think an adversary will spell the difference between victory and defeat.

Until recently, the technology to take enhanced decision-making to the next level simply did not exist. Today, it does, and leveraging what big data, artificial intelligence, and machine learning can provide to warfighters may well lead to the next breakthrough in naval warfare, especially in the area of decision-making.

As the U.S. military and its defense industry partners shape their R&D investment decisions in the third decade of the twenty-first century, a modest investment in this area could achieve the greatest improvements in warfighting effectiveness by providing commanders with the coup d'oeil of superior decision-making and ensure that they can make better decisions more quickly and with fewer errors than their adversaries—especially in the stress of combat.

7

IS THE GENIE OUT
OF THE BOTTLE?

Is Weaponizing AI Inevitable?

We believe, strongly, that humans should be the only ones to
decide when to use lethal force. But when you're under attack,
especially at machine speeds, we want to have a machine that
can protect us.

ROBERT WORK[1]

Weapons autonomy undergirded by AI is the biggest thing in
military technology since nuclear weapons.

WILLIAM ROPER[2]

THE ASTRONAUT DAVE BOWMAN is on a spacewalk. He must bypass
the defenses of the artificial general intelligence HAL (Heuristically programmed Algorithmic) computer that controls the spacecraft on which he
is voyaging. Possessing self-awareness as well as consciousness, HAL refuses
to allow itself to be shut down and reprogrammed after making a mistake

in reporting the presence of a fault in the spacecraft's communications antenna. Like human perfectionists whose self-worth is defined by correct actions, HAL is unable to admit even the smallest mistake and is ready to defend itself against critics and those who would interfere in its decisions. It has already killed Bowman's astronaut partner, Frank Poole, despite the fact that the astronauts had hidden their plan to shut HAL down by conversing outside the spacecraft. Unknown to them, by using its outside video monitoring system, HAL can read lips.

As Bowman works to shut down the computer controls, HAL begins to plead with him: "I know I've made some very poor decisions recently, but I can give you my complete assurance that my work will be back to normal. I've still got the greatest enthusiasm and confidence in the mission. And I want to help you. Dave, stop it. Stop, will you? Stop Dave. Will you stop, Dave? Stop Dave. I'm afraid. I'm afraid, Dave. Dave, my mind is going. I can feel it."

This scene is from one of the most iconic films of the last century, Stanley Kubrick's *2001: A Space Odyssey*. Its central theme is the issue of autonomy of robots (the unmanned vehicles of the time) and the potential hazard of general or strong artificial intelligence. HAL's primary fault is that it has become too human-like, adopting on its own some of the worst aspects of human psychology.

More recently, some of the technology celebrities of the twenty-first century—including Elon Musk and Apple co-founder Steve Wozniak—along with AI scientists and academics have identified AI as a potential danger to the future of humanity.[3] Metaphorically, they want to put the AI genie back into the bottle.

MOMENTUM AND CONCERNS

A powerful momentum is driving militaries to design and field semiautonomous, supervised autonomous, or fully autonomous weapons systems. Those responsible for the security of their nation recognize the value of these systems for a number of reasons, not the least of which is to keep warfighters out of harm's way when it comes to conducting dangerous missions.

We have already seen the use of semiautonomous and supervised autonomous weapons systems in warfare—especially in the course of Russia's invasion of Ukraine. What nations and military organizations are grappling with today are the risks and rewards of developing and employing fully autonomous lethal weapons systems. Indeed, Israel has fielded and demonstrated the Harpy systems described in a previous chapter but thus far has not deployed it in combat.[4]

There are divergent views, especially in the United States, regarding the efficacy of fielding fully autonomous lethal weapons systems. The National Security Commission on Artificial Intelligence *Final Report* notes that "we will not be able to defend against AI-enabled threats without ubiquitous AI capabilities and new warfighting paradigms."[5] Conversely, the American public (and even a few individuals such as Musk who have profited from commercial AI) has spent decades reading novels and seeing films with dystopian scenarios in which robots run amok and have become fully sensitized to the potential dangers of fully autonomous lethal weapons systems. Thus, the public has not yet demonstrated a buy-in regarding what the report recommends.

Why can't the public separate the wheat from the chaff and accept the findings of the National Security Commission on Artificial Intelligence? Or respond to the vision of Secretary of Defense Lloyd Austin for DoD to "successfully lead the AI revolution"?[6] The goal of going all in on lethal autonomous systems is to ensure that the United States does not fall behind adversaries who have no qualms about employing these weapons. Given the potential wars we have identified and the intent of the Chinese and Russian authoritarian leadership to fight them, isn't some degree of adapting lethal autonomous systems justified?

RELUCTANCE AND REALITY

The reason for public reluctance is, at once, straightforward yet complex. It is easy to see how a public that came of age reading H. G. Wells and watching such films as *2001* could be leery of the military losing control of its fully autonomous lethal weapons systems.

While few today worry that a twenty-first-century HAL will turn on its masters, the issues involved with fielding increasingly autonomous unmanned systems are complex, challenging, and contentious. Kubrick's 1968 movie was prescient. More than a half-century later, while we accept advances in other aspects of unmanned systems improvements such as pro-pulsion, payload, stealth, speed, endurance, and other attributes, we are still coming to grips with how much autonomy is enough, how much may be too much, and whether fully autonomous lethal weapons systems should be developed and used in conflicts. This is arguably *the* most important issue we need to address with respect to these systems over the next decade. These ongoing debates have spawned a cottage industry of books that attempt to address the complex issues of AI, autonomy, and unmanned systems, espe-cially armed military unmanned systems, in a thoughtful manner.[7]

The reality is that unmanned systems will become more autonomous in direct proportion to their ability to sense the environment and adapt to it. This capability enables unmanned systems to achieve enhanced speed in decision-making and allows friendly forces to act within an adversary's OODA loop. As the environment or mission changes, the ability to sense and adapt will allow unmanned systems to find the optimal solution for achieving their mission without the need to rely on constant human oper-ator oversight, input, and decision-making. Nevertheless, while we need unmanned systems, especially fully autonomous lethal weapons systems, to operate inside the enemy's OODA loop, are we ready to operate them inside *our* OODA loops at speeds human decision-making cannot match?

ETHICAL DILEMMAS AND MORAL AGENCY

An article in *The Economist* entitled "Morals and the Machine" addressed the issue of autonomy and humans in the loop this way:

> As they become smarter and more widespread, autonomous machines are bound to end up making life-or-death decisions in unpredictable sit-uations, thus assuming—or at least appearing to assume—moral agency. Weapons systems currently have human operators "in-the-loop," but as they grow more sophisticated, it will be possible to shift to "on-the-loop" operation, with machines carrying out orders autonomously.
>
> As that happens, they will be presented with ethical dilemmas. Should a drone fire on a house where a target is known to be hiding, which may also be sheltering civilians? Should a driverless car swerve to avoid pedes-trians if that means hitting other vehicles or endangering its occupants?

Should a robot involved in disaster recovery tell people the truth about what is happening if that risks causing a panic?

Such questions have led to the emergence of the field of "machine ethics," which aims to give machines the ability to make such choices appropriately—in other words—to tell right from wrong. More collaboration is required between engineers, ethicists, lawyers, and policymakers, all of whom would draw up very different types of rules if they were left to their own devices.[8]

In a 2013 op-ed in the *New York Times* entitled "Smart Drones," Bill Keller put the issue of autonomy for unmanned systems this way:

> If you find the use of remotely piloted warrior drones troubling, imagine that the decision to kill a suspected enemy is not made by an operator in a distant control room, but by the machine itself. Imagine that an aerial robot studies the landscape below, recognizes hostile activity, calculates that there is minimal risk of collateral damage, and then, with no human in the loop, pulls the trigger.
>
> Welcome to the future of warfare. While Americans are debating the president's power to order assassination by drone, powerful momentum—scientific, military, and commercial—is propelling us toward the day when we cede the same lethal authority to software.[9]

While it may seem counterintuitive, concerns about autonomous machines and artificial intelligence are also coming from the very industry that is most prominent in developing these technological capabilities. An article in the *New York Times* originally entitled "Robot Overlords? Maybe Not," quoted Alex Garland, director of the movie *Ex Machina*, who talked about artificial intelligence and quoted several tech industry leaders: "The theoretical physicist Stephen Hawking told us that 'the development of full artificial intelligence could spell the end of the human race.' Elon Musk, the chief executive of Tesla, told us that A.I. was 'potentially more dangerous than nukes.' Steve Wozniak, a co-founder of Apple, told us that 'computers are going to take over from humans' and that 'the future is scary and very bad for people.'[10]

In March 2023 Musk, Wozniak, and one thousand other scientists and concerned citizens signed an open letter calling for all labs to pause research in advanced AI for six months while a review of the future of AI was examined and debated.[11] Despite—or perhaps because of—immediate pushback by the CEOs of Alphabet/Google and Apple and former Microsoft CEO Bill Gates, the letter gained wide media attention.[12] Obviously, such a pause could not be enforced without federal government action, which the signatories sought. In April 2023 two AI experts argued in *The Economist* that the world needed an international agency for artificial intelligence.[13] However, how such an organization would function or convince nations to participate remains unclear.

For such reasons, the bar is extraordinarily high for the U.S. government, and especially the U.S. military, to prove to the American public that it will not lose control of its robots. Many have expressed apprehension that the U.S. military might lose control of its unmanned systems, and especially its armed ones. These fears have manifested themselves in many ways, such as Google discontinuing work on DoD's Algorithmic Warfare Cross-Functional Team, otherwise known as Project Maven, when thousands of Google employees protested working on "warfare technology."[14] This is especially concerning, as Project Maven had nothing to do with armed unmanned systems but rather with having AI search thousands of hours of surveillance video from unmanned air vehicles to tease out nuggets of useful information.

WHEN ROBOTS GO BAD

That said, incidents have occurred where military organizations have lost control of their fully autonomous lethal weapons systems. One of the most infamous instances occurred in 2007 in South Africa during the military's annual Seboka training exercise. During this major event, the 10th Anti-Aircraft Regiment's automated Mk5 antiaircraft system appeared to jam. Suddenly, the gun began firing wildly, spitting explosive shells at over five hundred rounds a minute in a 360-degree arc. The gun finally stopped firing when it had exhausted its magazine of shells, but not before nine soldiers were dead and fifteen more were seriously injured.[15]

In the case of the Seboka incident, the machine malfunctioned for a number of unique factors, including improper settings following maintenance.

One commentator called it a "mechanical failure," since the weapon was set to remote control but no controller was present. But what would happen if an adversary took action to purposefully cause a fully autonomous lethal weapons system to turn on its operators? It is easy to understand how widely reported cyberattacks on governments, industry, and other entities can lead to concerns that nations—especially U.S. peer adversaries—could fully take control of autonomous lethal weapons systems fielded by the United States and turn them against U.S. forces.

This kind of hacking of one government by another is ubiquitous. For example, in a 2015 attack attributed to China, a hack of the U.S. Office of Personnel Management computers exposed security clearance investigation data of twenty-one million people.[16] Farther afield, other hacking, especially denial of service attacks, has caused havoc in many nations. Russia's denial of service attacks on Estonia crushed that nation's electronic infrastructure, knocking banks, automated teller machines, communications, and media offline. Similar Russian attacks on Georgia did comparable damage to that nation's infrastructure. Nor are U.S. peer adversaries the only entities capable of inflicting this kind of damage. Iran launched cyberattacks against Saudi Arabia and the United States and destroyed data on thousands of computers owned by a Saudi oil company as well as those of U.S. banks doing business with these companies.[17]

To be fair, the United States, along with Israel, is suspected to have conducted the same kind of attacks in the military realm, most famously with the Stuxnet virus. This virus targeted Iran's Natanz nuclear facility, specifically the centrifuges that enriched the uranium. The attack knocked a large percentage of those centrifuges offline and seriously damaged Iran's enrichment capabilities.[18]

Given the ongoing cyber-hacking incidents, to say nothing of how adversaries are fielding increasingly sophisticated methods to make attacks in cyberspace, it is easy to see how vulnerable semiautonomous, supervised autonomous, or fully autonomous weapons systems could be to this kind of hacking. These issues have added to the American public's concerns regarding the wisdom of fielding these systems.

These worries are not farfetched. For example, the U.S. Navy has been testing the autonomous carrier-based MQ-25 Stingray refueling aircraft for several years, and the system will reach its initial operating capability in 2025. The Stingray will ultimately populate every U.S. Navy aircraft carrier air wing. If hackers took control of the 45,000-pound Stingray, steered it back toward the carrier that launched it, and had it scream out of the sky and smash into the carrier's flight deck, it would inflict catastrophic—and perhaps fatal—damage on that irreplaceable ship.

Another factor causing skepticism among the American public regarding the efficacy of the U.S. military fielding semiautonomous, supervised autonomous, or fully autonomous weapons systems (especially the latter) is the track record of autonomous systems in the nonmilitary space. In the past three decades, industrial robots operating alongside humans in factories have caused more than thirty deaths or injuries.[19] While these numbers are modest compared to casualties in factories or warehouses without robots present but where human error caused injuries or death, the headline-grabbing reports of these rare events have induced fears about the potential of fully autonomous lethal weapons systems running amok.

One area in which the American public is being sensitized to the inability of those writing the code to "first do no harm" is in the field of self-driving cars. If one were trying to explain the technology needed to develop and employ fully autonomous lethal weapons systems, the most convenient nonmilitary analogy would be the journey to field self-driving cars.

Those responsible for the concepts, research, development, building, fielding, and use of fully autonomous lethal weapons systems might be well served to look into the commercial trade space, to the automobile industry, to understand not only the opportunities but especially the challenges that must be addressed. And while not a perfect one-to-one match, this analogy can suggest what kinds of factors must be considered if fully autonomous lethal weapons systems are to be successfully fielded by the U.S. military.[20]

SECOND THOUGHTS ON SELF-DRIVING CARS

In 2004 the Defense Advanced Research Projects Agency held its first grand challenge. DARPA offered a $1 million prize to any team of robotic engineers that could create an autonomous car capable of finishing a 150-mile course in the Mojave Desert. No team was successful in completing the course.

The next year, the second DARPA grand challenge was again held in a desert environment, and five vehicles completed the course. This event spurred industry, the military, and academia to invest heavily in technologies that would lead to the manufacture and use of self-driving cars. However, with that substantial investment came a great deal of hype. By the 2010s, most "experts" predicted that by the early 2020s, self-driving cars would be nearly ubiquitous worldwide. Elon Musk went so far as to claim that he would have ten thousand Tesla robo-taxis on the road by 2020.

Unfortunately, progress with self-driving car technology has often been one step forward and two steps back, including accidents such as a Tesla Model S smashing into an 18-wheeler, killing the driver, and an Uber autonomous vehicle killing a woman pushing her bike through a crosswalk. While the number of fatalities and injuries due to self-driving cars has been relatively small (eight fatalities to date), these events have garnered international headlines and have caused substantial mistrust among the public as to the ability of those who write the code to get it right.[21] And even where engineers intervene in time before the code causes an accident (such as with Tesla's widely reported February 2023 recall of more than 360,000 vehicles equipped with its self-driving features), concerns remain about the wisdom of unleashing these vehicles onto the nation's highways, let alone in congested urban areas.

These worries run deeper. The initial enthusiasm for driverless cars has given way to second thoughts regarding drivers' willingness to be taken completely out of the loop. One article in the *New York Times*, "Whose Life Should Your Car Save?" addressed the apprehensions of many about driverless cars and, by extension, other fully autonomous systems:

> We presented people with hypothetical situations that forced them to choose between "self-protective" autonomous cars that protected their passengers at all costs, and "utilitarian" autonomous cars that impartially minimized overall casualties, even if it meant harming their passengers. (Our vignettes featured stark, either-or choices between saving one group of people and killing another, but the same basic trade-offs hold in more realistic situations involving gradations of risk.)

A large majority of our respondents agreed that cars that impartially minimized overall casualties were more ethical, and were the type they would like to see on the road. But most people also indicated that they would refuse to purchase such a car, expressing a strong preference for buying the self-protective one. In other words, people refused to buy the car they found to be more ethical.[22]

As this study and an increasing number of analyses and reports indicate, there is a growing consensus among consumers that drivers want to be "in the loop" and that they want semi- and not fully autonomous cars. Indeed, experts in this area have taken self-driving car manufacturers to task for even suggesting that their cars are "self-driving," pointing out that "the legal fine print requires drivers to keep their hands on the steering wheel and be ready to take control of the vehicle at any time."[23]

Given these concerns about benign civilian systems, there is little wonder that fears continue to surface regarding fielding fully autonomous lethal weapons systems. At the core of these concerns is the issue of accountability. In the case of a self-driving car, who is held liable: the human driver who is supposed to intervene if his vehicle appears to be on the verge of killing or injuring someone, the automobile manufacturer, the subcontractor who delivered the self-driving software, or the sub-sub-contractor who wrote a particular segment of the code? Or is everyone in the value chain liable? These civilian-sector concerns regarding accountability translate directly to the military space with fully autonomous lethal weapons systems. With these systems, as long as there is a human in the loop, there is clear accountability if mistakes are made. However, as in the case of self-driving cars, the use of fully autonomous lethal weapons systems opens up tremendously complex legal and ethical questions regarding accountability and where blame should be assigned.

Self-driving cars are not the only technologies causing public concerns that black box technologies could misfunction in both the civilian and military sectors, causing harm to friendly forces or other innocent people. We have already discussed Microsoft Corporation's travails with its Tay artificial intelligence chatter bot. More recently, the app ChatGPT, created to have open-ended text conversations designed to mimic human cognition and provide a Turing test–like result, has instead had conversations that have made humans extremely uncomfortable.[24] One *New York Times* reporter conducted a five-hour conversation with Bing's Chatbot where the AI declared that it loved him, suggested that he didn't love his wife, and said that the reporter would be happier without her. Even more concerning, the chatbot declared its intention to steal nuclear codes, persuade bank employees to hand over customers' information, and incite people to argue until they kill one another.[25]

RESPONSIBLE AI AND DOD POLICIES

With these concerns in the public gestalt, the U.S. military is under intense pressure to convince Congress and the American public that it will maintain control of its fully autonomous lethal weapons systems.

As part of this effort, in a May 2021 memorandum, "Implementing Responsible Artificial Intelligence in the Department of Defense," the deputy secretary of defense reinforced the department's commitment to ensuring a culture of ethical and responsible AI use across DoD. The memorandum notes,

> As the DoD embraces artificial intelligence (AI), it is imperative that we adopt responsible behavior, processes, and outcomes in a manner that reflects the Department's commitment to its ethical principles, including the protection of privacy and civil liberties. A trusted ecosystem not only enhances our military capabilities, but also builds confidence with end-users, warfighters, and the American public. By leading in military ethics and AI safety, we reflect our Nation's values, encourage Responsible AI (RAI) development globally, and strengthen partnerships around the world. To that end, I reaffirm the DoD AI Ethical Principles adopted by the Department on February 21, 2020, for the design, development, deployment, and use of AI capabilities.[26]

More recently, in early 2023 the DoD updated and reissued Directive 3000.09, "Autonomy in Weapon Systems," designed to demonstrate that DoD was dedicated to responsible policies regarding military uses of autonomous systems and artificial intelligence. This commitment was articulated in a press release, "DoD Announces Update to Directive 3000.09, 'Autonomy in Weapon Systems,'" whose language, quoting Deputy Secretary of Defense Kathleen Hicks, is instructive: "DoD is committed to developing and employing all weapon systems, including those with autonomous features and functions, in a responsible and lawful manner. Given the dramatic advances in technology happening all around us, the update to our Autonomy in Weapon Systems directive will help ensure we remain the global leader of not only developing and deploying new systems, but also safety."[27]

This public-facing document was issued to provide assurances that DoD would take all necessary steps to minimize the probability and consequences of failures in semiautonomous, supervised autonomous, and fully autonomous weapons systems that could lead to unintended engagements. This represents the department's—and by extension, the nation's—commitment to keeping the genie in the bottle as autonomous systems are weaponized.

One paragraph in this directive provides the strongest language regarding accountability when operating these systems: "Persons who authorize the use of, direct the use of, or operate autonomous and semi-autonomous weapon systems will do so with appropriate care and in accordance with the law of war, applicable treaties, weapon system safety rules, and applicable rules of engagement."[28]

Importantly, the United States did not stop at just one or two directives—no matter how powerfully worded—to guide its forces and ensure the public that these systems would be closely controlled. Soon after the issuance of DoD Directive 3000.09, at an international conference at The Hague, the United States launched an initiative designed to promote international cooperation on the responsible use of artificial intelligence and autonomous weapons by militaries. This event was inspired by the extensive use of unmanned systems during Russia's invasion of Ukraine.

The U.S. State Department's under secretary for arms control and international security, Bonnie Jenkins, put the purpose of the initiative this way: "As a rapidly changing technology, we have an obligation to create strong norms of responsible behavior concerning military uses of AI and in a way that keeps in mind that applications of AI by militaries will undoubtedly change in the coming years."[29] However, while offered as a potential focal point for international cooperation, the U.S. proposal only contained non–legally binding guidelines outlining best practices for responsible military use of AI.

In spite of these national and international efforts to assure governments and individual citizens that legitimate concerns regarding militaries fielding and maintaining control of fully autonomous lethal weapons systems are addressed, the jury is still out as to whether these efforts will be successful. Fears persist that AI weapons development cannot be controlled and that this momentum will result in an AI arms race with these systems proliferating worldwide. One of the primary challenges of slowing the AI arms race is the fact that while there has been rhetorical progress, principally under the auspices of the United Nations, to at least begin to address the issue, the pace of AI technology development has vastly outpaced the slow process of diplomacy. Without action, speeches do not trump technology.

LESSONS FROM UKRAINE?

Does Russia's invasion of Ukraine presage changes in the character of warfare enabled by the use of semiautonomous, supervised autonomous, and fully autonomous weapons systems? The war has witnessed the use of drone-on-drone attacks where Ukrainian suicide drones impaled themselves on attacking Russian drones, attacks on Ukraine's power grid by Iranian-supplied Shahed-136 loitering munitions, and the nearly ubiquitous use of small, cheap quadcopters as improvised bombers.[30]

There is compelling evidence that, due to the successful use of autonomous weapons by both nations, the genie is indeed out of the bottle, and there is little chance of turning back the clock to a point where nations and their militaries don't look to the use of these systems as weapons of first resort. General David Petraeus, former head of U.S. Central Command and later director of the Central Intelligence Agency, described the changes seen during this war and their impact on the future of warfare:

> We are, however, seeing some glimpses and hints of what the future of warfare might look like. We see the Ukrainian use of drones (of only modest range and capability) as aerial observers identifying Russian headquarters and other targets for the precision munitions the U.S. has

provided. And there would be incomparably greater numbers of vastly more capable unmanned systems (some remotely piloted, others operating according to algorithms) in every domain—not just in the air, but also at sea, sub-sea, on the ground, in outer space, and in cyberspace, and operating in swarms, not just individually.[31]

In the face of the predicted exponential growth in the use of semiautonomous, supervised autonomous, and fully autonomous weapons systems and concerns regarding the ability of military forces to maintain control of them, there is little wonder that many individuals, governments, and nongovernmental organizations have called for a complete ban on fully autonomous lethal weapons systems. More than sixty organizations, under the umbrella of the Campaign to Stop Killer Robots, have called for this ban, as have more than three thousand robotics and artificial intelligence experts, among them such high-profile technology experts as Elon Musk, Stephen Hawking, and Steve Wozniak.[32]

This raises the crucial question: Can these concerns be eliminated—or at least mitigated—by current laws such as the law of armed conflict or international humanitarian law? If not, are new international agreements, such as those governing chemical weapons and land mines, needed to ensure international cooperation to keep the AI weapons genie in the bottle, or is the underlying technology that enables autonomous weapons too diffuse, too readily available, and too easy to replicate to stop its proliferation? We address these issues in the next chapter.

8
—

THE LAWS OF WAR

Will AI-Enabled Weapons Change Them?

Before any strike is taken, there must be near-certainty that
no civilians will be killed or injured—the highest standard we
can set.

PRESIDENT BARACK OBAMA[1]

DODD 3000.09 defines LAWS [lethal autonomous weapon
systems] as "weapons systems that, once activated, can select
and engage targets without further intervention by a human
operator. This concept of autonomy is also known as 'human
out of the loop' or 'full autonomy.'"

DEFENSE PRIMER: U.S. POLICY ON LETHAL
AUTONOMOUS WEAPONS SYSTEMS,
November 14, 2022 [2]

IT IS SAID THAT WAR IS too important to be left to the generals and
admirals. So also are treaties and international law too important to be left
to diplomats and lawyers. Questions remain as to how the current laws
of war apply to fully autonomous lethal weapons systems. The ability of

international agreements to govern their use is uncertain. These important issues must be addressed, as they affect how laws and agreements might
keep the AI genie in the bottle.

As U.S. naval officers with over a half-century of active-duty experience
between us, our actions at sea, especially in command of naval vessels, were
governed by these laws and agreements. They provided us with extensive
guidance during the time that we served in uniform, whether it involved
putting ordnance on targets declared hostile by appropriate authority;
maintaining forward presence in areas of potential crises; enforcing sanctions and dealing with those who trafficked in persons, weapons, or drugs;
rendering humanitarian aid in disasters overseas and to mariners in distress;
or other activities too numerous to mention here.

In all these activities, laws and agreements provided a structure to deal
with both anticipated and unanticipated events and were undergirded by
decades of work by legal and diplomatic experts, followed by their application in military-to-military confrontations and crises. As we applied these
laws and agreements at sea, there was little ambiguity regarding which
actions were allowed and which actions were proscribed.

However, given the rapid advances in the technology that supports AI-
enabled semiautonomous, supervised autonomous, or fully autonomous
weapons systems, one must ask whether the existing laws of warfare, as well
as extant international agreements, are sufficient to govern the use of these
emerging weapons systems in the conflicts of today and tomorrow.[3] Indeed,
as Gen. Stanley McChrystal, former commander of the International Security Assistance Force in Afghanistan, observed, "Technology has only made
law more relevant to the battlefield."[4] We believe that technology has also
revolutionized the impact of law on war.

Others also see this as one of the most pressing issues in warfare. A
report from the Atlantic Council's Scowcroft Center, *A Candle in the
Dark: U.S. National Security Strategy for Artificial Intelligence*, states, "The
most discussed application of AI for defense and security has traditionally been enhanced autonomy, including autonomy that over time will
allow platforms and systems to respond and adapt to dynamic and complex environments either with greatly reduced human intervention or
absent it altogether. . . . The quest for heightened autonomy of individual

unmanned air, ground, surface, and undersea vehicles has long been a priority for militaries."[5]

The fact that fully autonomous lethal weapons systems driven by AI can select and engage targets without human involvement once the weapon is launched presages the most fundamental change in warfare in generations. It is long past time to engage in thoughtful analysis and discussions regarding their use.

IMPERATIVE FOR AN EXAMINATION

The imperative for a wide spectrum of stakeholders to engage in a dialogue on this issue now is a matter of urgency. In "Lethal Autonomous Weapon Systems: Translating Geek Speak for Lawyers" in the journal *International Law Studies*, Linell Letendre explained,

> Why can engineers not just keep designing systems based on operator requirements and military lawyers not just keep evaluating the legality of the weapons systems once the systems are built? The simple answer is that autonomy is different. Advances in autonomy have the potential to move the human warrior further and further out of the control loop and to leave more and more decisions up to the machine. The catch is that the laws of war are to be assessed and implemented by people, not machines.
>
> Translating the legal requirements for the use of force cannot be an afterthought in the development of autonomous weapon systems; it must be built-in from the beginning. The better engineers understand international law requirements and lawyers understand the technical limitations of autonomous systems, the more likely we are to develop lethal autonomous weapon systems that comply with the law.[6]

It is clear that the law has become central element to twenty-first-century conflict, even though there are armed forces—primarily terrorist groups—that have routinely violated it. Nevertheless, the laws of war are intended to reduce suffering caused by and during combat, particular the suffering of noncombatants. At a minimum, the laws of warfare must be reviewed to determine if the use of autonomous weapons is adequately addressed. Failing to do so will likely result in hardened stances by two opposing camps—those calling for a preemptive prohibition on these systems versus those who opine that current laws are completely adequate.

Political groups calling for preemptive prohibition have already become active. But their campaign to "ban killer drones" generally conflates unmanned/uncrewed aerial vehicles under the full remote control of a human operator with autonomous weapons that do not have humans in or on the loop. Obviously, these two methods of employing unmanned or uncrewed systems are very different.

There is a vast body of work regarding international laws and agreements that apply to warfare, some of which date back to antiquity. Our purpose is not to provide a tutorial on these subjects but rather to examine the adequacy of these laws and agreements to govern the use of semiautonomous, supervised autonomous, and fully autonomous weapons systems. To accomplish this, it is helpful to have a basic understanding of why these pacts exist in the first place.

MAKING WAR LESS HORRIFIC

For millennia, mankind has understood the horrors of war and has attempted to seek agreements to make it less so. These notions go as far back as the King of Babylon's Code of Hammurabi, issued in 1750 BCE, which simply stated, "I prescribe these laws so that the strong do not oppress the weak."[7]

During the ensuing centuries, nations and other entities tried, with varying success, to make war less horrific, largely by proscribing the use of certain weapons as well as by seeking some modest degree of agreement as to how wars would be conducted. In 1139 Pope Innocent banned the use of the crossbow against Christians based on the belief that it made conflict more abhorrent because it could inflict more damage than contemporaneous weapons such as the bow and arrow.[8]

The early seventeenth century saw the emergence of the idea that nations should cooperate both during armed conflict and also to avoid competition below the threshold of conventional military clashes. Hugo Grotius, generally recognized as the father of modern international law, promoted the idea of freedom of the seas, a concept that was formalized in 1982 with the United Nations Convention on the Law of the Sea.[9]

By the mid-nineteenth century, as warfare became more mechanized and new weapons were designed and fielded that could kill, main, or wound combatants more efficiently, nations forged agreements that attempted to govern the conduct of war. These efforts were instantiated in several conventions that carry forward to today, such as the Geneva Conventions and The Hague Conventions.[10]

In the contemporary context, we are primarily concerned with the laws governing adversaries during an armed conflict. The north star in this area is international humanitarian law (IHL), also known as the law of war or the law of armed conflict. This body of law seeks to mitigate the horrors of war by limiting certain methods of warfare as well as protecting those who are innocents, including combatants who can no longer fight.

International humanitarian law attempts to draw, if not clear lines in the sand, then at least boundaries regarding who may be attacked and who must not be harmed and also prescribes requirements and restrictions as to collateral damage that civilians and civilian objects might suffer. And while not every nation, especially rogue regimes, will comply with IHL, having these laws on the books makes it more straightforward to call out offending parties with sanctions and other forms of censure.

International humanitarian law consists not of a single document but rather a corpus of treaties, customary international law, and general principles of law. While there are numerous aspects of IHL that impact the entire scope of warfare, we are primarily concerned with the facets of these laws that govern the use of weapons and methods of their employment, and especially how these laws apply to the use of AI-enabled semiautonomous, supervised autonomous, or fully autonomous weapons systems.

NECESSITY, DISTINCTION, PROPORTIONALITY, AND PRECAUTIONS

Boiled down to its essential elements, international humanitarian law and the law of armed conflict rest on four pillars governing the use of force. The use of force must be necessary, it must be discriminate, it must be proportional, and it must take into account precautions required when conducting an attack. In the main, those authorizing or conducting war have had little trouble concluding whether what they were about to do met these criteria. However, with AI-enabled weapons systems, the picture is a bit muddled.

Before examining the adequacy of these rule sets that govern AI-enabled weapons, we need to briefly explain what these terms mean in all aspects of war. Since most examples of unmanned systems used in combat involve unmanned aerial systems, we will use the example of the ability of a pilot in a tactical jet to weigh these criteria versus an AI-enabled semiautonomous, supervised autonomous, or fully autonomous weapons system to do the same.

Necessity is the first criteria, and one that applies to all aspects of warfare. Simply put, necessity requires that force only be used lawfully and to the level needed to achieve the military objective. For example, in a naval engagement, if one side achieved a mission kill on an adversary (for example, destroying the flight deck of an aircraft carrier rendering it completely unable to launch aircraft), the principle of necessity would mitigate against further attacks to sink the vessel and doom its five thousand sailors to a watery grave.

Distinction is the ability of a combatant or weapon to distinguish between legitimate military and protected entities such as civilians who are not taking part in hostilities. This is typically not an easy task, even for a manned aircraft. First, a person is rarely alone but is enveloped by a background of other people, moving and stationary objects, and other distractions that often make it difficult to single out a person and determine if he or she is a combatant or an innocent civilian. That said, civilians may be targeted if they are directly participating in hostilities, such as ferrying ammunition to soldiers on the front lines.

Additionally, the principle of distinction charges armed forces to distinguish and separate themselves and their military equipment from the civilian population. This is not a hypothetical issue. During Operation Enduring Freedom in Afghanistan, the Taliban was notorious for the unlawful positioning of forces in or around protected places in hopes of deterring attacks.[11]

Centuries ago, soldiers wore distinctive and often brightly colored uniforms, making it easy to distinguish them from civilians. This is no longer the case, as combatants, especially terrorists, now wear a wide variety of clothing that makes them nearly indistinguishable from noncombatants. Whether by a pilot in an aircraft travelling hundreds of miles an hour or a fully autonomous lethal weapons system, distinction is rarely easy to accomplish.

Proportionality means that the military necessity of an attack must outweigh the potential for civilian collateral damage. In some aspects of warfare, such as combat at sea, proportionality typically does not come into play. However, in dense urban environments, there rarely is this certainty, and often determining what is proportionate involves making a judgment call that might be imperfect. Said another way, proportionality requires that collateral damage be limited to a level proportional to the military objective sought.

If the pilot in a tactical aircraft is directed to attack an enemy vehicle that is one in a force of dozens of trucks and tanks and the bomb does not land precisely on the intended vehicle, other adversary assets will likely be damaged, resulting in a successful attack. However, if the adversary parks that vehicle adjacent to an elementary school, an attack on that enemy asset would likely be egregiously disproportionate.

Precautions required when conducting an attack address a number of issues that must be considered in warfare. First, these precautions seek to avoid the use of weapons that cause unnecessary suffering beyond taking the enemy combatant out of action. This is one of the reasons behind prohibitions on the use of chemical and biological weapons, exploding bullets, blinding lasers, and other weapons.

Another precaution that is supported by most civilized nations is the imperative to not harm enemy combatants who have surrendered or who are so incapacitated that they are no longer capable of fighting. While some nations have flouted this aspect of international humanitarian law to terrorize opponents by declaring that it will take no prisoners and instead execute surrendering or incapacitated opponents, this precaution is generally followed.[12]

These short definitions make clear that when fully autonomous lethal weapons systems are employed in combat, a host of questions arise as to whether these new weapons can discriminate, can conduct an attack that is proportional, and can take into account precautions required when conducting an attack. While there is no point solution or yes-or-no answer, there is a great deal that we can unpack regarding the ability of fully autonomous lethal weapons systems to comply with international humanitarian law.

CAN AUTONOMOUS WEAPONS COMPLY?

Can a fully autonomous lethal weapons system exercise *distinction*? Doing so would require the weapon to distinguish between military and civilian targets. On the one hand, an AI-enabled weapons system that also employed machine learning could enable sensor fusion from multiple sources, making target recognition more reliable than what could be achieved by an aviator in a tactical aircraft. The technology to accomplish this is advancing with programs such as DARPA's Collaborative Operations in Denied Environment program, which seeks to design higher levels of sensor fusion.[13]

Conversely, AI-enabled weapons systems have significant limitations in their ability to distinguish between military and civilian targets, especially when the entity is dual-use such as a truck. Additionally, while an aircraft pilot might have the experience to find a target in a cluttered background, it is unlikely that an AI-enabled weapons system could be trained to ferret out a target, given the universe of all possible backgrounds.

There is ample evidence that AI systems can be "fooled" by a ruse as simple as placing a piece of duct tape on a traffic sign.[14] An enemy could use commonly available tools to sow enough doubt in the AI-enabled fully autonomous lethal weapons system to keep it from performing its mission.

Regarding *proportionality*, while an AI-enabled weapon could be trained to have some (but unlikely complete) success in targeting only military assets such as command centers, ships in port or at sea, ammunition dumps, or military vehicles, determining the requisite level of proportionality is an order of magnitude more difficult for autonomous weapons. This is due largely to the fact that, in many (perhaps most) cases, proportionality depends on a judgment call. A pilot in an aircraft travelling hundreds of miles an hour might have only seconds to make such a call. However, rightly or wrongly, we generally accept the fact that in the stress of combat, the pilot might make the wrong decision and conduct an attack that is disproportionate. This acceptance is common in virtually all other methods of lethal targeting—ship-launched Tomahawk land attack missiles, artillery batteries, special operations forces, and others—that are not subject to the same controversy or pressure for greater legitimacy that applies to fully autonomous lethal weapons systems.

We tend to be less forgiving if an autonomous weapon makes a disproportionate attack. First, it is doubtful that such a system could be trained to determine how much collateral damage is disproportionate. That said, those employing fully autonomous lethal weapons systems can decide to use them in areas such as oceans or deserts where targets typically stand out rather than in dense urban areas. While this would limit the use of such systems and even provide an adversary with some comfort knowing that it could operate in dense urban areas without fear of being targeted, it strikes us that if these systems are used in ways that fully exploit their capabilities, then they will have the most value.

Finally, the *precaution* to not cause unnecessary suffering can generally be complied with when employing fully autonomous lethal weapons systems. The system can employ the same types of weapons a tactical jet would carry, none of which presumably would cause unnecessary suffering. This is good as far as it goes, especially when targeting an object such as a ship, a tank, or an aircraft on the ground.

RISE OF DRONE WARFARE

When it comes to individual people, effectively employing the fully autonomous lethal weapons systems and taking appropriate precautions becomes more challenging. Combatants can wear a variety of outfits that do not fit the customary definition of uniforms. Additionally, while a human pilot or other warfighter can likely distinguish a combatant who has surrendered or who can no longer fight, it is highly unlikely that a fully autonomous lethal weapons system could make such a distinction. Compounding this challenge would be an occurrence such as enemy troops who feign surrender (for example, waving a white flag) in an effort to have a fully autonomous lethal weapons system terminate an attack.

This is not new ground for the United States. For two decades in the wake of the September 11, 2001, terrorist attacks, America employed a vast array of semiautonomous and supervised lethal autonomous weapons systems to hunt down and kill terrorists. An understanding of the often fraught process the United States engaged in during two decades following the 9/11 attacks can help us understand and anticipate what issues will need to be addressed if the nation intends to deploy fully autonomous lethal weapons systems.

As the United States embarked on a campaign to leverage semiautonomous and supervised lethal autonomous weapons systems, using drones (the popular name at the time for unmanned aerial vehicles) fielded by the U.S. military and other government agencies such as the Central Intelligence Agency (CIA), the government stated unequivocally that the use of drone strikes was consistent with international law. Concurrently, the United Nations Security Council passed a resolution condemning the 9/11 attacks and noting a nation's right to self-defense.[15]

As the nation that, rather suddenly, brought "drone warfare" to the attention of the international community, and as the United States sought to employ semiautonomous and supervised lethal autonomous weapons systems in a legal and ethical manner as a matter of course, the nation was mindful of the precedents that it was setting. Here is how then-CIA Director John Brennan put this imperative: "If we want other nations to use these technologies [semiautonomous and supervised lethal autonomous weapons systems] responsibly, we must use them responsibly. If we want other nations to adhere to high and rigorous standards for their use, then we must do so as well."[16]

Gen. David Petraeus highlighted the importance of the United States complying with international humanitarian law, the law of war, and the law of armed conflict by explaining how violations of these laws impact what happens on the battlefield: "Whenever we have, perhaps, taken expedient measures, they have turned around and bitten us in the backside. Whenever Americans have used methods that violated the Geneva Conventions or the standards of the International Committee of the Red Cross, we end up paying the price for it ultimately. Abu Ghraib and other situations like that are non-biodegradable. They don't go away. The enemy continues to beat you with them like a stick."[17]

While international humanitarian law, the law of war, or the law of armed conflict do not expressly prohibit the use of fully autonomous lethal weapons systems and, indeed, have little to say about them, there are considerations that most nations should—and will likely—comply with. We say "most" advisedly, as Russia's invasion of Ukraine has included the indiscriminate use of unmanned aerial vehicles to attack a wide array of Ukrainian civilian and infrastructure targets such as that nation's power grid. These attacks were expressly designed to cause "unnecessary suffering" by cutting off electricity and heat to large swaths of the Ukrainian population.

If international humanitarian law, the law of war, or the law of armed conflict are not fully adequate to address all of the issues involved in the use of fully autonomous lethal weapons systems, this raises the question as to whether international agreements ratified by the majority of states could put the proper guardrails in place to govern their use.

ROLE OF INTERNATIONAL AGREEMENTS

As with the case on IHL, there is a rich history of nations crafting international agreements designed to put limits on the production or use of weapons of war. Some of these agreements or treaties were drawn up between major powers that had the capacity to produce and deploy the most destructive weapons of the day, while others, many under the auspices of the United Nations, were crafted to have worldwide applicability.

One of the most well-known treaties designed to govern weapons of war was the 1922 Washington Naval Treaty, also known as the Five-Power Treaty, which was negotiated among the major allies of World War I. This agreement sought to prevent an arms race by limiting naval construction. It was signed, and later ratified, by the governments of the United Kingdom, United States, France, Italy, and Japan. The five signatories agreed to limit the construction of battleships, battle cruisers, and aircraft carriers.[18]

The Washington Naval Treaty is an example of a discrete agreement designed to address an important but narrow aspect of weapons of war. It is also an example of a treaty that did not stand the test of time. In 1934 Japan denounced the treaty's terms and began a major naval buildup. Soon thereafter, Italy announced that it would no longer abide by the treaty. In 1935 France laid down the hulls of several battleships, substantially violating their quota of tonnage. As with any agreement or treaty, these pacts are brittle because they depend on all parties continuing to comply with their strictures.

Among the more well-known international agreements and treaties that have governed the use of military weapons are the 1972 Biological Weapons Treaty, several Strategic Arms Reduction Treaties (STARTs) between 1972 and 1993, the 1993 Chemical Weapons Convention, the 1994 Anti-Ballistic Missile Treaty, the 1996 Comprehensive Test Ban Treaty, the 1997 Mine Ban Treaty, the 2010 New Strategic Arms Reduction Treaty, and the 2022 Treaty on the Prohibition of Nuclear Weapons. As with the Washington Naval Treaty, these agreements were discrete and focused on specific weapons, and the parties signing them could—and did—decide to cease compliance with the treaty for any reason. As one example, in February 2023 Russian President Vladimir Putin declared that Moscow was suspending its participation in the New START, the last remaining nuclear arms control pact with the United States, sharply upping the ante amid tensions with Washington over the fighting in Ukraine. The fact that he issued this declaration in a pique one day after U.S. President Joseph Biden made a surprise visit to Ukraine was lost on no one.[19]

AI is a dual-use technology that has been developed by industry and that is now being leveraged for military use. One among a vast array of potential applications of this technology is to enable fully autonomous lethal weapons systems. Herein lays the difficulty of crafting an international agreement to modulate its use. Beyond the voices of organizations such as the Campaign to Stop Killer Robots, Human Rights Watch, Amnesty International, and others, it is highly unlikely that the nations that possess the technology to develop and deploy fully autonomous lethal weapons systems would agree to a treaty that would control their use, let alone proscribe employing these weapons completely.[20]

It is difficult to overstate the momentum that is building to control fully autonomous lethal weapons systems. The Group of Governmental Experts of the High Contracting Parties to the Convention on Certain Conventional Weapons concluded its 2019 deliberations on lethal autonomous weapons systems with the simple statement: "The potential use of weapons systems based on emerging technologies in the area of lethal autonomous weapons systems must be conducted in accordance with applicable international law, in particular international humanitarian law and its requirements and principles, including inter alia distinction, proportionality and precautions in attack."[21]

However, just two years later, calls for a treaty—any treaty—that would completely ban "killer robots" gained purchase. At a United Nations conclave in December 2021, for the first time, a majority of the 125 nations that are party to the Convention on Certain Conventional Weapons said they wanted curbs on killer robots. However, these efforts are unlikely to succeed, as they were opposed by members that are developing these weapons, most notably the United States and Russia.[22] Indeed, as James Kraska has suggested, "The CCW group of governmental experts effort is unlikely to produce detailed, widely accepted rules."[23]

U.S. POLICY ON AUTONOMOUS WEAPONS

The United States has gone on record opposing any ban on fully autonomous lethal weapons systems, even suggesting that these systems might be more humane than those controlled by humans. The *Defense Primer: U.S. Policy on Lethal Autonomous Weapons Systems* puts it this way: "The U.S. government does not currently support a ban on LAWS [lethal autonomous weapons systems] and has addressed ethical concerns about the systems in a March 2018 white paper, 'Humanitarian Benefits of Emerging Technologies in the Area of Lethal Autonomous Weapons.' The paper notes that automated target identification, tracking, selection, and engagement functions can allow weapons to strike military objectives more accurately and with less risk of collateral damage or civilian casualties."[24]

The reasons for this stance should be abundantly clear. For example, a nation would be justifiably reluctant to send piloted aircraft on an attack mission to hit a target where the adversary has robust anti-access/area denial capabilities, fearing the chances of the pilot's survival might be small. However, it would be sanguine about attacking the target with a fully autonomous lethal weapons system, since no friendly life would be lost if enemy systems destroyed a pilotless aircraft.

That said, the United States has been forward-leaning in offering generally agreed principles to govern the responsible use of AI in weapons systems. At an international conference at The Hague in February 2023, the

U.S. Department of State issued a "Political Declaration on Responsible Military Use of Artificial Intelligence and Autonomy" for two primary reasons: to differentiate the U.S. position from those of Russia and China, as well as to expand the discussion of these issues to a broader range of nations. The declaration stated, in part:

> An increasing number of States are developing military AI capabilities, which may include using AI to enable autonomous systems. Military use of AI can and should be ethical, responsible, and enhance international security. Use of AI in armed conflict must be in accord with applicable international humanitarian law, including its fundamental principles. Military use of AI capabilities needs to be accountable, including through such use during military operations within a responsible human chain of command and control.
>
> A principled approach to the military use of AI should include careful consideration of risks and benefits, and it should also minimize unintended bias and accidents. States should take appropriate measures to ensure the responsible development, deployment, and use of their military AI capabilities, including those enabling autonomous systems. These measures should be applied across the life cycle of military AI capabilities.[25]

U.S. Undersecretary for Arms Control and International Security Bonnie Jenkins put the reason for this U.S. initiative this way: "The aim of the political declaration is to promote responsible behavior in the application of AI and autonomy in the military domain, to develop an international consensus around this issue, and put in place measures to increase transparency, communication, and reduce risks of inadvertent conflict and escalation."[26]

DIFFICULTIES PREVENTING AGREEMENT

Because the progress of AI technology in the civilian realm is truly breathtaking, international agreements that attempt to slow the development of AI-enabled weapons systems are fraught with difficulty. There is no agreement or treaty that will slow the progress of AI in the civilian sector, and militaries can simply leverage this technology in any stage of its development. The U.S. military has a wide array of semiautonomous and supervised autonomous weapons systems (especially unmanned aircraft systems such as Predator, Reaper, Stingray, Fire Scout, Global Hawk, Triton, and others). Any of these systems could be fitted with the code to make them fully autonomous in a relatively short time, far faster than the (often) clunky wheels of diplomacy could fashion an agreement or treaty to proscribe their use.

While not a one-to-one analogy, it is instructive to remember that the proximate reason for the United States invading Iraq in 2003 was the belief that Saddam Hussein had vast supplies of chemical and biological weapons of mass destruction (WMD). U.S. troops expected to find massive stores of WMD hidden throughout the country. None were found, and U.S. certainties that Iraq possessed WMD were found to be false. That said, what was true was that Iraq possessed the scientists and the technicians with the know-how to create these chemical and biological weapons and that, unlike nuclear weapons, the ingredients to make these WMD were readily available and their production could have been completed in a relatively short time.

It is difficult to imagine a scenario in which nations and militaries that have the capability and the will to build and employ fully autonomous lethal weapons systems will cease to do so, given the manifest military benefits of such systems, in spite of a growing number of organizations calling for their ban. That said, the international community—and especially the United States, which has arguably the most experience in dealing with the complex issues involved with lethal weapons systems possessing somewhat less autonomy—will need to evolve agreed upon principles governing their use. At the time of this writing, extant international law says nothing about the use of autonomous weapons systems.

In spite of this lack of specificity, some say that current international humanitarian law, the law of war, and the law of armed conflict provide adequate governance for the use of fully autonomous lethal weapons systems.[27] It may be true that IHL is adequate at the moment, but only because these weapons are so emergent that there is no real evidence to examine to determine whether their use is lawful. However, given the momentum to build these systems, it is likely only a matter of time before they will be used.

The *Defense Primer: U.S. Policy on Lethal Autonomous Weapons Systems* sums up the opposing sides, especially the likelihood that DoD will develop and deploy these weapons even in the face of attempts to proscribe their use: "Contrary to a number of news reports, U.S. policy does not prohibit the development or employment of LAWS. Although the United States does not currently have LAWS in its inventory, some senior military and defense leaders have stated that the United States may be compelled to develop LAWS in the future if U.S. competitors choose to do so. At the same time, a growing number of states and nongovernmental organizations are appealing to the international community for regulation of, or a ban on, LAWS due to ethical concerns."[28]

We believe that depending on current IHL to address the use of fully autonomous lethal weapons systems is a head-in-the-sand approach that avoids an issue that must ultimately be addressed. Whether it is a law, an agreement, or a treaty, reaching some kind of international consensus on the use of these systems will be crucial.

"Crucial" is a strong word. We use it advisedly for this reason. While the current controversy regarding the use of fully autonomous lethal weapons systems is focused on their ability (or lack thereof) to comply with principles of IHL such as necessity, distinction, proportionality, and precautions, they obscure another issue that is vastly more important.

If many nations possess fully autonomous lethal weapons systems, fielded either for operational advantage or explicitly to keep their warfighters out of harm's way, the natural expectation arises that war could be almost bloodless. If no human lives are at stake, the temptation to embark upon conflict may increase for those nations that contemplate it. When nations believe that robotic armies will do their fighting for them, will war be inevitable? And if robots are doing the fighting, is there any incentive to eventually end the conflict? We address these issues and the role of military AI overall in the following chapters.

9
___

WORLD WAR III

How Will It Start?

We need to become again the country that breaks the hard problems, that sees the virtue in innovation and the reward in risk. . . . If we do not succeed, then I worry that all is truly lost.

FROM *GHOST FLEET: A NOVEL OF THE NEXT WORLD WAR*[1]

Chinese cyber dominance of the American forces was complete. A highly sophisticated artificial intelligence capability allowed the *Zheng He* to employ its cyber tools at precisely the right moment to infiltrate U.S. systems. . . . [I]t was the massive discrepancy in offensive cyber capabilities—an invisible advantage—that allowed the *Zheng He* to consign a far larger force to the depths of the South China Sea.

FROM *2034: A NOVEL OF THE NEXT WORLD WAR*[2]

SCENARIO: SOME YEAR IN THE NEAR FUTURE

It was the bolt from the blue that the Americans and allies had feared and trained for but had never actually expected. The octogenarian general secretary of the Chinese Communist Party had determined—with the assistance of an artificial intelligence decision support system—that the "reunification" of Taiwan with the mainland by force now had the highest probability of success. Never in history had the full unification of China been accomplished, and the one to achieve it would be regarded as the greatest Chinese leader of all time.

The general secretary's AI decision support system was capable of simulating and assessing millions of war-gaming moves in seconds while correlating actual intelligence data so as to predict their outcome. Tied to it were the thousands of information sensors of the vast PLA intelligence, surveillance, and reconnaissance network—located in satellites, at ground bases on the mainland and forward bases in other countries, on crewed ships, submarines, and aircraft, and within thousands of controlled or autonomous unmanned vehicles in all domains, coupled with a constantly updating cyber database.

Accepting the recommendations of the AI-controlled network, made by compiling big data beyond what could be comprehended by hundreds of human decision-makers, required considerable trust on the part of the single human on the loop. But for the world's leading AI and cyber war power—dwarfing the military capabilities of potential opponents—trust in a high-technology, tightly connected, and logistically well-supported military might be considerable.

It was the same trust in their systems that was held by previous national leaders who launched what became world wars.[3] And like its Pacific war predecessor, the goal was not invasion of the opposing great power, but a limited fait accompli followed by a negotiated agreement to cement the results. This is one of the premises behind the novel *Ghost Fleet*.

Let's isolate and examine a part of the conflict. At 0702 local time—amidst the background of cyber and antisatellite battles—the remaining U.S. satellites scanning the Western Pacific detected the simultaneous launch of twenty-four PLA DF-26 antiship ballistic missiles toward the U.S. Navy strike group operating at sea to the east of Taiwan.[4] The missiles were a new variant, each carrying a multiple independently targetable reentry vehicle that dispersed eight warheads. Thus, a total of 192 individual warheads would strike at a small combined group of manned and unmanned vessels, with their focus on the vessel hosting its central decision-making network.

With the ballistic missiles having an exoatmospheric flight speed of 15,000 miles per hour, the U.S. Navy strike group would have approximately four minutes warning time, enough to ready its systems and crews for the attack. Yet to defeat an incoming raid of 192 warheads would be impossible without a machine-speed combination of antiballistic missile launches, electronic warfare attacks, decoy deployments, defensive maneuvering—and all the other elements of battle management that in the past would be decided and conducted by Sailors.

Experimentation and experience indicate that a human-controlled or human-in-the-loop defense might be able to defeat the simultaneous attack of perhaps twenty warheads. Using human-machine teaming and moving human control to on the loop might increase that number to forty.

Against 192 warheads, and with the probability of follow-on attacks by hypersonic edge-of-atmosphere missiles and gathering swarms of kamikaze UAVs—as well as the possibility of launching counterstrikes—a defense of the strike group would be beyond the speed of human response. The strike group commander would have no choice but to flip the switch to "autonomous" and turn over battle management to a machine-speed AI system in order to survive.

Taking control of the battle, the U.S. naval AI system launched antiballistic missiles and decoys, used electronic warfare to paint false targets and cover the real ones, and dispersed the ships into positions that optimized stealth characteristics and made the strike group a hard target to hit. Not every incoming ballistic missile could be downed or diverted, but casualties were much lighter than would be expected if humans were in control.

Going on the offensive, the naval AI system rapidly repositioned the ships into the optimal positions to mass and launch kinetic, electromagnetic, and cyber weapons against the remaining mobile ballistic missile transporter-erector-launchers (TELs), hypersonic missile TELS, and fixed sites, and seeded a cloud of aerial mines impenetrable to the slower-moving, loitering UAVs.

Yet there is an alternative scenario. The commander flips the switch to "autonomous" and turns over battle management to a machine-speed AI system in order to survive. But nothing happened. The AI system failed to engage, and the Sailors on board the human-crewed vessels were left to defeat the incoming missile raid as best as they could. Fortunately, they were able to override the stalled AI system controls since the designers had allowed for manual control of individual combat systems and weapons. A few ships survived.

The battle's after-action report acknowledged that it was difficult to determine whether there were design flaws in the system software, the opponents had a means of penetrating the AI decision-maker process, or a PLA sleeper agent within the parts supply chain was able to install a Trojan horse. This alternative drives the plot of *2034: A Novel of the Next World War*.

There is a third alternative. It was a bolt from the blue that shocked the entire world. Just a month before, the global community celebrated a diplomatic triumph: After years of negotiations, the last holdout member of the United Nations finally acceded to the treaty on retaining human control over the use of deadly force. This was the result of many years of lobbying and activism on the part of nongovernmental organizations—primarily in the Western democracies—dedicated to banning "killer robots." Celebratory remarks concerning "moving nearer to world peace" echoed throughout social media.

Scant attention was paid to the practicalities of enforcing the treaty. Throughout the negotiations process, defense analysts pointed out that it would be nearly impossible to ensure that nations did not retain the capability and capacity to shift combat decision-making from human controlled to exclusively AI controlled in order to speed their OODA loops. Unlike nuclear weapons, which can be counted by national technical means based on installations and radiation emissions, AI-embedded computers cannot be distinguished from non-AI computers by outside means. Few, if any, nations would allow another to directly examine their defense networks lest all their information be compromised by a potential enemy.

As with the Versailles Treaty, Munich Agreement, and many UN human rights declarations, it was assumed that signatories would honor the agreement. However, a number of the signatories retained AI-driven autonomous weapons capabilities—some to hedge against cheating by potential opponents, some because they considered treaties to be subject to flexible interpretations or conveniently disregarded if an issue of greater importance arose.

Unification of Taiwan with the People's Republic of China was considered an issue of greater importance than a treaty. AI-driven autonomous weapons were used for both tactical and terror operations. A large number of Taiwanese citizens were killed or wounded in the attack, some by autonomous weapons. Those left needed to be processed—like the Uyghurs.

ISSUES OF MILITARY AI IN THE REAL WORLD

These scenarios are intended to examine four particular questions concerning the probable course of military AI development. First is the question of whether AI could initiate a war, particularly in times of international tension. Second is the question of whether the use of AI would make the war more or less destructive for civilians as well as combatants. Third is the question of whether the use of AI in war can be prevented. Fourth is the question of whether AI could prevent war. We will use the information presented in the previous chapters and logic to attempt to answer these questions.

COULD AI INITIATE A WAR?

The answer can be no or yes, depending on if the question is whether AI in itself could start a war or whether it could simply provide information that leads humans to go to war.

The "No" Answer

Every war has been initiated by humans. Scholars have argued that certain wars have been caused by "accident" or "miscalculation." Some see World War I as occurring almost by accident; once one European great power mobilized its troops—which included almost all military-age males—all counterparts had to do likewise. Each believed that the first nation that could mass its forces and move them to the borders (primarily by railroad) would be in a position to attack and achieve a quick victory. The only way to prevent this would be to quickly mobilize one's own troops. However, maintaining large armies in the field was expensive and difficult. The first nation that demobilized might be defeated by the one that did not demobilize. Theorists argue that once mobilization occurred—even by mistake—war would be impossible to avoid, whether leaders wanted it or not.

These scholars are wrong as to war being an accident. Some of the statesmen of Europe wanted a quick and victorious war that would allow their nations to dominate the continent. Aggressors who have initiated hostilities have often miscalculated as to whether the opponent would fight or surrender, with most calculating that surrender of the enemy would occur in short order. In deciding to invade Ukraine, Vladimir Putin is but one in a long line of those who expected a swift victory with relatively low costs. But miscalculating the length of war or its outcome does not represent an accident or a mistake in choosing an act of war.

Carl von Clausewitz maintained that "war is not merely a political act but a real political instrument, a continuation of political intercourse, a carrying out of the same by other means."[5] War is an attempt to bend an opponent to one's will by force of arms. Many humans may regret the fact that war occurs and that it might possibly be considered a "political intercourse . . . by other means." Yet as such, it entails a deliberate choice by a political leader to use violence. (Under international law, that political leader should be the head of state of a recognized nation.)

The current state of AI is narrow—systems that can make decisions normally relegated to humans but are limited as to task. Some people dream of AGI, a machine capable of experiencing consciousness. Although a staple of science fiction, the ability to create AGI is questionable and certainly is not at hand. Current algorithms cannot replicate the multitasking ability of humans. Therefore, it is impossible, at least for now and the foreseeable future, that an AI machine—in essence a robot set to a narrow task—could replace the decision-making of a head of state who could declare war.

It is also unlikely that modern humans would blindly follow without question the directions of a machine that issued such a directive any more than they would other directions devised from a nonhuman source, such as a book, a gamble, or an omen. It is possible, but the human would have to comprehend the information provided and decide to choose war. Even if it could be done, turning over control of an entire war-making force without a human somewhere in the decision loop would be a choice that the decision-maker would know is fraught with danger.

Current autonomous weapons systems could—on the tactical level—malfunction and attack the persons or property of another nation. However, the same has been done by humans. Yet the historical record indicates that none of these individual mistaken attacks actually caused a war.

From the perspective of AI making an unsupervised choice, the answer to the first question is *no*. It is impossible for current and near-term AI to choose on its own to initiate a war. (Please note the words "current" and "near-term.")

A Possible (Old) Exception

However, there is a potential exception—the "dead hand" (*Mertvaya Ruka*) retaliatory second-strike strategic nuclear missile launch system created by the Soviet Union and now operated by Russia.[6] Development of this system, called Perimeter (also spelled Perimetr), began in 1967, and it became operational sometime before 1986. Its purpose was to be able to broadcast an order to the Strategic Rocket Forces to launch a second-strike nuclear attack even if the Soviet military leadership were killed in an attack on Moscow. Details concerning its method of operation still remain murky and disputed, and statements by Soviet and Russian officials have been contradictory. The system was supposedly designed to detect the impact of nuclear weapons on Russian soil via seismic, overpressure, light, and radioactivity sensors, and launch a signal rocket that would wirelessly broadcast orders to all Strategic Rocket Forces personnel in nuclear missile silos to commence an attack. In an interview in the United States, Valery Yarynich, one of its developers, explained,

> It was designed to lie semi-dormant until switched on by a high official in a crisis. Then it would begin monitoring a network of seismic, radiation, and air pressure sensors for signs of nuclear explosions. Before launching any retaliatory strike, the system had to check off four if/then propositions: If it was turned on, then it would try to determine that a nuclear weapon had hit Soviet soil. If it seemed that one had, the system would check to see if any communication links to the war room of the Soviet General Staff remained. If they did, and if some amount of time—likely ranging from 15 minutes to an hour—passed without further indications

of attack, the machine would assume officials were still living who could order the counterattack and shut down. But if the line to the General Staff went dead, then Perimeter would infer that apocalypse had arrived. It would immediately transfer launch authority to whoever was manning the system at that moment deep inside a protected bunker—bypassing layers and layers of normal command authority.[7]

Does such a system constitute AI? Under our first definition of AI in chapter one as "the capability of a machine to imitate human behavior," the answer is yes. However, under the second definition of "the set of statistical techniques that teaches software to make decisions on past data," the answer appears to be no. Perimeter is clearly not a learning system.

Most books and articles on AI published since 2000 make no mention of the Perimeter system, perhaps because it seems too old, predating the renewal of AI interest in the 1990s. Is Perimeter an autonomous weapons system as described in chapter four? Since it was intended that a Soviet/Russian leader would only switch it on if a major great power crisis was threatening, it would fall in the supervised autonomous system category. Activating it would be a human decision. Following its orders to launch missiles would also be a human decision by the Strategic Rocket Force personnel on watch in the silos. Thus, we can say that there are indeed humans sitting on the loop.

However, the late Dr. Bruce Blair, longtime fellow of the Brookings Institution and leader of the Global Zero movement to eliminate nuclear weapons, maintained—based on research and interviews with former Soviet officials—that Perimeter did have the capability to launch missiles autonomously, bypassing the remaining human watchstanders at the launch sites.[8] Other experts maintain that the autonomous capability of the dead-hand system is a myth.[9] But most sources insist that it still exists in some form.[10]

If it received a faulty set of signals from its sensors, could Perimeter launch a (nuclear) war on its own? Has it been upgraded with modern AI features? It seems impossible to determine based on open sources. However, there is a report that Vladimir Putin switched the system back on in 2011.[11]

The "Yes" Answer

It is possible for AI systems to provide decision-makers with erroneous (or even correct) information that could encourage them to start a war, providing they already have an inclination to do so. From that perspective, one could say AI *initiated* the war. Perhaps *originated* would be a better word to use. Again, however, the situation would be one in which the human utilized AI as a decision aid or, at most, teamed with the machine.

The point of human-machine teaming is to facilitate enhanced decision-making by the human partner, not to remove the possibility of choice. If the possibility of human choice is removed, the situation is not one of human-machine teaming. Rather, it is the same as simply operating a machine without a human involved. But that is not the situation we are envisioning.

Information provided by AI could convince an aggressor that they could win a war. However, information provided by other sources could do likewise. Yet a prime purpose of AI is to speed the OODA loop; thus, information would be compiled rapidly and might be acted on rapidly.

During the Cold War, leaders of the Soviet Union sought to calculate and continuously update an assessment of the "correlation of forces" that could indicate whether the Warsaw Pact or NATO would prevail in a war. The information for this correlation was gathered through all types of intelligence sources. It included global political, diplomatic, and economic data as well as military data. Many analysts in the West assumed that correlation of forces was merely a term for a "standard" intelligence assessment.

However, some analysts feared that the Soviets sought to create an algorithm that could predict—based on the correlation of forces—the optimal moment to go to war and be victorious. Claiming that their actions were determined by "scientific socialism" derived from natural logic, it is possible that the Soviet leadership could indeed base its decision on such an algorithm   particularly during an ongoing international crisis. This algorithm would be (or was) developed through the use of computer software run on the most powerful computers. But in the 1960s, '70s, and '80s, managing the big data to be compiled would still be a labor-intensive task since information had to be sorted and fed to the machine.

Could AI be programmed with such an algorithm and compile and assess the big data required? One of the three definitions for AI that we identified is "the set of statistical techniques that teaches software to make decisions based on past data." This is the *yes* part of the answer. It is theoretically possible to develop an algorithm of Armageddon that could convince a previously deterred aggressor that the greatest chance for victory had arrived. This is a significant factor in the scenarios we have described above.

Those who would dispute the idea that any leader would be tempted to launch a war based largely on statistics has to look no further than Imperial Japan prior to the Pearl Harbor attack of World War II. At one of the last their meetings before deciding to attack, the Imperial cabinet was provided very accurate information concerning a correlation of forces between the Japanese empire and the United States. If its full industrial potential was utilized, the United States was estimated as being seven to eight times more powerful than Japan.[12] However, the analysis also concluded that American strength would continue to increase, so that it would be even more difficult—perhaps impossible—to win a war against it in the future. Although the correlation was negative, it would become even worse. Statistically, the window for victory was closing, so the cabinet chose war.[13]

Is this an algorithm of Armageddon to be utilized by AI to tempt the warlike?

An additional issue would be the question of whether to trust an AI-driven compilation of information. This compilation could be utilized by AI systems to run hundreds of thousands of war games to determine the probable outcome of hostilities. If AI systems were provided false information and concluded that a nation just launched a strategic nuclear attack on the United States, how would the American leadership react? Would they base their decision on advice from AI?

In the introduction, we stated that our greatest fear was not that AI would control humans, but that some humans would use AI to control other humans (which, in China and elsewhere, they already do). Such an algorithm of Armageddon could be one of the most useful tools in encouraging an effort at control.

WILL AI MAKE WAR LESS DESTRUCTIVE?

The answer is: not necessarily. At the beginning of the second offset, a number of defense analysts speculated that the development of precision weapons and more intensive ISR would make war less deadly. Attacks could be pinpointed so as to avoid collateral damage and minimize casualties. Some thought that the "fog of war"—the fact that commanders do not have a complete image of the battlefield—was being lifted.[14] Media speculated on the possibility of "bloodless wars" in which machines fought machines and humans were not involved. Critics lamented that the effect would be to make leaders less reluctant to go to war—and to normalize warfare as a routine element of international relations rather than a catastrophe to be avoided.

But that is not quite how modern warfare developed. There have indeed been fewer civilian casualties since World War II, in which cities were carpet-bombed in order to land at least one bomb on a key military-industrial weapons production facility or fuel stockpile. Once released, the unguided bombs of that time were affected by wind, weather conditions, or the aircraft's inaccurate navigation or avoidance of enemy's air defenses, and they hit places other than the target. One needed to drop a considerable number to ensure the target was destroyed. A survey suggests that only 20 percent of air-dropped ordnance fell within range of the intended target (the "target area").[15] Others claim less.[16] Nazi Germany attempted to produce a small number of "precision weapons," but the technology of the time only raised the chance of a hit to 30 percent.[17]

However, the necessary technology has advanced greatly. The second offset of the 1960s through the 1980s represented a search (with claimed success) for a "one weapon, one hit" capability. Operation Desert Storm in 1991 appeared to prove this capability was possible with precision weapons (although many "dumb bombs" were also used). Iraqi military infrastructure and combat formations were destroyed with comparable low numbers of ordnance expended. This certainly lowered the number of American and coalition nations' military personnel killed in comparison with previous engagements. However, it may have increased the numbers of Iraqi military killed, since there was less chance of escaping a long-range strike. The number of Iraqi military casualties in that conflict remains unknown, but estimates range up to 100,000.

Precision weapons appear to have performed well in more recent conflicts, but up until the Russian invasion of Ukraine, all operations in which precision weapons were employed were decidedly one-sided. One of the combatant forces (such as Iraq, the Taliban, Serbia, Libya, and Syrian opposition) did not possess precision weapons. Thus, we do not know how they would perform in a war against the People's Republic of China or Russia, or what level of lethality they would have in a contested electromagnetic environment.

Employing AI would probably increase the effectiveness of existing precision weapons. But the greatest effect would likely be in speeding up the OODA loop of the combatants and managing big data derived from ISR sensors so that the weapons are employed at the optimum moment. Whether advanced AI systems actually installed in the ordnance would make "smart" weapons even "smarter"—and at a reasonable cost—is still questionable. Existing fire-and-forget weapons—those that do not have to be guided continuously onto the intended target but have a technical mechanism to track the target (such as by detecting radar emissions)—are essentially autonomous once they are launched. But they are not normally considered AI-enabled.

From that perspective, a weapon such as the Cold War–era Captor naval mine can be considered autonomous AI. Captor, intended as a weapon against opposing submarines, was designed to distinguish potential targets and launch a torpedo against a specific target profile. Once emplaced, the weapon—not an operator—determined the actual target it would destroy. The human-on-the-loop role is in deciding where to place the mine. Clearly, the weapon is not a learning system; the target profiles have to be preloaded. But it acts in a similar fashion to a crewed submarine in its particular mission.

Did those existing AI-like systems appear to make war less destructive? Not at all.

WHAT WOULD BE THE EFFECTS ON CIVILIANS?

It all depends on the opponent's objectives and intended target. AI could make ordnance more precise by improving firing solutions and human-machine control. AI-enabled precision attacks on military targets in civilian areas might result in less collateral damage. But that depends on whether the attacker intends to avoid civilians. Despite the supposed advancement of international humanitarian laws, Russia made no effort to reduce civilian casualties in Ukraine—it repeatedly targeted nonmilitary facilities so as to maintain a sense of fear throughout the civilian population.

As previously noted, an image of bloodless future wars fought by autonomous systems without human involvement remains in the minds of individuals influenced by its long use in science fiction. Presumably this would mean that civilians would be safer from harm. But what happens when one side wins the war? The application of AI on the (civilian) Uyghur population bodes ill. Since AI can help control populations through surveillance and monitoring almost every association and behavior, could this information be used for even more evil purposes?

The destruction of the Jewish people during the Nazi Holocaust (along with Christian pacifists, anti-Nazis of all stripes, and others dubbed subhuman) was the most barbarous event of the past century. That it occurred in a nation long considered one of the most civilized—with centuries of contributing much to science and the arts—gives one pause. For the killers, however, this activity required information, administration, and resources that were taken away from the Nazi war effort. People had to be identified and sorted and the demographics of conquered nations understood. Big data had to be recorded. Still, a few people escaped, and a small number survived.

One can imagine how much "more efficient and accurate" such a process could be utilizing AI. Many have speculated as to what the outcome of World War II would have been if the Nazis succeeded in their effort to develop nuclear weapons. Perhaps it is now time to consider what an Adolph Hitler (or Joseph Stalin or Mao Zedong) could have done with AI. It all depends on the opponent's objectives and intended target.

COULD THE USE OF AI IN WAR BE PREVENTED?

This is a question that will inevitably be discussed within the sphere of international law and diplomacy. Right now, the answer is: very unlikely. The more AI becomes a feature of everyday life, the more it will be used in military applications. Siri cannot give much advice about conducting a battle. ChatGPT and equivalent systems mine the Internet for answers, and much information on the web is wrong. However—and as we have frequently noted—systems that compile intelligence data that help with military decision-making already exist. As civilian systems are functionally improved and add new features, it seems inevitable that military applications will also improve. The genie is out of the bottle and is already proliferating.

AI is a key component being built into the next generation of weapons, a process already under way. Chapters three and four discussed some of the systems extant or in development. Chapter eight outlined the laws of war and asked whether AI will change them. A great deal of momentum has built, and outside some concerns expressed in Western democracies (where concerns can actually be expressed), nations whose cooperation would be essential for any ban or treaty do not appear to be favorable to controls.

As in the third fictional alternative, there is no known mechanism of determining whether a weapons system contains AI (however it is defined) without intrusive monitoring. One literally has to get within the system's digital code. Another way would be to monitor the production of weapons systems. However, the intrusiveness makes it unlikely that potential opponents would agree to such monitoring, since the same tools useful for monitoring could be used to insert malware. Preventing the use of AI does not seem part of the probable future.

COULD AI PREVENT WAR?

It is unlikely in itself. It is conceivable that as a tool of analysis, AI could be an additional element of deterrence by advising a leader that there was a low likelihood of victory. Gathering all possible big data, such a system could identify the cost and risks involved in the same manner it could advise financiers whether a particular investment was likely to turn a profit in the future. However, such a calculation would be dependent on the actual balance between opposing armed forces. AI might perceive the correlation of forces, but it could not necessarily change it.

Thus, preventing wars falls back on the traditional elements of deterrence as it has been practiced throughout history. AI would simply be a decision-making (or, hopefully, non-decision-making) tool. Utilizing the ideas of Clausewitz, AI might change the "character of war" (tactics and operations) but not the "nature" of war.

WHAT WILL THE ROLE OF AI BE AT THE START OF WAR?

History is replete with improbable events. It is always possible for the unlikely to occur. However, through research and knowledge of human affairs, one can identify the most probable future.

It is unlikely that AI would, on its own, initiate a war. The most threatening situation would occur if a nuclear weapons power placed control of its arsenal exclusively with an AI command and control system. It holds the potential for an accidental launch. Although the Soviet Union built the "dead hand" system to guarantee a retaliatory nuclear strike if the military leadership was decapitated, most reports regard it as a communications system in which humans remained in actual control of the weapons. Even if that is accurate, it is unfortunate that the system has reportedly been reactivated by Vladimir Putin as part of his campaign of intimidation.

The primary role for AI in the period in which a decision is made to go to war is more likely to be as an enabler for analysis and advisory features. AI would facilitate the compilation of big data that could convince a decision-maker that a victory is likely. Siri may not prompt a world leader to "go to war now." But the modeling and simulation—with an AI system running hundreds of thousands of war games including all possible factors—might persuade an aggressor that the risk is low. At that point, there would be a failure in deterrence. Ultimately, however, it will be a human choice to trust the data, have the desire to fight, and commence the conflict.

During the actual conflict, AI would be utilized for human-machine teaming in conducting military operations. As engineering improves the capabilities of autonomous platforms, it is probable that fully autonomous systems would also be deployed. How these systems operate raises the question of whether autonomous systems would be permitted to use deadly force in a manner totally unsupervised by humans.

Thus far, the U.S. government has set a firm policy that fully autonomous systems—those without a human in the loop—will not be permitted to kill. Unfortunately, neither China nor Russia has indicated it will adopt the same policy. Both have incentives—particularly Russia—to allow full autonomy of combat systems. All three nations are conducting experiments as to how AI-driven weapons systems could operate autonomously in an effective manner. As of now, the engineering has not caught up with the expectation of those envisioning autonomous systems dominating the battlefield. But there is no reason to suspect it will not.

The overriding question becomes whether the United States and its allies can defend themselves while holding the firm principle of humans in the loop while the potential opponents do not. Are we literally "driven to autonomy" as far as combat operations since the human OODA loop cannot keep up?

Perhaps there is a metaphorical algorithm of Armageddon developing that will force future wars to be autonomous from the start. This is an idea worthy of a national dialogue.

WILL WORLD WAR III EVER END?

If So, How?

Those with the power to start a war frequently come to discover that they lack the power to stop it.... Thousands of man-years are absorbed by calculations on specific military operations or pieces of equipment, and by intelligence estimates of enemy strength in this or that local area. Usually very few military officers or civilian analysts are given the time or opportunity to pull all these pieces together and to prepare estimates that bear directly on the over-all strategy and that will show how the entire undertaking might be brought to a satisfactory end.

FRED CHARLES IKLE
Every War Must End, 1971

IF, IN THE NEAR TERM, the primary purpose of military AI will be intelligence assessment, iterative war gaming, and aiding human decision-making, and it does convince the aggression-minded that their objectives can be achieved, does it also hold the potential to advise decision-makers on how to *end* a war?

ALGORITHMS OF PEACE?

The late Fred Ikle, who served as a defense official in the Ronald Reagan administration, points out that ending a war—particularly if it might result in an apparent defeat—involves a different form of thought and emotion than displayed at the start of the conflict. AI systems are designed to provide capabilities such as "estimates of enemy strength" quickly without the need for "thousands of man-years." They are intended to replace the requirement for human analysts to work those thousands of man-years. Presumably, an AI system that is given the time (it might need little) to calculate the probable outcome at the start of the war should be able to calculate a more accurate assessment of that outcome once the war progresses and more big data concerning the reality of operations becomes available.

However, it is not clear whether the same algorithm that can "make predictions on past data" in a static situation (the relative calm before the start of hostilities) can do the same in the dynamic environment of actual combat. It would seem that it would require (thousands) more lines of additional coding and labeling. It would have to be able to make an accurate assessment amidst the fog of war—in other words, calculations based on only partial and likely inaccurate data. But, additionally, how does one label "peace?" Moreover, why should a decision-maker trust the outcome of AI algorithmic calculations as to when to stop a war if its predictions concerning the outcome of the war at the start were incorrect?

Such calculations would likely come via human-machine teaming. It is doubtful that humans would simply follow the predictions of what is essentially a black box without participating in the calculations. But man-machine teaming introduces human elements into the calculus, such as cultural imperatives to fight to the last, a desire not to appear a traitor to one's cause or people, or the romantic perception of fighting forever for a lost cause. The idea that a decision-maker would dispassionately accept the advice of a machine that he or she needed to surrender or seek a negotiated settlement with a "hated" enemy remains unlikely.

This is reflected in the fact that there are wars that have never ended. Ikle's study is based on wars fought between 1914 and 1956. The totalitarian government of North Korea has never acceded that the Korean War, which saw its most active (and bloody) combat between 1950 and 1953, has ended. The present day is just a temporary truce. The fact that combat might break out tomorrow is its justification for prioritizing the military and letting parts of its civilian population starve.

The Chinese civil war between the Chinese Communist Party and the Nationalist Party (Kuomintang) has never ended. Despite the fact that the Kuomintang is no longer in power in Taiwan, the CCP's obsession with Taiwan is largely its desire to end the civil war with an absolute victory that truly displays it has the mandate from heaven to rule China.

Imagine an AI system that could gather, compile, and analyze all possible information in the universe; could a negative prediction achieve the historical result of causing either side to give up the thought of war?

Return to the Near-Future Scenario

The general secretary's AI decision support system was capable of simulating and assessing millions of war-gaming moves in seconds while correlating actual intelligence data so as to predict their outcome. Tied to it were the thousands of information sensors of the vast PLA intelligence, surveillance, and reconnaissance network—located in satellites, at ground bases in the mainland and forward bases in other countries, on crewed ships, submarines, and aircraft, and within thousands of controlled or autonomous unmanned vehicles in all domains, coupled with a constantly updating cyber database.

Having calculated a high probability of success, the general secretary chose to go to war. In the initial bloody stages, combat appeared to be proceeding in a favorable direction. But fog, friction, and chance are always present in war. The fog comes from a lack of information or reliance on false information. Many of the sensors that constitute the general secretary's ISR network are destroyed and their information curtailed. He is becoming uncertain about the quality of his information.

The friction is the breakdown of combat systems, not only from the fire of the enemy, but also due to their complexity and through encountering an environment or event for which they were not designed. Imagine pushing a heavy weight across a smooth floor and then encountering a carpet that was not expected. Friction increases. As friction increases, the outcome of the event becomes less certain.

Although the general secretary's AI decision aid has taken the possibility of friction into consideration from the start, there were obstacles and unexpected actions taken by the enemy that created unexpected friction. There was a carpet hidden somewhere on the smooth floor. He is becoming frustrated because progress is not following his detailed plan.

Chance is the occurrence of random events that could not truly be anticipated. AI systems can assess probability and identify possibilities by running through thousands of simulations. Perhaps this can account for every element of chance, but chance often flows against calculated logic. Effective planners know that chance must be accounted for. But to do that, the planners must—in effect—not trust their own judgment. Is it possible to teach an AI algorithm not to trust its answer? How difficult is it to train a computer not to trust itself? No one as yet has been able to successfully do that, a situation we will discuss in more detail later.

After more unexpected/uncalculated events occur, AI intelligence systems now predict that defeat of the general secretary's forces has become probable. Does he end the war? If defeated, it is possible that—in traditional Chinese culture—he no longer possesses the mandate to rule, and it will be time for others to challenge his authority (this is likely to happen regardless of whether there is a traditional culture). Or does he fight on, despite the knowledge that his defeat is almost assured?

That was the decision made by the government of Imperial Japan after recognizing in late 1942 that there was no plausible way to defeat the United States and its allies. Japan fought on in the hope that its opponents would just stop fighting (perhaps to conclude a truce). When it was apparent that its opponents would not stop, desperate measures were taken: kamikazes, suicide charges and sorties, and civilians killing themselves rather than be taken prisoner. It took two nuclear bombs to convince Imperial Japanese forces to stop fighting.

Ironically, the kamikazes can be seen as the ultimate human-machine teaming—the pilot was integrated as the guidance system within the ordnance. This is not exactly what is envisioned in utilizing AI but is interesting to ponder.

SCENARIO VERSUS AGI

Our point is that there is no convincing logic that AI in itself could either prevent or end a war. Perhaps the even more important point is that AI in and of itself is nothing. Militarized AI is a tool for humans to control other humans.

We contend that artificial general intelligence will not arrive in the near future, but others might disagree. So the question should be asked: If AGI—the extreme form of AI that requires no human intervention—were given the power of decision-making, would the war end? In fact, would there be any wars at all?

There are extreme proponents of AGI who would consider turning over all decision-making to the machine. As one proponent maintains, AI "could run the world better than humans ever could."[1] Does that mean AI could start, conduct, and end war better than humans could? It could potentially end war better than a human; once it calculates that the objective cannot be achieved, defeat is imminent, or the financial costs involved outweigh the benefits, it would have no emotion-based reason not to stop.

Of course, most proponents of AGI believe that such an AI machine could develop self-awareness, consciousness, or singularity (their preferred term) similar to that demonstrated by the fictional HAL. So maybe—to avoid admitting mistakes—it would *not* end the war until there were no combatants left (whether autonomous systems or humans). Worse yet, it might end the war—with all due logic—by ending the (human) combatants.

This is a potential for AGI that could be included in the ones Musk, Wozniak, the late Stephen Hawking, and others have raised concerning the future of AGI.

Scenario: AI and Autonomy in a More Distant Future

The bolt from the blue took both humans and machines by surprise. Both authoritarian states and democracies had maximized their investment in military AI and assembled fleets of autonomous uncrewed aerial vehicles, uncrewed surface vehicles (both ships and tanks), uncrewed undersea vehicles, and an uncrewed satellite network and machine-speed cyber war tool. Justification for a near-total reliance on autonomous systems included:

- the speed necessary to complete the required OODA loop to successfully fight autonomous systems
- the desire to keep humans off the battlefields to reduce the loss of life
- the promise that autonomous systems would successfully deter war or provide a quick victory
- a shortfall in military-age citizens or an inability to recruit military personnel
- the view that machines would be "more politically reliable"
- the assumption that a war between autonomous systems would be isolated from civil society and thereby protect the lives and property of civilians
- the perception that a war of autonomous systems would prove less bloody
- the hope that war would be less likely since it would be stripped of its entanglement with human emotions, no longer an activity driven by the fear, honor, or ambitions of individuals
- the illusion if that the robot armies and navies of one side were defeated, the defeated side would peacefully submit to the (hopefully) modest demands of an enemy that would not impose an oppressive regime on the defeated.

Such justifications prompted the ultimate in revolutions in military affairs—a near-complete replacement of human combatants by machines. This was perceived as a clear step toward the larger goal of a peaceful world. But whether the combatants are human or machine, the strategic goals of the opponents do not change. Nations that have launched wars *have* sought peace (eventually), but one in which their objectives dominate and are fulfilled.

And in this continuing scenario, strategic goals did not change. The general secretary desired a peace that only the end of the Chinese civil war would bring. His enormous armada of autonomous uncrewed ships, aircraft, missiles, amphibious landing forces, and ground combat vehicles is poised to rapidly strike across the 100-nautical-mile width of the Taiwan Strait.

Positioned as a deterrent is an undersea fleet of uncrewed vehicles and weapons belonging to the United States, Japan, Australia, and other allies. But this force is designed to function as a trip-wire to delay the crossing until more autonomous uncrewed weapons systems can deploy into the theater. However, like all mechanical equipment, autonomous weapons must be maintained, overhauled, refurbished, and upgraded. The costs of these activities can be quite high, and they are often deferred during periods of tight or overextended defense budgets that have to compete with other government priorities. (Current human-crewed ships and aircraft face exactly that sort of backlog today in maintaining readiness following years of deferred maintenance as most defense dollars were directed to operations in Iraq and Afghanistan.)

Sensing a similar circumstance in the future, the general secretary's AI decision support system predicts the moment at which the opponent's maintenance backlog is the greatest and readiness is the lowest. This calculus presents a logical moment for an aggressor to strike, but it surprised the opponent's machines as well as humans nevertheless.

Such surprise does not necessarily provide a long-term advantage—perhaps just enough to tilt the balance, since many of the allied autonomous systems must be moved long distances to enter the region of combat. Long transits make them more vulnerable to long-range attacks guided by satellite reconnaissance strike networks optimized by AI. In combat between the autonomous systems of technological near-peers, the battle becomes one of attrition as systems destroy opposing systems in complex, but finely AI-calculated, operational plans.

However, at a certain point in the conflict, the autonomous systems are expended. Systems have destroyed systems. The defense industrial bases of both nations attempt to build replacements, but the systems are complex. Just-in-time business techniques mean there is no great stock of replacement parts on the shelf. In fact, the parts and electronic circuitry originally utilized were originally supplied by the opponent. Supply cannot match even a modest demand.

So how does it end? Do both sides just stop fighting and accept the status quo? Or does the war enter a second phase in which humans fight humans once again?

Going further into the scenario: human marines start loading into human-controlled vessels to make the 100-nautical-mile crossing. Those on the endangered island need to decide if, as in the promise of British Prime Minister Winston Churchill in World War II, they will "fight on the beaches . . . fight in the landing grounds, fight in the fields and in the streets [and] never surrender." Or, having chosen surrender, do they fathom what the occupying army, armed with the AI social control system they have perfected with their own population, will do to their society?

ACCEPTING THE FOG OF WAR: DOUBT AND INCOMPLETE INFORMATION

Doubt is a human ability that, as of today, AI systems have not demonstrated. Given that AI is designed to make predictions and provide decision support based on past data in an environment where data is so vast that no human can correlate all of it, is there any logical reason for such a system to be programmed to experience doubt? The point of AI is to assist in making decisions at near–machine speed. The OODA loop is not the OODDA loop (observe-orient-decide-doubt and think again-act). Doubt would seem to be contradictory to the whole purpose of having AI.

This is where human-machine teaming proves its great value—superior to the machine alone. In the first scenario above, we added the fog of war—the effect of friction generated when two opposing forces, with two opposing plans, encounter each other. Chance also becomes a factor, particularly when humans do illogical things. As previously noted, some military analysts have suggested that the use of modern technologies—such as networks of sensors, communications systems transmitting data between computers, and AI decision-making tools—can literally lift the fog of war. But those who proposed that possibility in the 1990s would be disappointed by the subsequent two decades. The fog is still there, despite significant technological advances. Their answer might be that we need even more technology; eventually, we will have the right capabilities.

But that answer raises two more questions: Can AI systems operate effectively with limited access to information? Is there a point at which information is so limited that a human—able to accept the reality of the fog and doubt one's own plan—is more effective at correlating and understanding the available information than AI?

Current AI systems operate under the assumption of open access to large amounts of information—in other words, free big data. Those systems such as Deep Blue, DeepMind, and IBM's Watson, which have defeated humans in the TV game show *Jeopardy!*, chess, and iGo, have operated (and still do) under conditions of complete information. All the rules of the game are known. There are no changes in the rules during the competition. The AI is trained to learn and know every possible move. The point of utilizing AI is to determine all the possibilities by gaming move after move, thousands, perhaps millions, of times, until every possible combination (allowed under the rules) is identified and, in effect, practiced.

No human can do that. As Noam Chomsky said, it is like a bulldozer competing against a weightlifter. Even in Texas Hold'em poker, where luck can play a role, the number of cards played is finite. The computer knows which cards have been played and which are still held and can calculate all the possible upcoming plays. It can also "count cards" better than any human.

However, what happens when the rules change in the middle of the game? Instead of a pawn being a mere tool, it is now as valuable as the king. Can the same algorithm adapt? Or, more complex still, what if the human player suddenly pulls out a checkerboard in the middle of the chess game? The AI machine has never played checkers. It is not trained to calculate all possible checker combinations; it doesn't even recognize the game. It now faces an environment of incomplete information. A human playing another human could likely adapt to checkers since it is a well-known human game. The human can respond to the completely unexpected move.

As of today, no one has built an AI system that can do that. Theoretically, one could combine multiple AI systems, each individually trained on an individual game, until one had a combined AI engine that could handle every known game ever played. Still, each game has a fixed rule set. Rules are not supposed to change in the middle of the contest.

To ask a tangential question: even if it were possible to actually construct such a machine, could anyone afford to do so when the total costs were added up—not just coding, parts, and personnel, but loans, venture capital, and lost financial opportunities? It cost $1 billion to beat the iGo master.

War, however, is an endeavor in which one fights in an environment of incomplete information. Even with advanced sensors, one can never fully know what is in the mind of the opponent. The opponent doesn't have to do the expected. There are no fixed rules. The opponent doesn't even have to obey any particular law of war. (Fighters who belong to terrorist groups don't obey them.) The use of autonomous AI systems might convince humans that the laws of war need to be adjusted, but it is the humans that are doing the adjusting, and there is no guarantee that other humans will obey the adjustment.

ADDING IN DECEPTION

What will happen when technological near-peers fight each other—two forces that have equivalent capabilities that attempt to lift the fog? Meanwhile, each is attempting to utilize deception techniques to create more fog. An attempt to lift the fog might simply introduce more deception.

Sun Tzu, the great ancient Chinese sage and author of *The Art of War* states definitively that "all war is deception." Deception is an unexplored element in the examination of AI. Most commercial users of AI have no incentive to deal with it. Google, for example, assumes that you are actually interested in the websites on which you click. It does not assume you might be deceiving its AI engine by clicking on sites that you have no interest in just to throw off its algorithms. Google could handle a single user doing that; it's a drop in a vast ocean of data. But if millions of users did it, how could Google guarantee its paying advertisers that it is delivering potential customers inclined to purchase their products? Why advertise with Google when you might be reaching millions of the wrong customers? For Google to admit that deception is an issue would be to admit that its business model is flawed. Therefore, there is little incentive to deeply investigate deception.

We do not know if Google has ever contemplated the above situation. But we have discussed the impact of deception on AI systems with a number of leaders in the AI community. Some have argued that deception is virtually impossible since AI algorithms are designed to look for patterns and identify anomalies. All one needs to penetrate deception is more big data. With enough accurate data, one could find the outliers that do not fit the "true" pattern.

In theory that might be so, but it presumes one has the biggest trove of accurate data at the commencement of a war. Where can more "accurate" big data be obtained in the midst of a conflict in which the enemy is generating deceptive data and all the data one is working with is incomplete?

Others have conceded that the commercial world has no incentive to spend large amounts of resources—cutting into profits—to solve a problem that they assume has no impact on their business. It costs money to solve problems. However, it is certainly an issue that should receive a great deal of attention by the intelligence community.

ADDING UP THE REACH OF AI IN WAR

In the final chapter, we will summarize all the issues concerning the military application of AI and its role in war. But we will begin to work toward that here in the context of our question of how a World War III—with heavy use of AI—will end.

AI in the form of a decision-making aid utilized by human-machine teaming (as opposed to giving it the sole power of decision) is not going to start a war on its own. Similarly, it is not going to end one. We can examine a whole range of plausible scenarios (besides the People's Republic of China invading Taiwan) in which AI could play an increasing role—a Putinized Russia continues to try to conquer Ukraine, Iran clashes with Saudi Arabia (perhaps using proxies such as Houthis in Yemen), Pakistan again fights with India, and other scenarios too numerous to mention here. But nowhere does it seem that decision-makers would stop a war because of analysis by AI. There are too many internal political factors and emotions.

AI in the form of autonomous systems will play an increasingly significant role in future wars. Will these wars ever be a clash of autonomous systems alone, with no humans directly involved in fighting other humans? This image, projected by countless science fiction stories, will remain science fiction for some time. One can envision a small number of machine-machine engagements on the battlefield or at sea, but in the context of a (largely) human-human fight.

Just as in the *Star Wars* series of movies and other media, the most probable far-future combat scenario will be humans fighting other humans alongside autonomous systems. A concept we have discussed is the loyal wingman, an initiative the U.S. Air Force is developing where a fleet of unmanned "collaborative combat aircraft" will be wingmen to Air Force F-35 Joint Strike Fighters.[2] Whether the human would be the lead with the machine as the wingman (as is being developed now) or the human would be the wingman to a machine that would lead and be the enemy's first target will depend on AI's future capabilities. But it definitely constitutes a continuing collaboration between warrior and weapon.

AUTONOMOUS WEAPONS AND THE DEFENSE INDUSTRIAL AND INNOVATION BASE

One of the limitations in machine-machine or even human-machine teaming combat is the ability of the defense industry to replace losses. It is a significant issue for the United States today due to the tremendous consolidation in the defense industry and the outsourcing of parts manufacturing to other countries. According to DoD, following the end of the Cold War, the number of U.S. aerospace and prime defense contractors shrunk from fifty-one to five.[3] This reduction in capacity has been highlighted by the difficulty of weapons production in NATO nations to keep up with Ukraine's ordnance expenditure in its defense against Russia.

The question applying to the more distant future scenario is whether it would be possible for any nation to keep up with the demand for autonomous systems in a machine-machine war with high attrition. In terms of cost, sophisticated AI-controlled combat platforms might not be less expensive than crewed vehicles. Many of the most capable UAVs, such as Predator and Triton, approximate the size of conventional aircraft. One of the reason DoD is eager to adopt AI is to reduce long-term personnel cost. This, of course, parallels the primary use of AI in the commercial world—to reduce staff.

The rate of replacement of damaged or destroyed autonomous systems could become the deciding factor in a machine-to-machine war. The side that can manufacture to replace losses quicker than the opponent would gradually have the advantage. The defense industrial base would thereby be the most important weapon in the conflict. Or, perhaps, if production of autonomous systems cannot keep up with attrition, the war would revert to combat between human personnel.

That is the most likely outcome today. Analysts have speculated that in a war with the People's Republic of China, the United States would expend its inventory of precision weapons in as little as two weeks, depending on the intensity of combat operations. Such smart weapons could be assessed as proxies for future AI-controlled autonomous weapons, and AI weapons would face a similar expenditure rate. However, neither side indicates that it would consider a stop to fighting once all (or at least most) precision weapons are used up. Rather, the fight would shift to "dumber" bombs. This would be the likely situation in the future if the inventory of autonomous weapons were depleted. The war would continue.

A contrary argument is made by some who see a lesson in the use of the Internet services that Starlink provided to the Ukrainian government in the war against Russia.[4] SpaceX has launched thousands of very small Starlink satellites to provide relayed Internet broadband services to remote areas of the world. SpaceX/Starlink's CEO, Elon Musk, gained considerable media attention when he began providing Starlink receivers to the Ukrainian government.[5] His later warning of ending services due to costs resulted in a public outcry, resulted in his acceding to continuing the Starlink service.

The argument is that, similar to the deployment of Starlink satellites, small autonomous weapons—nanoweapons—could be produced and deployed in great numbers prior to the conflict, lessening the strain to increase production during hostilities.[6] As of November 2022 there were 3,271 Starlink satellites in orbit, each weighing 573 pounds. SpaceX plans to launch a total of 42,000 of these satellites. However, the argument turns unpersuasive when comparing size capability and cost between what is essentially an Internet relay reflector and a sophisticated UAV such as Triton. In February 2023 a SpaceX official decried Ukraine's "weaponization" of Starlink, presumably for its use in transmitting orders and intelligence data.[7]

Our analysis concludes that capable autonomous weapons will remain comparatively expensive and inventories will remain relatively small in the near future. However, if the opposing sides are evenly matched in defense industrial capabilities, could a machine-to-machine war go on literally forever? Such is the plot of science fiction stories stretching back at least a century.

DOES THE WAR HAVE TO END?

Fred Ikle suggested that every war *must* end, but what about ones in which AI plays a significant role? Ikle's analysis was completed in the 1980s, prior to the expansive growth of the public Internet and increasing commercial dependence on the medium called cyberspace. Since then, cyberspace has become a domain of conflict as well as a means of espionage. Cyber conflict involves the protection of national cyber infrastructure—particularly national security systems—against malicious actors, which include other nations as well as criminal groups of many stripes. Massive Russian cyberattacks on Estonia's government and financial systems prompted NATO to create a Cooperative Cyber Defence Centre of Excellence in Tallinn, that country's capital, in 2022. The NATO general secretary, Jens Stoltenberg, suggested that such a future cyberattack against a NATO member might result in declaration of Article 5, the prelude to NATO military operations against an enemy.

Since 1996 U.S. defense networks and civilian infrastructure have been under near-constant cyberattack by such entities as Fancy Bear, linked to Russian military intelligence; Cozy Bear, linked to the Russian Foreign Intelligence Agency; and Byzantine Candor, linked to the Chinese PLA Unit 61398. Cyberattacks on DoD networks have originated from Beijing and Guangdong, China. Such attacks have gone beyond espionage and included malware attacks designed to wipe computer memories.

Does this persistent struggle constitute a war? If so, it appears to be never ending. Unlike depleted inventories of autonomous weapons, operations in cyberspace seem inexhaustible—an undeclared, mostly hidden, but endless war. AI is undoubtedly used in cyber warfare operations as a natural evolution of the level of computing required to access cyberspace. It also seems a natural tool for cryptologic operation to encrypt and decrypt code at machine speed.

From this perspective, a war utilizing AI might never end. The cyber combat systems could operate autonomously forever. Victory might eventually come to the side that persisted or possessed superior AI capability with a faster OODA loop than that of the opponent. Or victory just might never come in a war continued by AI.

11

TOWARD A NATIONAL DIALOGUE ON MILITARY AI

The coming era of Artificial Intelligence will not be the era of war, but be the era of deep compassion, non-violence, and love.

AMIT RAY[1]

AI has the power to throw us back into the Dark Ages.

REV. DR. DEBORAH L. H. MARIYA[2]

HAVING READ THE PREVIOUS chapters and gained an understanding of the military applications of AI, the question is: what should we do as a nation? The U.S. Department of Defense is trying to integrate AI into information and combat systems in what it sees as a responsible manner. Their intent is to keep humans in the loop on any decision to use deadly force. All DoD directives state that particular precept, and none of the autonomous systems—whether currently or potentially driven by AI— appear to have been designed to violate it.

Contrary to novels, movies, and some people's fears, there are no "Dr. Strangeloves" lurking in the deep confines of the Pentagon and singlehandedly creating a "Terminator." For one thing, it is currently impossible. And for another, all large defense programs (as opposed to R&D of prototypes or improvements to current systems) are known to Congress and eventually become known, even with classification and safeguards, to the public. Indeed, the money for these programs is appropriated by Congress. Building a Terminator would cost many billions of dollars and could not be hidden for long.

Even black programs—those classified at the highest levels of top secret, special compartmented information, or special access—require oversight by at least a select group of Congressional members and, most obviously, the senior-most civilian officials in the presidential administration. Their particulars may be—and should be—unknown beyond a small group and not to the public or even the majority of servicemembers; however, analysts and citizens can generally discern, by knowledge of research and logic, the types (not the details) of programs being secretly worked. There are no indications of an unexpected breakthrough in AI weaponry.

Rather than new methods of combat, military AI is currently directed at improving the old. As a decision-making aid, it is intended to provide the combatants with more information more rapidly in order to be able to speed the OODA cycle. As the controller for autonomous systems, AI is trying to perfect what is already operating by remote control.

Even in the spiritual perspectives of the epigraphs, expectations on the impact of AI on humans vary wildly. Perhaps the best way to approach a necessary public dialogue on what we should do is to first identify and deal with the facts. Not everyone will agree with the facts, so that is where the discussion needs to begin. Others do not want to believe them because they can be frightening. In any event, there needs to be a common understanding of the possibilities, vulnerabilities, and practicalities of military application of AI. That has been our intent with this book. Only with facts can we generate the necessary discussion.

To summarize the details of our previous chapters, we will break the facts into three categories: basic facts about AI, AI at war, and dangers and issues that we need to collectively discuss. In AI speak, we will *label* the facts and bin them into three categories, but with the understanding that all the data (facts) are interrelated. The categories are artificial constructs to help us think humanly.

BASIC FACTS ABOUT AI

AI leverages advanced computing methodologies with advantages and vulnerabilities. By now this is obvious, but it is important to repeat this observation to dispel the notion that AI is some sort of magic unrelated to all other advances in computing—software, hardware, chips, and other components. It is important to acknowledge that it has the same vulnerabilities that impact all computers:

- AI can be hacked
- AI is dependent on access to the electrical grid (or some other continuous power source)
- the development and supply chain are easily penetrated by those with malicious intent
- only a small percentage of people know how to do it (so they can make claims that are difficult to judge)
- as with all commercial computing, AI is subject to hype and promotion.

These vulnerabilities must be acknowledged and balanced against the capabilities that the adoption of any AI system brings.

For example, ChatGPT and its competitors—which, as of the time of writing, are the AI research tool and chatbots of greatest public interest—may be great tools for assembling data in an apparently effortless manner and crafting an information paper with considerable ease. Not much time needs to be spent in the library. But such programs have to acquire the information from a source, and if that source is the Internet (the most readily available and cheapest source of information), some amount of inaccurate or false information is likely to be incorporated into the text at some point. Anyone with a website can place any information—true or false—on the Internet that a search engine will eventually encounter. Corporate websites extol virtues that might not exactly match reality. This behavior is not insidious when one considers that the web is primarily an advertising tool, but it is a fact that many users forget due to the usefulness of search engines.

Experts who have tested such AI information tools by prompting them to provide increasing amounts of information of greater specificity have found that the more details are added, the more inaccuracies are included. One can argue that is true of all research, whether by human or machine. But the hype surrounding these tools has given them an aura of accuracy that is not valid. Hype always expands when serious investments are made and tremendous profits are expected.

As an example, ChatGPT is expected to generate huge profits by developing specialized apps for individual companies at a cost of $100,000 to $500,000. Microsoft has invested at least $11 billion in OpenAI, the formerly nonprofit organization that developed ChatGPT (and which is now valued at over $20 billion). One estimate is that it costs OpenAI $700,000 per day ($255 million per year) to provide ChatGPT services. That does not include development or other corporate costs. A staggering amount of money is involved. Hence, a staggering amount of hype is generated.

Nevertheless, it is still necessary to acknowledge that advanced chatbots—and all AI—have the same vulnerabilities of all computing. AI has been set apart from "standard" computer and software hardware development, but in reality, that separation is somewhat artificial. Garbage in equals garbage out, even if the garbage load is much bigger and arrives much faster. Such AI-driven data compilers will eventually become more accurate. However, there is no common lie detector for the Internet, despite efforts to create programs that can detect "fake news." Consider what this means when utilizing military AI against an opponent that is doing everything possible to generate false information.

AI tricks us to think it is thinking. Here we return to the Turing test or, as we have called it, the Turing trick. Turing never claimed that a machine could actually be made to think in the same manner as humans. He simply maintained that if the human believes a machine to be intelligent, then it is. This is an important observation to remember when assessing the future of AI—for good or for ill. Many foresee a day when AI will experience consciousness in the same manner of a human and will bring in a glorious new age for humanity. Others see it as creating a HAL or, even more scary, a Terminator. However, this remains speculation based on one's desires or fears.

AGI will not happen tomorrow. In fact, it may never happen. AGI (which would need autonomy) could trick us into believing it is human-like by linking a tremendous number of AI processes (along with biomechanical technology), but there is no evidence that humans can create consciousness in a machine. We barely know what consciousness is, let alone how it is created. Consciousness is self-awareness as a living being and requires biochemical processes. It incorporates a sense of the spiritual. If a machine had self-awareness installed through a biochemical process, it would no longer be a machine. In accordance with our constant refrain concerning human-machine teaming, it is much more likely that cyborgs—AI systems embedded in humans—could be developed rather than AGI (but that too is some time away and generates many ethical concerns). Even among AI scientists, a significant number believe AGI is an impossibility.

This has an implication for starting a public dialogue on AI in general and military AI in particular. If AI ever "replaces humans," it will not be AI replacing humans. It will be humans using AI to "replace" other humans, perhaps in a violent manner. This means any effort to control the future of AI is actually an effort to solve a human problem much bigger than just AI. This also leads to a fundamental question about the imperative in developing military applications, such as autonomous systems. Do we need to develop military AI simply in order to deter others with military AI from controlling us? Will we have any choice?

AI is developed (in democracies) to make money. Elsewhere, money is a secondary concern. In democracies, AI development currently depends on profitability. It is hyped for the purpose of making money (or getting more resources to make money). AI will undoubtedly eliminate some jobs and maybe create a few new ones. Its impact on jobs and employment deserves considerable public debate in itself, but we will leave developing that to others.

We will argue that two related observations need to be recognized. First, in authoritarian countries, AI is not being developed solely or even primarily to make money. It is being developed for social control and aggressive purposes. Anyone who disputes that observation merely needs to read the 2017 *Next Generation Artificial Intelligence Development Plan* of the People's

Republic of China State Council. Or perhaps juxtapose Vladimir Putin's views on the future importance of AI and his invasion of Ukraine. They do want to make money, but that is not why they view AI as so powerful.

This places democracies in the difficult position of determining how to respond. Do they need to change priorities in AI development from a free market profit-dominant approach to a more restricted national security–focused approach? And if so, how can that been done without interfering with the free and open marketplaces that democratic governments were created to preserve?

Also, how can we interest the biggest AI developers in seriously supporting national defense? Is it a problem of patriotism (hard to maintain in companies that think of themselves as global corporations)? Or is it the problem of profit?

Why should top AI developers forego the potential for immense commercial profits to develop applications for a single customer in a highly regulated environment and with a legislatively directed low profit margin? Many within the defense community assume that future AI "breakthroughs" will come from small start-ups or researchers supported in some measure by government. DoD maintains the Defense Innovation Unit in Silicon Valley, a small office to discover, encourage, and finance small companies that could produce AI and other computing products with military applications. However, most AI breakthroughs—even those that originate in university laboratories—are brought to full development by firms that can attract at least $1 billion in venture capital. Perhaps the only answer is direct government involvement in commercial AI—not on the scale of the PRC or Russia, but certainly larger than today.

As chair of the 2018–21 National Security Commission on Artificial Intelligence, former Google CEO Eric Schmidt demonstrated a strong commitment to encouraging U.S. government investment in AI as an essential element of national security. He has continued this effort by funding nongovernmental commissions and studies. From our perspective, this is a public service example that many other former and current CEOs of high-tech firms should be following.

Nevertheless, the example that also appears to be needed is that of the U.S. government's commitment to the space race in the 1960s–70s. An epigraph in an earlier chapter compared AI to the space race rather than being a technology. During the space race, the National Aeronautics and Space Administration did not make money. Neither did military support for space exploration, which cost money. However, products spun off from these efforts, including solar panels, microwave ovens, laptop computers, global positioning systems, the Internet, and cell phones, were further developed and commercialized by civilian companies. Perhaps this is the model we should follow. It certainly appears that it is the model the PRC is following.

Autonomy is not a technology but a combination of technologies. When they are truly developed, self-driving cars will not be solely the result of advances in AI. They will need AI systems, but they will be the result of a combination of technologies that produce the sensors that provide the data to AI, control mechanisms that respond to the directions of AI, and power systems that can be integrated with AI. The AI will not come to life if an alternator or other power source is not started. All of these technologies require modifications to optimize the capabilities of AI to perform the task: driving.

So too is the situation with developing military autonomous systems. We have argued that sensors are the critical elements that provide the big data that fuels AI. In combat, destruction of sensors appears more important than the destruction of AI control systems in order to blind the enemy.

Autonomous military land systems will benefit from commercial advances in self-driving; autonomous systems in other environments, perhaps not as much. Conducting undersea warfare is a bit different than driving safely on the highway.

AI IN WAR

We will not belabor many of the facts concerning AI at war since we have covered them all before with perhaps one exception.

AI's primary military use today is to compile and analyze information faster. The U.S. military is pursuing autonomy and doing so in a responsible manner as directed by civilian authority. But the current focus is on speeding the OODA loop.

Big data, not AI, is the most necessary ingredient. We have highlighted that many times. But with regard to the public impression of AI, it cannot be said enough. In battle, there may be too much information for a human commander to absorb and understand. But there also might be too little information for AI to make a difference. Deception is the enemy of useful big data.

AI will be increasingly used to develop autonomous systems. This perhaps is obvious but is a fact to mention. Effective autonomous systems require AI; AI is designed to provide machines with a degree of autonomy, if only in making predictions based on past data.

AI will give uncrewed (unmanned) systems more autonomy. This has certainly been discussed—particularly in the case of the U.S. Navy's Triton UAV. Utilizing AI does not have to result in complete autonomy. It can be used to provide only the level of autonomy needed to make human-machine teaming effective.

Human-machine teaming appears the optimal use of military AI. AI systems—like all machines—do not have the flexibility, the creativity, the initiative, or the capacity for doubt to function effectively on their own. They operate most effectively when supporting human teammates. AI brings vulnerabilities along with advantages. It is the human who makes up for the vulnerabilities.

Military AI will cost more money than commercial AI because there are a limited number of customers (one and perhaps a handful of allies). We have not discussed the financial costs of AI in this book beyond noting that they could be huge, and they remain a barrier that can disincentivize companies—beyond the existing military industrial base—from pursuing military applications. We need to explore this a bit more.

Developing a military innovation base (again, outside traditional defense corporations) remains difficult as concerns AI. DoD can easily purchase commercial-off-the-shelf AI systems, but they are not tailored to military operations. Companies that have poured resources into systems that win at chess and iGo do so to demonstrate their AI capabilities in order to persuade potential clients to use their services for solving practical problems. In essence, it is advertising; they do not expect to turn a profit with chess or iGo. They are willing to expend resources—perhaps up to $1 billion—under the assumption that they will make tremendous amounts of money in the future. This is also their incentive in their granting money to universities and institutes that conduct basic research. Sometimes it pays off; sometimes it doesn't, which is why venture capital financing can be a gamble for all involved.

But to generate profits following such expenditure requires a large volume of customers. The more clients means more income. One can take a gamble on producing AI-powered cell phones if one expects to have millions of customers. Investment is recouped by many purchases, and in a competitive environment, lower prices can be the result.

That is not the reality for businesses in the defense industry. They are dependent on one primary customer in a highly regulated environment in which Congress scrutinizes their level of profit. There is often limited economy of scale to decrease the cost of production.

Critics often lambast the Pentagon for paying too much for what purportedly costs commercial customers less. That might be valid criticism for simple consumables, but not for systems that have little or no civilian use. Waste, fraud, and abuse aside, simple economics explains why things cost more, and this will include military applications of AI.

Military applications *will* cost more—perhaps more than initially expected. The overruns in large military programs prominently discussed in the media are often the result of underestimating the cost of doing things that are really hard to do. Building, for example, an uncrewed vehicle that can survive in combat by avoiding enemy fire and conducting its mission makes the challenge of developing a self-driving car for city streets seem comparatively small—which it, in fact, is.

Congress and critics urge DoD to run itself like a business. But it is not a business. It doesn't turn a profit. It cannot choose components in the way that any commercial firm does. Rather, it is a necessity.

AI cannot start a war (unless we let it). We have discussed this fear at length. The bottom line is that humans might use AI to analyze information (big data) in support of decision-making, but it is a human who makes the decision to go to war. If human decision-makers are actually willing to turn that decision over to machines, the possibility of war might be the least of our (global) problems. Autonomous systems might operate inadvertently or even go rogue. But as indicated by our list of such lethal accidents, they have never by themselves caused a war. They might be an excuse but have never been a cause. Algorithms of Armageddon are temptations to war, not inevitable outcomes.

AI cannot stop a war (unless we let it). Compiling big data utilizing AI methods might tell a commander that he or she is losing. But many nations, insurgents, and violent groups have fought on even when defeat stared them in the face. So knowing through AI that there is little hope of victory does not automatically end a war. Whole squadrons of AI-controlled autonomous weapons systems might fail. But that does not mean the side experiencing the failure just packs it in.

Some might argue that—for the sake of humanity—all militaries should adopt an AI system that immediately ceases hostilities when defeat is apparent; thereby, less bloodshed and suffering would occur. But what about deception? How would such a system ever know defeat was certain? Would a military commander trust such a recommendation? It would seem that force commanders would have to make their own conclusions. If human emotions play a role—as they always do—the answer might not be based on logic. Left to themselves, algorithms of Armageddon are just algorithms.

Deception is an issue that has not been sufficiently examined. Sun Tzu says that all wars are deception—meaning that deception is an element in all aspects of warfighting. Both warriors and those who study war generally agree. In applying AI to military operations, deception must be taken into account. But this causes a conundrum. AI is all about analyzing big data to make a decision. If the big data is false, then the wrong decision would be recommended. And if little data is available, then AI begins to lose its advantage as a decision-making tool.

In order to penetrate deception, one must doubt what others are presenting as facts. Humans can second-guess themselves in analysis and then begin again with different assumptions. AI might be able to calculate thousands of analytic options in the same way it can identify thousands of possible alternatives for a move in chess. However, can it doubt the information it has been trained with? Can it look at what might be a turtle or might be a gun and choose an option based on incomplete and contradictory information? In theory, it can. But as has been pointed out by commercial AI leaders, what is needed to crack a pattern of deception is more big data.

So where, in the midst of war, does the commander get more big data? With sensors and information nodes being destroyed in battle, the commander is likely to be getting diminishing amounts of big data. If more is obtained, it is likely to be incorrect data, perhaps poisoned by the enemy. Given these factors, at a certain point AI seems to lose its value because the astute commander will have less trust that the answers he or she might be getting are valid.

Commercial AI does not have to deal with this conundrum. Customers and component suppliers usually are not out to deceive. If the majority of customers are deceptive, you are out of business. If a component supplier is knowingly shipping false parts, they can go to jail. The result is that there is little commercial incentive to tackle the possibility of deception. If DoD and the intelligence agencies don't take an aggressive lead in this challenge, it isn't going to just bubble up out of Silicon Valley.

DANGERS AND CRITICAL ISSUES THAT WE NEED TO DISCUSS

Now we come to the heart of the matter: the dangers and issues—derived from the above facts—that all Americans should be discussing.

AI makes tyranny more effective. This is a reality of which every corporation, every coder, every scientist, and every citizen needs to be aware. Corporations that are sharing data or technologies with PRC "counterparts" or that maintain mainland Chinese subsidiaries are playing a role in perpetuating the CCP dictatorship. Hundreds of excuses can be made— "we are neutral," "we are only answerable to our shareholders," "we are global," "somebody else would be doing it anyway," "they could develop these capabilities on their own," "our economy is so intertwined with China that there is nothing we can do"—but at the end of the day, the reality remains that those who supply the tools of repression have a hand in the repression. CEOs and shareholders need to examine their consciences. The public needs to pressure them to do so. This issue is not about whether AI should be developed, but about how critical knowledge should be shared with those who have a track record of utilizing that knowledge for what most humans would see as evil purposes.

The general consensus among leaders and influencers in democratic nations in the heady days of 1990s globalization was that the technology revolution in information—Internet, wireless communications, the global reach of social media—would naturally bring democracy to China and other authoritarian states. It was only a matter of time.

The time has passed, and the opposite has occurred. Advanced technologies have brought even greater authoritarian control over individuals. AI is playing a major role in this by facilitating the processing of the necessary big data. The question becomes: What should we as American citizens do about this? Should all or most AI development be regulated and controlled? Should algorithms be placed under the authority of the existing U.S. International Traffic in Arms Regulations (ITAR) regime, in which the Department of State and the Department of Defense determine whether a proposed export identified under the regulation would harm national security or U.S. law and thus be restricted? ITAR was designed to prevent the export of weapons and weapons technology except to allies and partners. Even when exported to them, ITAR restrictions apply: the recipient cannot subsequently transfer the technology to a third party without U.S. permission. Militarily weaker nations have more to fear from AI, so this is not an issue for the United States alone.

There is not going to be a global consensus concerning AI. Opponents of the United States and allies are not concerned with our perspective, and we should not expect them to be. The CCP is a dictatorial regime that seeks to perpetuate its control over the Chinese people. If it were not, it would not be developing an AI-based social control system, starting with registration of minority groups. There is no CCP concern with human rights issues as regards AI.

Like their Western counterparts, Chinese AI companies want to make money. But unlike Western companies, Chinese AI companies act as agents of the state when called upon to do so by the CCP. There is no AI development that is not shared with the People's Liberation Army. It might take some time for the PLA to effectively apply whatever techniques are provided, but it has open access.

No matter what rhetorical justifications are offered, Western AI companies that share algorithms or data with PRC-based companies or universities are helping to perpetuate the dictatorial regime. With more than 1.3 billion people, China is a potential market coveted by Western corporations. But with state requirements for technology sharing as an entry requirement, those Western companies that become dependent on a Chinese market as it is structured today eventually go bankrupt (witness WorldCom and Nortel systems). Serving China is short-term thinking concerning a long-term gamble.[3]

Since the acceptance of state capitalism by CCP leader Deng Xiaoping in the 1980s, many expected the PRC to become a democracy. Western theory suggests that the influx of democratic ideas and growing wealth would naturally result in greater public participation in government decision-making. It has not. As current trends flow, it will not. AI will play a significant role in assuring it does not.

Arms control treaties cannot effectively constrain AI. Many question whether arms control treaties have ever been effective in preventing war. They were a key component of Cold War diplomacy, but there were many other factors that created the deterrence situation that prevented it from going hot. Nevertheless, past arms control regimes were about counting tangible items—battleships, nuclear missiles, antiballistic missile sites, and other weapons of war. AI is not a tangible item. In itself, it cannot be counted so as to compare balances between nations or verify that cheating does not occur.

One can argue that we could count autonomous weapons systems. But without a detailed inspection, how does one determine whether an uncrewed vehicle is autonomously controlled by AI or controlled remotely by a human? One would likely have to take it apart, something nations concerned with their security would not allow. And if one weapons system was examined, how would an inspector know that the hundred-plus systems in the same class are all controlled in the same way? Adherence to the treaty could never be effectively verified. AI does not cause an uncrewed vehicle to look different.

Are there any alternatives to arms control efforts to control military AI? This must be the premise for the national dialogue, not shrill demands to "ban killer drones." Such demands are counterproductive in creating a national dialogue on this issue. The genie is out of the bottle. No one can stuff it back in. Authoritarian regimes do not want to stuff it back in.

Silicon Valley seems somewhat ambivalent on defense issues, which means they are somewhat ambivalent about our national security. This is a harsh criticism, but a necessary one. Eric Schmidt and a handful of former CEOs of high-tech firms along with a number of AI scientists have made major efforts to publicize the national security issues raised by AI. With the financial resources available to him, Schmidt has taken a public lead in these efforts. But it is does not appear that there is a large line of current CEOs, venture capitalists, or major investors in AI forming up behind him. Rather, it has been former defense officials and some members of the scientific community who have joined this line.

Of course there are AI developers willing to sell technology to the Pentagon. Many are start-ups that have not yet penetrated the overall commercial market or see a niche for themselves with the defense industry. Quite a few of the companies are eventually bought by existing defense corporations. But within the overall environment of commercial AI development—with expanding profits as the goal—there is no sense of threat or urgency. Perhaps it is assumed that national security is solely the government's problem. But individual efforts also contribute to national security. Avoiding selling dual-use technologies to authoritarian nations that are hostile or potentially hostile is a first step.

Inaction by major AI developers will eventually bring the very regulations on their market activities that they seek to avoid. As one venture capitalist confided to us, "I conduct my investing in Chinese technology companies in accordance to the laws of the United States. If the U.S. government did not want me to do it, it needs to pass a law to prevent it." It is in the enlightened self-interest of Silicon Valley to take the dangers that we have described seriously.

The United States will lose the military AI race without a direct, significant effort. This is our penultimate observation. The PRC and Russia believe that there has been an AI arms race under way. They are going to race in it whether we do or not. They see military AI as the key to defeating the United States whenever they determine that expansion is necessary.

Right now, Vladimir Putin is having a difficult time in his expansion into Ukraine. Not only are Russian high-tech weapons inventories low, but also many in his human military forces appear unwilling to risk the dangers that initiative requires. Most will fight when ordered to, but not without doubts concerning the outcome. As a result, Putin has had to outsource much of the fighting to the Wagner mercenary company and entice fighters out of Russian prisons. For a major power to have to rely on mercenaries would have been unthinkable just a few years ago. Mercenary companies that exist focus on small wars—primarily against insurgents—in the pay of governments (or prospective governments) without significant military assets. Large mercenary armies seem like a throwback to the Middle Ages.

The lesson Putin is undoubtedly learning is that AI-driven autonomous systems (along with more nuclear weapons) are the way to create willing Russian military power. As he has already said, he who controls AI will control the world. Current sanctions against Russia will thwart his efforts in the near term; there is little access to outside technology and capital. However, in the same way that sanctions have not influenced Putin to end the war with Ukraine, they are not going to end the Russian quest for military AI systems.

The PRC has the strongest incentive of any nation in the world to perfect military AI. A possible exception is North Korea, history's most successful totalitarian state, but fortunately it lacks the resources. AI is an exceptionally important tool for the CCP to use to control Chinese society. Its sees investments in military AI as stimuli to commercial AI—the complete opposite to the commercial-focused approach in the United States.

As of the writing of this book, Chinese military literature maintains that the United States still retains superior military force capabilities, particularly in the high-tech–intensive areas such as undersea warfare and joint force command and control. The literature clearly indicates that investment in AI is seen as the best method to counter U.S. advantages, particularly when they will attempt to cross the Taiwan Strait.[4] Some analysts believe they will never try. But, on the other hand, some analysts believed Vladimir Putin would never invade the rest of Ukraine.

Meanwhile, the United States is approaching this apparent race in a rather undisciplined and haphazard manner. Military services are pursuing AI and autonomous systems with some enthusiasm. However, overall American AI innovation does not have enhancing national security as a primary goal, and AI technology is a trickle-down process with respect to military requirements. This would be perfectly fine if our prospective opponents were doing the same. They are not.

HOW CAN THESE ISSUES BE ADDRESSED?

Public discussion is necessary, and we encourage it greatly. The primary purpose of this book is to stimulate the public debate over military AI—but in a responsible, not a combative or confrontational, manner. However, our own ultimate conclusion goes beyond that. In short: the United States does not need just an AI policy; it needs a national AI program.

This conclusion corresponds to the recommendation by experts such as those who served on the National Security Commission on Artificial Intelligence. Yet most studies have envisioned the U.S. government being a stimulator and regulator of future AI development. We envision stronger actions.

In 1962 President John F. Kennedy publicly announced to a joint session of Congress his goal, "before this decade is out, of landing a man on the moon and returning him safely to the earth." The United States channeled both government and commercial resources to accomplish that goal. It is time for us to pursue a similar national program in which the U.S. government encourages the responsible development of AI while also setting the standards and regulating the outcome. The freewheeling commercial AI market and its manner of development have made tremendous profits for individual entrepreneurs and venture capitalists as well as for many people whose retirement depends on their stock market investments. However, given the investment in military AI by the authoritarian powers that is fueled by the diffusion of our own research and development, the time for unpurposed and unregulated development of AI must come to a close.

The huge profits have been made. It is time for national security to be a priority. If not, profits will naturally dwindle once the world perceives that the United States can no longer defend the world order in an autonomous military environment and the dollar is no longer the world's reserve currency. Under such a government-industry partnership, profits might not be as huge as in the generally unregulated AI market today. But following the pattern of industry and jobs during the space race, they will be steady.

The four overarching objectives of an AI program would be to

1. ensure the responsible development of both commercial and military AI

2. prevent the transfer of dual-use AI technologies to any nations except for strong U.S. allies in NATO and the Asia-Pacific

3. monitor the AI and autonomous systems supply chains to eliminate dependence on foreign suppliers and prevent foreign penetration of U.S. production

4. develop autonomous systems that match or surpass those of potential enemies.

Developing autonomous military systems does not mean discarding a human-based defense. Humans will obviously build and deploy these systems. More importantly, only humans can determine victory or defeat and the postconflict order.

This is indeed an arms race, but the only alternative appears to be to let the CCP and Russian government race by themselves; they have no incentive to stop.

IF WE DO HAVE SUCH A PROGRAM, WHAT GUIDELINES CAN WE ADOPT?

Instead of humans *in* the loop, should the humans-*on*-the-loop method for employing AI-controlled autonomous weapons systems be adopted—that is, deciding when and where to employ them but not directly controlling their activities? That debate has been ongoing within the White House, DoD, and Congress. Although few like the thought of "killer robots" taking lethal actions, we are at the point that we will be facing opposing systems that will not have humans in the loop.

The strict rule on requiring a human to make every decision to use lethal force seems ethical and makes a lot of sense—if you are the only side that is operating unmanned/uncrewed systems. The rule is designed to prevent civilian casualties. It is highly appropriate when hunting terrorists with drones in an environment containing innocent civilians. It is primarily effective in conditions where the enemy has limited means of fighting back—a situation of small arms versus unmanned vehicles. But in a conflict between technological near-peers with developed AI capabilities, the ability of human combatants to defend against saturation attacks at machine speed will always be limited.

One of the very first books written on the probable course of a nuclear war and the strategy of nuclear deterrence, published in 1946, has a very apt title—*There Will Be No Time: The Revolution in Strategy*.[5] This is also an apt description of a war dominated by AI-controlled autonomous systems. There will be no time to make individual decisions on the use of lethal force as we have been able to for the past thirty years. There indeed needs to be another revolution in strategy. The prospect of a war against a "great power" that is a technological near-peer is literally driving us to share decision-making with autonomous systems—not because we want to, but because we have to.

In his book, *I, Warbot*, Kenneth Payne offers three rules that should be integrated into all AI-controlled autonomous systems:[6]

- A warbot (autonomous weapons system) should only kill those I want it to, and as humanely as possible.
- A warbot should understand the intent of its (human) commander and operate solely under that intent.
- A warbot should protect the humans on my side, sacrificing itself to do so—but not at the expense of the mission.

We agree with all these principles; they are already the principles guiding the human military personnel in the U.S. armed forces and those of other (but not all) nations. They conform to the laws of war as they currently exist.

However, we see them as guidelines on how humans should direct the use of autonomous systems rather than rules that can be currently programmed into AI systems. How does a machine know it is acting humanely? A practical factor is that for the conceivable future, most autonomous systems will have only one method of killing. One could suppose that autonomous tanks have an option to either shoot or run over a target, but in the reality of combat, that is not an either-or choice but rather depends on the situation. To know what is humane requires consciousness, and we are not close to having AGI that can anticipate that—likely not in the current century (if at all).

Operating under the intent of the commander is a de facto reality. Autonomous systems are programmed with the functions (rather than the mission) that the commanders desire. Intent in this case is all about how the commander intends to deploy them. The responsibility for the result remains with the commander. The law of war may have to change, but the responsibility of the human should not and need not be discarded.

The development of AI-driven autonomous systems does not in itself mean more or less war, more or fewer military casualties, more or fewer civilians killed, more or less cruelty, higher or lower defense budgets. Any of those results will be the result of human choices as to how autonomous military systems will be used. However, if one side has autonomous weapons and the other does not, the choices become very one-sided indeed.

A PROBLEMATIC CONCLUSION

Again, the real issue of AI is not about AI controlling humans. It is about humans using AI to control other humans. In a very subtle way, AI has been used commercially to control the purchasing habits of humans. In a very direct way, AI is being used to perpetuate dictatorial control over humans.

Many scientists, celebrities, and public influencers have spoken openly about the future dangers of AGI to the human race. That may be a worthy discussion, but it is theoretical, and few practical actions beyond calling for more government regulations have been offered. Fortunately, we are a long way from achieving AGI (if ever). But we are practically moments away from narrow AI being used in war in a big way. That is the real danger that we face now.

AI will be used in war, both as a decision-making tool and to control autonomous systems. The genie *is* out of the bottle. Previous efforts in arms control—which relied on counting things—do not seem applicable to controlling the military use of AI.

We have laid out a proposal. It needs to be seriously addressed. We don't want to have to face an algorithm of Armageddon. But we don't want other nations to be able to use military AI to control *us*.

That is the dilemma we as Americans—along with our democratic allies—need to discuss and need to resolve.

CONCLUSION

MOST PEOPLE AGREE that war is a terrible thing—a blot upon humanity. One only need read the reporting of Russia's invasion of Ukraine to understand the horrors of war, not just for combatants, but for civilians as well. Sadly, as Plato is quoted as saying, "Only the dead have seen the end of the war." Sometime later, Roman general Vegetius noted: "If you want peace, prepare for war," a phrase that most American presidents adopted during the Cold War.

One of the ways that nations prepare for war is to ensure that their military services are equipped with emerging technologies. If we have established anything during the course of this book, it is the fact that the technological peer competitors of the United States—the PRC and Russia—are investing enormous sums of money in developing AI-enabled systems and adapting them for military use. The quotes by the leaders of China and Russia presented earlier in this book do not represent vacuous hyperbole, but rather bedrock beliefs that both authoritarian nations are now pursuing.

Spurred by the findings of documents such as the National Security Commission on Artificial Intelligence *Final Report*, U.S. national security officials have acknowledged the importance of leveraging big data, artificial intelligence, and machine learning in U.S. military platforms, systems, sensors, and weapons. They have also recognized the need for a defense innovation base consisting of high-technology companies not normally considered part of the defense industrial base, which is why DoD has established organizations such as Defense Innovation Units in high-tech hubs such as San Jose, California.

What DoD perceives as an obvious need for applying AI to military systems is worthy of an important public discussion. Unfortunately, it is overshadowed—and perhaps being swallowed up—by what is becoming a shrill but unfocused debate on the overall dangers posed by AI. A significant number of influencers have called for a reexamination of the costs versus benefits of unbridled AI development.

These calls are not specifically about military applications, but they reflect fears concerning the commercial and social uses of AI and of artificial general intelligence—the potential HALs of the future. Geoffrey Hinton, widely recognized as the "godfather of AI," quit his job at Google in order to "freely speak out about the risks of AI." Among other statements, Hinton said: "AI technologies pose profound risks to society and humanity. . . . Future versions of AI technology pose a threat to humanity because they often learn unexpected behavior from the vast amount of data they analyze, and not only generate their own computer code but run that code on their own. . . . It is hard to see how you can prevent the bad actors from using it [AI] for bad things."[1] Unsurprisingly, Dr. Hinton is opposed to the use of AI on the battlefield by what he terms "robot soldiers," noting that he fears a day when truly autonomous weapons—those killer robots—become reality. In other words, he fears a Terminator.

The problem is that the bad international actors *already* have AI. They have the capacity to develop it on their own—perhaps not as fast as the Silicon Valley corporations, but steadily. They currently are developing autonomous weapons to be controlled by AI, and they don't care what Hinton, Elon Musk, Steve Wozniak, or any other public influencer in the United States or other democracy says about it.

Perhaps no tech leader has been more vocal regarding the dangers of AI than Elon Musk, who opines on multiple media platforms, for example, that poorly built artificial intelligence could have catastrophic effects on humanity and that chatbots, such as OpenAI's ChatGPT could lead AI to become too powerful for humans to control.[2] Perhaps most dramatically, Musk has stated, "With artificial intelligence we are summoning the demon."[3]

We share concerns about any demon that AGI can summon, although we don't believe it is possible without the development of technologies even more complex than AI. However, we don't want other nations to use AI to control us, particularly nations that deny human rights to their own people.

Hinton and Musk are not the only tech leaders urging caution in developing AI. In a wide-ranging interview, Google CEO Sundar Pixhai expressed worry about the state of the "AI race," noting, for example, that the open letter signed by nearly 200 technology leaders and researchers urging companies to pause development of powerful AI systems for at least six months "was a cautionary message and deserved to be out there." Later in the interview, he declared, "We are working with a technology that has the potential to cause harm in a deep way."[4]

It is ironic that some of those expressing their concern nevertheless continue working to develop AI or invest in companies that do. Beyond anything else, we wish that Google and the other corporate developers of AI *stop* sharing or selling their knowledge to China.

Concurrently, the U.S. government is also considering regulating AI tools.[5] Some (but not all) of this demand for governmental intervention came from the widely published promise and perils of apps such as ChatGPT, as even the app's developers admit that they don't always fully understand why the black box does what it does.

According to a *New York Times* article, the Biden administration "is confronting the rapidly expanding use of artificial intelligence, warning of the dangers the technology poses to public safety, privacy, and democracy while having limited authority to regulate it."[6] The Commerce Department put out a formal public request for comment on what it called accountability measures, including whether potentially risky new AI models should go through a certification process before they are released.[7] Federal Trade Commission chair Lina Khan pledged that the commission would regulate AI and not let companies that produce this technology use "business models or practices involving the mass exploitation of their users." She noted further that "enforcers have the dual responsibility of watching out for the dangers posed by new AI technologies while promoting the fair competition needed to ensure the market for these technologies develops lawfully."[8]

Following a meeting with AI technology leaders, the White House stated that it impressed upon the companies that they should address the risks of new AI developments and that there had been frank and constructive discussions about the desire for the companies to be more open about their products, the need for AI systems to be subjected to outside scrutiny, and the importance that those products be kept away from bad actors. The White House called on these leaders to "model responsible behavior" and to take action to "ensure responsible innovation and appropriate safeguards, and protect people's rights and safety."[9] How can we ensure that our authoritarian rivals will take similar action?

Others have pushed back on the concerns about a dire AI-induced future. Eric Schmidt contends that policymakers should take care not to blunt America's technological edge, while still fostering development and innovation to be consistent with democratic values: "Let American ingenuity, American scientists, the American government, American corporations invent this future, and we'll get something pretty close to what we want."[10]

Sam Altman, CEO of OpenAI, noted: "The hype over these systems—even if everything we hope for is right long term—is totally out of control for the short term."[11] This sentiment was echoed on other fronts, with most experts agreeing that concerns that AI could slip outside of human control are "wildly overblown."[12]

Such arguments ignore the wealth of evidence we have presented in the chapters of this book, much of it supported by the findings in the National Security Commission on Artificial Intelligence *Final Report*—that America's peer competitors are racing forward to militarize AI to gain a war-winning advantage over the United States.

Senior DoD leaders have pointed to the existential threat peer competitors with AI-enabled military forces pose if the U.S. military cannot counter them with similar platforms, systems, sensors, and weapons. In an address at the Reagan National Defense Forum, U.S. Secretary of Defense Lloyd Austin stated that DoD "wants to successfully lead the AI Revolution."[13] Deputy Secretary of Defense Dr. Kathleen Hicks emphasized the importance of AI technologies to the U.S. military in order to "provide operational commanders with data-driven technologies, including artificial intelligence, machine learning, and automation."[14]

A front-page *New York Times* article quoted the Pentagon's chief information officer, John Sherman, regarding the national security imperative to continue AI development: "If we stop, guess who's not going to stop: potential adversaries overseas. We've got to keep moving." The article went on to say that Pentagon officials thought the idea of a six-month pause in developing the next generations of ChatGPT and similar software was a bad idea because the Chinese won't wait, and neither will the Russians.[15]

As we said in chapter eleven, America needs a national dialogue to determine the risks and rewards of AI development, and a large part of that discussion should be focused on the need for the U.S. military to have access to the latest AI-enabled technology in order to provide for the security and prosperity of the American people. But successful debate would be based on the facts identified in that chapter and about the threat that already exists, not just the fear of what corporations or researchers might do in creating AGI in the farther future.

As Paul Scharre notes in the conclusion of his recent book *Four Battlegrounds: Power in the Age of Artificial Intelligence*: "Authoritarian uses of AI for surveillance, disinformation, and repression pose a profound challenge to freedom around the globe. Democracies have tremendous advantages in this competition, but they must find ways to harness these advantages."[16]

We will leave it to you to decide where you fit in this national dialogue. But the algorithms of war are here. Humans are going to try to use AI to control other humans. Mere words are not going to stop it. We believe that America needs to have the capabilities to deter other nations from turning algorithms of war into algorithms of our Armageddon.

NOTES

INTRODUCTION

1. "'Whoever Leads in AI Will Rule the World': Putin to Russian Children on Knowledge Day," *RT*, September 1, 2017, https://www.rt.com/news/401731-ai-rule-world-putin/.
2. Elon Musk, comments at National Governors Association 2017 Summer Meeting, Providence, RI, July 15, 2017, https://www.c-span.org/video/?c4676772/user-clip-elon-musk-national-governors-association-2017-summer-meeting.
3. The theme of AI inevitably transforming every aspect of warfare is expounded throughout National Security Commission on Artificial Intelligence, *Final Report*, March 2021, https://nscai.wpenginepowered.com/wp-content/uploads/2021/03/Full-Report-Digital-1.pdf.
4. Andrew Eversden, "Autonomy on a Stryker? 'It Will Be Challenging,' General Says," *Breaking Defense*, June 16, 2022, https://breakingdefense.com/2022/06/autonomy-on-a-stryker-itll-be-challenging-general-says/.
5. Margarita Konaev and Samuel Bendett, "Russian AI-Enabled Combat: Coming to a City Near You?" *War on the Rocks*, July 31, 2019, https://warontherocks.com/2019/07/russian-ai-enabled-combat-coming-to-a-city-near-you/.
6. People's Republic of China, *Notice of the State Council Issuing the Next Generation of Artificial Intelligence Development Plan*, State Council Document (2017) no. 35, trans. Foundation for Law and International Affairs, https://flia.org/wp-content/uploads/2017/07/A-New-Generation-of-Artificial-Intelligence-Development-Plan-1.pdf.
7. Apoorva Komarraju, "China Will Become the AI Superpower Surpassing the U.S. How Long?" *Analytics Insight*, February 19, 2021, https://www.analyticsinsight.net/china-will-become-the-ai-superpower-surpassing-u-s-how-long/.
8. E. Glen Weyl and Jaron Lanier, "AI Is an Ideology, Not a Technology," *Wired*, March 15, 2020, https://www.wired.com/story/opinion-ai-is-an-ideology-not-a-technology/.

CHAPTER 1. WHAT IS AI, AND WHY IS IT IMPORTANT?

1. Shana Lynch, "Andrew Ng: Why AI Is the New Electricity," *Insights by Stanford Business School*, March 11, 2017, https://www.gsb.stanford.edu/insights/andrew-ng-why-ai-new-electricity.

2. Orison Swett Marden, *How They Succeeded: Life Stories of Successful Men Told by Themselves* (New York: Lothrop Publishing Company, 2015).

3. Any new technology can lead to unhappy second-order effects. Electricity helped power the second Industrial Revolution, but that period was replete with brutal working and living conditions in cities, child labor, etc. (as illustrated in the novels of Charles Dickens and others). See, for example, "Industrial Revolution," History.com, October 29, 2009, https://www.history.com/topics/industrial-revolution/industrial -revolution. Eventually, these problems were remedied. However, AI already has many downsides and is likely to have more. Whether they outweigh the benefits is the underlying issue.

4. Lt. Cdr. Connor S. McLemore, remarks at "Beyond the Hype: Artificial Intelligence in Naval and Joint Operations" conference, U.S. Naval War College, Newport, RI, October 24, 2019.

5. Aliya Ram, "Europe's AI Start-Ups Often Do Not Use AI, Study Finds," *Financial Times*, March 4, 2019, https://www.ft.com/content/21b19010-3e9f-11e9-b896-fe36 ec32aece.

6. Skymind Inc., "Artificial Intelligence (AI) vs. Machine Learning vs. Deep Learning," A.I. Wiki, https://skymind.ai/wiki/ai-vs-machine-learning-vs-deep-learning.

7. FORTRAN was the first computer language.

8. Aaron Ricardela, "Best Way to Realize AI Benefits: Don't Shoot the Moon," *Forbes*, October 2, 2019, https://www.forbes.com/sits/oracle/2019/10/02/best-way-to-realize -ai-benefits-dont-shoot-the-moon/. The quote is by Clive Swan.

9. AI-enabled machines beating humans at their own games have become a strong thread in popular culture over the last decade, with IBM's Watson beating *Jeopardy!* champions and machines beating humans in chess and AlphaGo. The latest (but likely not the last) machine victory occurred in 2019 where the Pluribus machine beat six professional players at no-limit Texas Hold'em poker. For a short descriptive article on why poker required a far higher level of AI than that trained to excel at chess or AlphaGo see, for example, Noam Brown and Tuomas Sandholm, "Superhuman AI for Multiplayer Poker," *Science* 365 (August 30, 2019): 885–90, https://science.sciencemag.org/content/ 365/6456/885.

10. *A Framework for Developing a National Artificial Intelligence Strategy* (Geneva, Switzerland: World Economic Forum, August 2019).

11. Nathan Strout, "Intelligence Agency Takes Over Project Maven, the Pentagon's Signature AI Scheme," C4ISRNET, April 27, 2022, https://www.c4isrnet.com/intel -geoint/2022/04/27/intelligence-agency-takes-over-project-maven-the-pentagons -signature-ai-scheme/.

12. We will return to Project Maven (officially the "Algorithmic Warfare Cross-Functional Team") in later chapters. It has an iconic place in the still-evolving relationship between the U.S. Department of Defense and the U.S. tech industry, as this was a well-publicized case of Google employees pressuring their corporate leadership to stop working on "killer robots." See, for example, Daisuke Wakabayashi and Scott Shane, "Google Will Not Renew Pentagon Contract That Upset Employees," *New York Times*, June 1, 2018,

https://www.nytimes.com/2018/06/01/technology/google-pentagon-project-maven .html.

13. The "if-then-else" statement is the bedrock of computer programming. The "statement" compares two or more sets of data and tests the results. "If" the results are true, the "then" instructions are taken. However, when the results are not true, the "else" instructions are taken.

14. Understanding deep learning is challenging for the layperson, and we hesitate to take the reader down the path to try to grasp this concept fully. However, for the interested reader, Maxim Lapan, *Deep Reinforcement Learning Hands-On* (Birmingham, UK: Packt Publishing, January 2020), is one of the more readable books on the subject.

15. Such as "Aud the Deep Minded," a wise woman in Norse sagas. See "Aud the Deep Minded," *The Lone Medievalist*, https://lonemedievalist.hcommons.org/women-of-the -middle-ages/aud-the-deep-minded/.

16. Skymind Inc., "A Beginner's Guide to Automated Machine Learning & AI," A.I. Wiki, https://skymind.ai/wiki/automl-automated-machine-learning-ai.

17. Skymind Inc., "A Beginner's Guide." Skymind Inc. notes in its more self-promotional material: "I know what you want to hear: 'You, too, can automate AI in your company, and never have to worry about those pesky data scientists again!' [but] it's not that simple."

18. Matt Bevilacqua, "Uber Was Warned before Self-Driving Car Crash that Killed Woman Walking Bicycle," *Bicycling*, December 18, 2018, https://www.bicycling.com/ news/a25616551/uber-self-driving-car-crash-cyclist/.

19. Will Knight, "The Dark Secret at the Heart of AI," *MIT Technology Review* 120, no. 3 (May/June 2017): 54–61, https://www.technologyreview.com/s/604087/the-dark -secret-at-the-heart-of-ai/.

20. Stephanie Pappas, "AI Has Created a 3D Replica of Our Universe. We Have No Idea How it Works," Space.com, July 3, 2019, https://www.space.com/ai-creates-model -universe-mysteriously.html.

21. National Security Commission on Artificial Intelligence, *Final Report*.

CHAPTER 2. HOW DID WE GET HERE?

1. "Artificial Intelligence Is Not a Technology," *Forbes*, November 1, 2018, https://www .forbes.com/sites/cognitiveworld/2018/11/01/artificial-intelligence-is-not-a-tech nology/?sh=71a30b6b5dcb.

2. Noam Chomsky, *Language and Thought* (New York: Moyer Bell, 1993), 92–93.

3. Quoted in Patrick Sullivan and the OCEANIT Team, "Theory and Conceptual History of Artificial Intelligence," in *AI at War: How Big Data, Artificial Intelligence, and Machine Learning Are Changing Naval Warfare*, ed. Sam J. Tangredi and George Galdorisi (Annapolis, MD: Naval Institute Press, 2021), 27.

4. Sullivan, 25.

5. Sullivan, 27.

6. As one indication of the fact that the computer has impacted society not as a stand-alone entity but as a means to an end, we are reminded of a line from the AMC series *Halt and Catch Fire*. The series chronicles the computer revolution in the early 1980s

and features as its stars hardware and software experts, as well as entrepreneurs and serial innovators. In the penultimate episode of the series, the entrepreneur character shares his epiphany with his colleagues: "Computers aren't the thing; they're the thing that gets you to the thing."

7. Many books have been written about this computer pioneer. For one of the best, see James Essinger, *Ada's Algorithm: How Lord Byron's Daughter Ada Lovelace Launched the Digital Age* (Brooklyn: Melville Publishing, October 2014).

8. Walter Isaacson, *The Innovators: How a Group of Hackers, Geniuses, and Geeks Created the Digital Revolution* (New York: Simon and Schuster, 2014), 29.

9. Michael Smith, *The Emperor's Codes: The Thrilling Story of the Allied Code Breakers Who Turned the Tide of World War I* (New York: Arcade Publishing, 2011).

10. Several excellent books have been written about the life and work of Alan Turing. Perhaps the best is David Leavitt's *The Man Who Knew Too Much: Alan Turing and the Invention of the Computer* (New York: W. W. Norton and Company, 2006). Turing's life was the subject of the critically acclaimed 2014 film *The Imitation Game*. Perhaps not coincidentally, another 2014 film, *Ex Machina*, revolved around a computer programmer who is invited to administer the Turing test to an intelligent (and strikingly attractive) humanoid robot.

11. The Turing test is a test of a machine's ability to exhibit intelligent behavior indistinguishable from that of a human. Turing proposed that a human evaluator would judge natural language conversations between a human and a machine designed to generate human-like responses. The conversation would be limited to a text-only channel such as a computer keyboard and screen so the result would not depend on the machine's ability to render words as speech. If the evaluator cannot reliably tell the machine from the human, the machine is said to have passed the test.

12. Andrew Hodges, *Alan Turing: The Enigma* (London: Burnett Books, 1983), 152–54.

13. It is difficult to overstate the iconic place this study holds in the annals of computer science and artificial intelligence. For a descriptive article on this event, including the actual proposal, see *AI Magazine* 27, no. 4 (2006).

14. Michael Wooldridge, *A Brief History of Artificial Intelligence: What It Is, Where We Are, and Where We Are Going* (San Francisco: Flatiron Books, 2021).

15. Although it is set a decade and a half after the start of the AI Spring, the turbulent nature and boom and bust cycle of the computer (hardware and software) industry is well presented in the AMC series *Halt and Catch Fire*.

16. *Her* received critical acclaim and achieved a worldwide box office gross of close to $50 million.

17. See, for example, SRI International's website (https://www.sri.com/?s=Shakey&order by=post_date&order=desc&post_type=all) for an interview with Bill Gates, where he describes Shakey as an invention that inspired him.

18. To be fair, AI research did not completely shut down during this three-decade period. Most recognize that a nascent AI Spring occurred in the early 1980s when the Japanese Fifth-Generation Project poured large sums into AI research and high-performance logic machines. Sadly, this initiative did not gain the required momentum, and the AI

Winter returned in force. See, for example, Peter J. Denning and Ted G. Lewis, "Intelligence May Not Be Computable," *American Scientist*, November–December 2019.

19. Isaacson, *The Innovators*, 470.

20. Isaacson.

21. Isaacson, 470–71.

22. Cade Metz, "A Tech-Military Revolution Away from Silicon Valley," *New York Times*, March 3, 2021. This article was the lead piece in the *New York Times* business section and noted, in part, "The military and intelligence communities have a long history with research labs and tech companies in Silicon Valley. ARPANET, the forerunner of the Internet, was funded by the Defense Department. David Packard, one of the founders of Hewlett-Packard, served as deputy secretary of defense under President Richard Nixon. Oracle, one of the biggest software companies, got its start writing computer code for the Central Intelligence Agency."

23. "How Big Tech Got Even Bigger," *Wall Street Journal*, February 6–7, 2021.

24. Max Boot, *War Made New: Technology, Warfare, and the Course of History 1500 to Today* (New York: Gotham Books, 2006), 318–51.

25. Bruce Berkowitz, *The New Face of War: How War Will Be Fought in the 21st Century* (New York: The Free Press, 2003), 2–3. Berkowitz does not restrict his examples of how disruptive military technology has led to victory on the battlefield to just one conflict, noting further: "The same thing happened when the United States fought Yugoslavia in 1999 and the Taliban regime in Afghanistan in 2001. Each time experts feared the worst; each time U.S. forces won a lopsided victory" (3).

26. James Pethokoukis, "U.S. Federal Research Spending Is at a 60-Year Low. Should We Be Concerned?" American Enterprise Institute, May 11, 2020. By way of comparison, federal research and development spending as a percentage of total federal spending peaked at nearly 12 percent at the height of the Cold War and the "Space Race" but is now less than 3 percent of total federal outlays.

27. The Department of Defense has attempted to develop a closer working relationship with Silicon Valley by establishing organizations like the Defense Innovation Unit (DIU) in Mountain View, California. DIU has satellite offices in Boston and Austin, all designed to enable easier access to high-technology companies.

28. For an example of the many articles pointing out the current—and anticipated future—disparity in AI spending, see Jonathan Ponciano, "Google Billionaire Eric Schmidt Warns of 'National Emergency' If China Overtakes U.S. in AI Technology," *Forbes*, March 7, 2021.

29. Analogies to the nuclear arms race and the AI arms race are made in convincing fashion in the National Security Commission on Artificial Intelligence *Final Report*.

CHAPTER 3. WHAT IS AT STAKE?

1. Samuel Bendett et al., *Advanced Military Technology in Russia* (London: Chatham House/ Royal Institute of International Affairs, September 2021), 76, https://www.chatham house.org/sites/default/files/2021-09/2021-09-23-advanced-military-technology -in-russia-bendett-et-al.pdf.

2. "China Has Won AI Battle with U.S., Pentagon's Ex-Software Chief Says," Reuters, October 11, 2021, https://www.reuters.com/technology/united-states-has-lost-ai-battle -china-pentagons-ex-software-chief-says-2021-10-11/.

3. Dan Robitzski, "Russia's Semi-Autonomous Tanks Were Utterly Useless in Syria: These Killer Robots Were a Glitchy Mess," *Futurism*, October 21, 2019, https:// futurism.com/the-byte/russia-semi-autonomous-robot-tanks-useless-syria; Sebastien Roblin, "This Is the Robot Tank the Russians Used in Syria," *The National Interest*, October 21, 2019, https://nationalinterest.org/blog/buzz/robot-tank-russia-used-syria -89866.

4. Paul Scharre, *Four Battlegrounds: Power in the Age of Artificial Intelligence* (New York: W. W. Norton, 2023).

5. Paul Mozur, "One Month, 500,000 Facial Scans: How China Is Using AI to Profile a Minority," *New York Times*, April 14, 2019, https://www.nytimes.com/2019/04/14/ technology/china-surveillance-artificial-intelligence-racial-profiling.html.

6. Derek Grossman et al., *Chinese Views of Big Data Analytics* (Santa Monica, CA: RAND, 2020), 16.

7. Vanessa Caldwell, "With Artificial Intelligence, We Have Nowhere to Hide. Don't You Think It's Horrifying?" *CBCDocs*, Canadian Broadcasting Corporation, September 27, 2021, https://www.cbc.ca/documentaries/the-passionate-eye/with-artificial-intellig ence-we-have-nowhere-to-hide-don-t-you-think-it-s-horrifying-1.6185448.

8. Joyce Huang, "China Boasts of 'Mind-reading' Artificial Intelligence that Supports 'AI-tocracy,'" VOANews.com, July 9, 2022, https://www.voanews.com/a/china -boasts-of-mind-reading-artificial-intelligence-that-supports-ai-tocracy-/6651986 .html.

9. "Russian Army to Use Unmanned Ground Robot Taifun-M to Protect Yars and Topol-M Missile Sites," *Army Recognition*, April 23, 2014, https://www.armyrecognition.com/ april_2014_global_defense_security_news_uk/russian_army_to_use_unmanned_ ground_robot_taifun-m_to_protect_yars_and_topol-m_missile_sites_2304143.html.

10. Bendett et al., *Advanced Military Technology*, 52–55.

11. Bendett et al.

12. The reason for the caveat "perhaps as much" is the fact that a significant amount of commercial technology products offered to customers originated as projects of the U.S. Department of Defense or the National Aeronautics and Space Administration that were funded by those agencies. This includes high-speed computing, satellite communications, the Internet, handheld wireless devices, and microwave ovens. Many large technology companies found initial success by commercializing the results of government research and development. From a financial perspective, it is relatively easy to determine whose money is being spent on current R&D. However, it is difficult to individually determine the relative value of commercial versus government R&D for many high-technology products.

13. Frank Kendell, *Getting Defense Acquisition Right* (Fort Belvoir, VA: Defense Acquisition University Press, 2017), 95, https://dod.defense.gov/Portals/1/Documents/pubs/ Getting-Acquisition-Right-Jan2017.pdf.

14. Gregory C. Allen, *Understanding China's AI Strategy: Clues to Chinese Strategic Thinking on Artificial Intelligence and National Security* (Washington, DC: Center for a New American Security, February 2019), 1.

15. Ben Wodecki, "China Set to More than Double AI Spending by 2026," Data Center Knowledge, October 14, 2022, https://www.datacenterknowledge.com/investing/china-set-more-double-ai-spending-2026.

16. Grossman et al., *Chinese Views of Big Data Analytics*, vii.

17. Quoted in Allen, *Understanding China's AI Strategy*, 1.

18. Emily S. Weinstein and Ngor Luong, *U.S. Outbound Investment into Chinese AI Companies* (Washington, DC: Center for Security and Emerging Technology, March 2023), 6, https://cset.georgetown.edu/publication/u-s-outbound-investment-into-chinese-ai-companies/.

19. Bendett et al., *Advanced Military Technology*.

20. Bendett et al.

21. Margarita Konaev and Samuel Bendett, "Russia's AI Disconnect: The War in Ukraine and the Looming Collapse of Russia's AI Industry," Institute for Technology and Security, April 28, 2022, https://www.youtube.com/watch?v=mFkN7cZnvxo.

22. Yasmin Tadjdeh, "Algorithmic Warfare: Russia Expanding Fleet of AI-Enabled Weapons," *National Defense*, July 20, 2021, https://www.nationaldefensemagazine.org/articles/2021/7/20/russia-expanding-fleet-of-ai-enabled-weapons.

23. Tadjdeh.

24. Tadjdeh.

25. Mozur, "One Month."

26. Sara Salinas and Jillian D'Onfro, "Google Employees: We No Longer Believe the Company Places Values over Profit," CNBC, November 27, 2018, https://www.cnbc.com/2018/11/27/read-google-employees-open-letter-protesting-project-dragonfly.html.

27. John Ruwitch, "Apple Is Accused of Limiting Crucial AirDrop Function in China Weeks before Protests," NPR, December 26, 2022, https://www.npr.org/2022/12/26/1145509265/apple-is-accused-of-limiting-crucial-airdrop-function-in-china-weeks-before-prot.

28. Katyanna Quach, "While Google Agonizes over Military AI, IBM Is Happy to Pick Up the Slack, Even for the Chinese Military," *The Register*, April 12, 2019, https://www.theregister.com/2019/04/12/ibm_ai_database/.

29. Melissa Heikkila, "The AI Myth Western Lawmakers Get Wrong," *The Algorithm*, November 28, 2022, https://www.technologyreview.com/2022/11/29/1063777/the-ai-myth-western-lawmakers-get-wrong/.

30. Heikkila. Quote is from Zeyi Yang.

31. Heikkila.

32. Ryan Fedasiuk, Jennifer Melot, and Ben Murphy, *Harnessed Lightning: How the Chinese Military Is Adopting Artificial Intelligence* (Washington, DC: Center for Security and Emerging Technology, October 2021), iii, https://cset.georgetown.edu/publication/harnessed-lightning/.

33. Fedasiuk, Melot, and Murphy, 10–11.

34. Fedasiuk, Melot, and Murphy, 37–38; Lyle J. Goldstein, "Beijing Confronts Long-Standing Weakness in Anti-Submarine Warfare," *China Brief* 11, no. 14 (July 29, 2011): 14–17, https://jamestown.org/program/beijing-confronts-long-standingweakness-in-anti-submarine-warfare; Lyle J. Goldstein and Shannon Knight, "Wired for Sound in the 'Near Seas'," U.S. Naval Institute *Proceedings* 140, no. 4 (April 2014): 56–61, https://www.usni.org/magazines/proceedings/2014/april/wired-sound-near -seas; Owen R. Cote Jr., "Assessing the Undersea Balance between the U.S. and China," U.S. Navy SSP Working Paper, February 2011, https://www.usni.org/sites/default/ files/inline-files/Undersea%20Balance%20WP11-1.pdf; and Eric Heginbotham et al., *The U.S.-China Military Scorecard*, RR 392 (Santa Monica: RAND Corporation, 2017), 186–200, https://www.rand.org/content/dam/rand/pubs/research_reports/RR300/ RR392/ RAND_RR392.pdf.

35. Fedasiuk, Melot, and Murphy, *Harnessed Lightning*, 38.

36. Jeffrey Engstrom, *Systems Confrontation and System Destruction Warfare: How the Chinese People's Liberation Army Seeks to Wage Modern Warfare*, RR1708 (Santa Monica: RAND Corporation, 2018), iii, https://www.rand.org/content/dam/rand/pubs/research_rep orts/RR1700/RR1708/RAND_RR1708.pdf.

37. Fedasiuk, Melot, and Murphy, *Harnessed Lightning*, 38–39.

38. Jeffrey Edmonds et al., *Artificial Intelligence and Autonomy in Russia*, DRM-2021-U -029303-Final (Arlington, VA: CNA, 2021), 123–26, https://www.cna.org/rep orts/2021/05/Artificial-Intelligence-and-Autonomy-in-Russia.pdf.

39. Margarita Konaev and Samuel Bendett, "Russian AI-Enabled Combat: Coming to a City Near You?" *War on the Rocks*, July 31, 2019, https://warontherocks.com/2019/07/ russian-ai-enabled-combat-coming-to-a-city-near-you/.

40. Konaev and Bendett.

41. Konaev and Bendett.

42. Ross Anderson, "The Panopticom Is Already Here," *Atlantic*, September 2020, www.the atlantic.com/magazine/archive/2020/09/china-ai-surveillance/614197.

43. Matt Shehan, "What China's Algorithm Registry Reveals about AI Governance," Carnegie Endowment for International Peace, December 9, 2022, https://carnegie endowment.org/2022/12/09/what-china-s-algorithm-registry-reveals-about-ai-gov ernance-pub-88606.

44. DL, TT, and YX (identities withheld), "Is China Emerging as the Global Leader in AI?" *Harvard Business Review*, February 18, 2021, https://hbr.org/2021/02/is-china -emerging-as-the-global-leader-in-ai.

45. Yasmin Tadjdeh, "China Threatens U.S. Primacy in Artificial Intelligence," *National Defense*, October 30, 2020, https://www.nationaldefensemagazine.org/articles/2020/ 10/30/china-threatens-us-primacy-in-artificial-intelligence.

46. National Security Commission on Artificial Intelligence, *Final Report*, 1.

47. Sharon Weinberger, Robert Wall, and Doug Cameron, "Pentagon Woos Silicon Valley to Join Ranks of Arms Makers," *Wall Street Journal*, March 26, 2023, https://www.wsj .com/articles/pentagon-woos-silicon-valley-to-join-ranks-of-arms-makers-38b1d 4c0?=q819s61u4azb57.

CHAPTER 4. WEAPONIZING AI

1. Boot, *War Made New.* Boot does not present technology as the only element determining victory or defeat, giving full acknowledgment to a host of other factors—geography, demography, economics, culture, leadership. However, he is firm in his contention of technology's huge impact, noting: "Some analysts may discount the importance of technology in determining the outcome of battles, but there is no denying the central importance of advanced weaponry in the rise of the West. . . . The way to gain military advantage, therefore, is not necessarily to be the first to produce a new tool or weapon. Often it is to figure out better than anyone else how to utilize a widely available tool or weapon" (458).

2. Andrew W. Marshall, "Some Thoughts on Military Revolutions—Second Version" (memorandum for record, August 23, 1993), in Owen Daniels, *The AI RMA: The Revolution Has Not Arrived (Yet)* (Washington, DC: Andrew W. Marshall Foundation, October 2022).

3. The characterization of the event as demonstrating the result of a revolution in military affairs is from P. W. Singer, *Wired for War: The Robotics Revolution and Conflict in the 21st Century* (New York: Penguin Press, 2009), 219–24. Contemporary records differ as to whether Pizarro's force numbered 168 or 180, but all agree that it was less than 200. Records are also unclear whether the entire 80,000-man Inca army was camped outside, but the force reportedly consisted of "the greater part of the Inca's forces." Sources also differ as to whether the Inca emperor expected an ambush. In North America, Hernán Cortés achieved similar results in his conquest of the Aztec empire; however, he was supported by thousands of Indian allies.

4. Since modern militaries consist of women as well as men, the term "unmanned" is gradually being replaced by "uncrewed." However, since "unmanned" is the term still in popular use, particularly throughout the media, we retain it in this volume.

5. Thomas Wildenberg, "Crewless Ghost Ships of the Inter-War Navy," *Naval History* (April 2014): 56–62, https://www.usni.org/magazines/naval-history-magazine/2014/march/crewless-ghost-ships-interwar-navy.

6. Additionally, DASH was outfitted with antisubmarine warfare torpedoes to deal with the rapidly growing Soviet submarine menace, the idea being that DASH would attack the submarine with Mk-44 homing torpedoes or Mk-57 nuclear depth charges at a distance that exceeded the range of the submarine's torpedoes. For one of the most complete descriptions of the U.S. Navy's DASH program, see Benjamin Armstrong, "Unmanned Naval Warfare: Retrospect and Prospect," *Armed Forces Journal*, December 20, 2013, http://armedforcesjournal.com/unmanned-naval-warfare-retrospect-prospect/. See also Thomas Pinney, "UAVs: Before Fire Scout There Was Dash," U.S. Naval Institute *Proceedings* 144, no. 8 (August 2018), https://www.usni.org/magazines/proceedings/2018/august/uavs-fire-scout-there-was-dash.

7. Douglas Main, "Robots to the Rescue," *Popular Science*, April 8, 2013, https://www.popsci.com/trp-sponsored-article-slideshow/.

8. As discussed throughout Tangredi and Galdorisi, *AI at War.*

9. Norman Polmar, "Historic Aircraft—The Pioneering Pioneer," *Naval History*, September 2013, https://www.usni.org/magazines/naval-history-magazine/2013/september/historic-aircraft-pioneering-pioneer.

10. Department of Defense, Office of the Under Secretary for Acquisition, *FY 2017–2042 Unmanned Systems Integrated Roadmap*, August 28, 2018, https://apps.dtic.mil/sti/citations/AD1059546.

11. Paul Scharre, *Army of None: Autonomous Weapons and the Future of War* (New York: W. W. Norton and Company, 2018), 313.

12. *FY 2017–2042 Unmanned Systems Integrated Roadmap.*

13. National Security Commission on Artificial Intelligence, *Final Report.*

14. See Harry Hillaker, "John Boyd, Father of the F-16," *Code One Magazine*, July 1997, quoted in George Galdorisi, "Warfighting Demands Better Decisions," U.S. Naval Institute *Proceedings* 146, no. 6 (June 2020): 32–35. Boyd's construct was originally a theory of achieving success in air-to-air combat, developed out of his energy-maneuverability theory and his observations on air-to-air combat between MiG-15s and North American F-86 Sabres in Korea. Harry Hillaker, chief designer of the F-16, said of the OODA theory: "Time is the dominant parameter. The pilot who goes through the OODA cycle in the shortest time prevails because his opponent is caught responding to situations that have already changed."

15. Amir Husain, "AI Is Shaping the Future of War," *Prism* 9, no. 3 (November 2021): 50–61. This article provides ten examples of autonomous systems—including lethal autonomous systems—in use by various militaries today.

16. Scharre, *Army of None*, 47–48.

17. Husain, "AI Is Shaping the Future," 56.

18. Karl Capek, *R. U. R. (Rossum's Universal Robots)* (New York: Samuel French, 1923), https://www.gutenberg.org/files/59112/59112-h/59112-h.htm.

19. For one of the most comprehensive reports on the impact of AI on military operations, see *The Militarization of Artificial Intelligence* (New York: United Nations, August 2019).

20. Department of Defense Directive 3000.09, "Autonomy in Weapon Systems," updated January 25, 2023.

21. Ralph Peters, "Bloodless Theories, Bloody Wars: Easy Win Concepts Crumble in Combat," *Armed Forces Journal*, April 1, 2006, http://armedforcesjournal.com/bloodless-theories-bloody-wars/.

CHAPTER 5. ROBOTS AT WAR

1. Paul Scharre, "Centaur Warfighting: The False Choice between Humans vs. Automation," *Temple International and Comparative Law Journal* 30, no. 1 (Spring 2016): 152, https://sites.temple.edu/ticlj/files/2017/02/30.1.Scharre-TICLJ.pdf.

2. John Arquilla and Peter Denning, "Automation Will Change Sea Power," U.S. Naval Institute *Proceedings* 145, no. 6 (June 2019), https://www.usni.org/magazines/proceedings/2019/june/automation-will-change-sea-power.

3. Scharre, *Army of None*, 321.

4. Jada Rivera, "A Flank Bell: The Importance of Manned-Unmanned Teaming," USNI blog, January 29, 2021, https://blog.usni.org/posts/2021/01/29/a-flank-bell-the-im portance-of-manned-unmanned-teaming.

5. Mike Cassidy, "Centaur Chess Brings Out the Best in Humans and Machines," Bloom-Reach blog, December 14, 2014, https://www.bloomreach.com/2014/centaur-chess -brings-best-humans-machines.

6. See, for example, the 1960 paper by J. C. R. Licklider, "Man-Computer Symbiosis," *IRE Transactions on Human Factors in Electronics*, vol. HFE-1 (March 1960): 4–11.

7. National Academies of Sciences, Engineering, and Medicine, *Human-AI Teaming: State of the Art and Research Needs* (Washington, DC: The National Academies Press, 2022), https://doi.org/10.17226/26355. See also Maria Jesus Saenz, Elena Revilla, and Cristina Simón, "Designing AI Systems with Human-Machine Teams," *MIT Sloan Management Review*, March 18, 2020, https://sloanreview.mit.edu/article/designing -ai-systems-with-human-machine-teams/, and Barry Strauch, "Ironies of Automation: Still Unresolved After All These Years," *IEEE Transactions on Human-Machine Systems*, April 2017, 1–15.

8. Berkowitz, *The New Face of War*. Berkowitz does not restrict his examples to just one conflict, noting further: "The same thing happened when the United States fought Yugoslavia in 1999 and the Taliban regime in Afghanistan in 2001. Each time experts feared the worst; each time U.S. forces won a lopsided victory" (3).

9. Robert Work, interview with David Ignatius at "Securing Tomorrow" forum, Washington, DC, March 30, 2016.

10. The importance of artificial intelligence and autonomy to all aspects of society, and especially to military operations, has been well documented at the international and national levels. See, for example, Executive Office of the President, National Science and Technology Council, Committee on Technology, *Preparing for the Future of Artificial Intelligence*, October 2016; Office of the Secretary of Defense for Acquisition, Technology, and Logistics, *Report of the Defense Science Board Summer Study on Autonomy*, June 2016; and more recently, the March 2021 National Security Commission on Artificial Intelligence *Final Report*.

11. Robert Work, remarks at the Center for New American Security Defense Forum, December 14, 2015.

12. Kris Osborn, "The Strategic Problem of Persistent Surveillance," *National Interest*, June 7, 2021, https://nationalinterest.org/blog/buzz/strategic-problem-%E2%80%98 persistent-surveillance%E2%80%99-187034.

13. George Galdorisi, "UAVs Can Fill the Navy's Scouting Gap," U.S. Naval Institute *Proceedings* 149, no. 1 (January 2023): 36–37, https://www.usni.org/magazines/proceed ings/2023/january/uavs-can-fill-navys-scouting-gap.

14. Audrey Decker, "Navy Eyes Stingray for Future Carrier-Based Aviation," *Inside the Navy*, September 9, 2022, https://insidedefense.com/daily-news/navy-eyes-stingray -future-carrier-based-unmanned-aviation. The article mentions what Navy leaders have said in a number of speeches and presentations, noting in part: "More than 4 out of every 10 aircraft would be unmanned."

15. Sherry Sontag, Christopher Drew, and Annette Lawrence Drew, *Blind Man's Bluff: The Untold Story of American Submarine Espionage* (New York: Public Affairs, 1998).

16. Sam Lagrone and Mallory Shelbourne, "CNO Gilday: 'We Need a Naval Force of over 500 Ships,'" *USNI News*, February 18, 2022, https://news.usni.org/2022/02/18/cno-gilday-we-need-a-naval-force-of-over-500-ships.

17. Department of the Navy, Chief of Naval Operations, *NAVPLAN 2022*, July 2022, https://news.usni.org/2022/07/26/2022-chief-of-naval-operations-navigation-plan-update; Sam Lagrone, "Updated: Navy's Force Design 2045 Plans for 373 Ship Fleet, 150 Unmanned Vessels," *USNI News*, July 26, 2022, https://news.usni.org/2022/07/26/navys-force-design-2045-plans-for-373-ship-fleet-150-unmanned-vessels.

18. Lagrone, "Updated: Navy's Force Design 2045."

19. Patrick Tucker, "Soldiers Don't Trust Robot Battle Buddies. Can Virtual Training Fix That?" *Defense One*, November 30, 2020, https://www.defenseone.com/technology/2020/11/soldiers-dont-trust-robot-battle-buddies-can-virtual-training-fix/170378/.

20. Javier Chagoya, "Researchers, Marines Explore Trust in Human-Machine Teams," Navy News Service, December 4, 2020, https://www.navy.mil/Press-Office/News-Stories/Article/2435883/researchers-marines-explore-trust-in-human-machine-teams/.

21. Megan Eckstein, "Berger: Marines Need to Trust Unmanned, AI Tools for Future Warfare," *USNI News*, February 2, 2021, https://news.usni.org/2021/02/02/berger-marines-need-to-trust-unmanned-ai-tools-for-future-warfare.

22. National Security Commission on Artificial Intelligence, *Final Report*. See also Joseph Chapa, "Trust and Tech: AI Education in the Military," *War on the Rocks*, March 2, 2021, https://warontherocks.com/2021/03/trust-and-tech-ai-education-in-the-military/, for a discussion of how trust in the aviation world can inform trust in AI-enabled weapons systems.

23. Scharre, *Army of None*, 229–30.

24. Scharre, "Centaur Warfighting."

CHAPTER 6. DECISION-MAKING

1. Gen. John Shanahan, remarks at the U.S. Naval War College Artificial Intelligence Symposium, December 10, 2019.

2. Department of Defense, Deputy Secretary of Defense Memo, "Accelerating Data and Artificial Intelligence for the Warfighter," June 21, 2021, https://media.defense.gov/2021/Jun/23/2002748007/-1/-1/1/MEMORANDUM-ON-ACCELERATING-DATA-AND-ARTIFICIAL-INTELLIGENCE-FOR-THE-WARFIGHTER.PDF.

3. One of the best references on the OODA loop is John Boyd, *Destruction and Creation* (Fort Leavenworth, KS: U.S. Army Command and General Staff College, 1976).

4. Galdorisi, "Warfighting Demands Better Decisions."

5. See, for example, Ian Toll, *Six Frigates: The Epic History of the Founding of the U.S. Navy* (New York: W. W. Norton and Company, 2006).

6. To be clear, the Navy suffered a number of setbacks during this timeframe, most notably the capture of USS *Philadelphia* by Tripoli in 1803 and the capture of USS *President* in the War of 1812.

7. The six original U.S. Navy frigates were USS *Constitution*, USS *Constellation*, USS *President*, USS *United States*, USS *Chesapeake*, and USS *Congress*.

8. The movie was loosely based on an incident in October 1962, shortly before the Cuban Missile Crisis, when the U.S. Navy was pursuing Soviet submarine B-59.

9. While there are a plethora of news reports regarding this tragic incident, one of the best is "Iran Plane Crash: Ukrainian Jet Was 'Unintentionally' Shot Down," BBC News, January 11, 2020, https://www.bbc.com/news/world-middle-east-51073621.

10. See John Cordle, "Design Systems That Work for People," U.S. Naval Institute *Proceedings* 144, no. 9 (September 2018), https://www.usni.org/magazines/proceedings/2018/september/design-systems-work-people. The author analyzes these two accidents and concludes that the lack of human systems integration in designing the systems that officers and Sailors onboard these ships used to make designs was an important causal factor in both accidents.

11. See, for example, Azmat Kahn, "Hidden Pentagon Records Reveal Pattern of Failure in Deadly Airstrikes," *New York Times*, December 21, 2021, https://www.nytimes.com/interactive/2021/12/18/us/airstrikes-pentagon-records-civilian-deaths.html; Azmat Kahn, "The Human Toll of America's Air Wars," *New York Times*, January 2, 2022, https://www.nytimes.com/2021/12/19/magazine/victims-airstrikes-middle-east-civilians.html; and Alex Horton, Dan Lamothe, and Karoun Demirjian, "Botched Drone Strike That Killed 10 Civilians in Kabul Was Not a Result of Criminal Negligence, Pentagon Says," *Washington Post*, November 3, 2021, https://www.washingtonpost.com/national-security/2021/11/03/kabul-drone-strike-inspector-general-report/. The first *New York Times* article identified "incomplete information or misinterpretation of the information available" as well as "failed intelligence and decision-making" as some of the root causes of these errant airstrikes.

12. Lee Bennett addressed this challenge in his article, "Fight Information Overload," where he noted, "There are human limits to quickly understanding, retaining, and implanting critical information." U.S. Naval Institute *Proceedings* 143, no. 7 (July 2017), https://www.usni.org/magazines/proceedings/2017/july/fight-information-overload.

13. U.S. Army Training and Doctrine Command, Mad Scientist blog, November 23, 2020, https://madsciblog.tradoc.army.mil/287-artificial-intelligence-an-emerging-game-changer/.

14. Dr. Alexander Kott, keynote address, 22d Command and Control Research and Technology Symposium, Los Angeles, November 7, 2017.

15. Dr. Eric Haseltine, keynote address, Office of Naval Research Applied Artificial Intelligence Summit, San Diego, October 15–18, 2018.

16. Department of the Air Force, *Technology Horizons: A Vision for Air Force Science and Technology 2010–2030*, September 2011, 156, http://www.defenseinnovationmarketplace.mil/resources/AF_TechnologyHorizons2010-2030.pdf.

17. A significant part of this emphasis on leveraging big data, artificial intelligence, and machine learning for U.S. military applications is the fact that potential adversaries are fielding this capability in their weapons systems, often faster than the U.S. military is

doing so. See, for example, the Naval Research Advisory Committee report *Autonomous and Unmanned Systems in the Department of the Navy* (Washington, DC: Naval Research Advisory Committee, September 2017).

18. As we noted above, a classic case where this did not happen was in July 1988 when USS *Vincennes* shot down Iran Air Flight 655. See Anthony Tingle, "The Human-Machine Team Failed Vincennes," U.S. Naval Institute *Proceedings* 144, no. 7 (July 2018), https://www.usni.org/magazines/proceedings/2018/july/human-machine-team-failed-vincennes. The author noted, "Technology must create time for the commander, mitigating compression while presenting the proper information to the warfighter, at the correct time, and in a useful and usable format."

19. Richard Burgess, "CNO: Precision Era Gives Way to Decision Era," *Seapower Magazine*, June 13, 2017, http://seapowermagazine.org/stories/20170613-CNO.html.

20. Discussions of the OODA loop are making a resurgence in professional journals. See, for example, Carl Governale, "Brain-Computer Interfaces Are Game-Changers," U.S. Naval Institute *Proceedings* 143, no. 8 (August 2017), https://www.usni.org/magazines/proceedings/2017/august/brain-computer-interfaces-are-game-changers; and John Allen and Amir Husain, "AI Will Change the Balance of Power," U.S. Naval Institute *Proceedings* 144, no. 8 (August 2018), https://www.usni.org/magazines/proceedings/2018/august/ai-will-change-balance-power.

21. Details of the Current Strategy Forum, held June 13–14, 2017, at the U.S. Naval War College can be found at https://www.youtube.com/playlist?list=PLam-yp5uUR1ZUIyggfS_xqbQ0wAUrGoSo. This includes a one-hour video of the CNO's remarks.

22. One of the best works that explains the TADMUS system is Janis Cannon-Bowers and Eduardo Salas, *Making Decisions Under Stress* (Washington, DC: American Psychological Association, October 1998).

23. Jeffrey Morrison, "Decision Support Displays for Military Command Centers: Enabling Knowledge-Centric Warfare for Fleet Decision-Makers," *Human Systems IAC Gateway* 11, no. 4 (2000).

24. See, for example, Glenn Osga et al., " 'Task-Managed' Watchstanding: Providing Decision Support for Multi-Task Naval Operations," Space and Naval Warfare Systems Center San Diego Biennial Review, 2001, and Jeffrey Morrison, *Global 2000 Knowledge Wall*, http://all.net/journal/deception/www-tadmus.spawar.navy.mil/www-tadmus.spawar.navy.mil/GlobalKW.pdf.

25. This was one of the principal findings in Bryan Clark, Dan Pratt, and Harrison Schramm, *Mosaic Warfare: Exploiting Artificial Intelligence and Autonomous System to Implement Decision-Centric Operations* (Washington, DC: Center for Strategic and Budgetary Assessments, 2020), https://csbaonline.org/uploads/documents/Mosaic_Warfare_Web.pdf.

26. Rear Admiral Dietrich Kuhlmann, remarks, AFCEA/U.S. Naval Institute WEST Conference, February 6, 2018.

27. The Honorable James Geurts, Assistant Secretary of the Navy for Research, Development, and Acquisition, keynote remarks, AFCEA/U.S. Naval Institute WEST Conference, February 6, 2018.

28. Admiral Michael Gilday, remarks on Project Overmatch, AFCEA/U.S. Naval Institute WEST Symposium, June 30, 2021.

29. Richard Burgess, "Adm. Trussler: Information Warfare 'All about Speed for Advantage,'" *Seapower Magazine*, November 13, 2020, https://seapowermagazine.org/adm -trussler-information-warfare-all-about-speed-for-advantage/.

30. Edward Lundquist, "DMO Is Navy's Operational Approach to Winning the High-End Fight at Sea," *Seapower Magazine*, February 2, 2021, https://seapowermagazine.org/ dmo-is-navys-operational-approach-to-winning-the-high-end-fight-at-sea/.

31. Department of the Navy, *CNO NAVPLAN 2022*, January 2023, https://media .defense.gov/2022/Jul/26/2003042388/-1/-1/1/NAVIGATION%20PLAN%20 2022%20ONE%20PAGER.PDF.

32. Sydney Freedberg, "Military AI Is Bigger Than Just the Kill Chain: JAIC Chief," *Breaking Defense*, November 4, 2020, https://breakingdefense.com/2020/11/military-ai-is -bigger-than-the-kill-chain-jaic-chief/.

33. U.S. Naval Institute *Proceedings* has hosted an extensive dialogue on the importance— and challenges—of decision-making in the stress of high-intensity naval operations. See, for example, Lee Bennett, "Fight Information Overload," U.S. Naval Institute *Proceedings* 144, no. 7 (July 2017), https://www.usni.org/magazines/proceedings/ 2017/july/fight-information-overload; Governale, "Brain-Computer Interfaces Are Game-Changers"; Gabe Harris, Cynthia Lamb, and Jerry Lamb, "Surf the Data Tsunami," U.S. Naval Institute *Proceedings* 145, no. 2 (February 2018), https://www.usni.org/ magazines/proceedings/2018/february/surf-data-tsunami; Jeff Benson, "Prepare for Decision-Making at Sea," U.S. Naval Institute *Proceedings* 145, no. 12 (December 2019), https://www.usni.org/magazines/proceedings/2019/december/prepare-decision -making-sea; Kevin Hoadley, "Achieving Decision Superiority in Great Power Competition," U.S. Naval Institute *Proceedings* 147, no. 2 (February 2021), https://www .usni.org/magazines/proceedings/2021/february/achieving-decision-superiority -great-power-competition; and Sam J. Tangredi, "Sun Tzu Versus AI: Why Artificial Intelligence Can Fail in Great Power Competition," U.S. Naval Institute *Proceedings* 147, no. 5 (May 2021), 20–25, https://www.usni.org/magazines/proceedings/2021/ may/sun-tzu-versus-ai-why-artificial-intelligence-can-fail-great-power.

34. K. C. Miller et al., "Merging Future Knowledgebase System of Systems with Artificial Intelligence/Machine Learning Engines to Maximize Reliability and Availability for Decision Support," Military Operations Research Society, 2021.

35. See, for example, Tangredi, "Sun Tzu Versus AI," for one of an increasing number of articles in the professional literature describing the importance of data in the big data, artificial intelligence, machine-learning continuum. The article points out, for example, "It is not the one who has the best AI who will dominate politico-military decision-making, but the one who has the most accurate, meaningful and deception free data" (24).

36. Office of Naval Research, "Command Decision Making (CDM)," https://www.nre .navy.mil/organization/departments/code-34/division-341/command-decision-mak ing-cdm.

37. Clark, Pratt, and Schramm, *Mosaic Warfare*, iv.

38. Scharre, *Army of None*, 244.

39. See, for example, "R2P2—Rapid Response Planning Process," The Lightning Press, https://www.thelightningpress.com/r2p2-rapid-response-planning-process/.

40. Christof Koch, "To Keep Up with AI, We'll Need High-Tech Brains," *Wall Street Journal*, October 27, 2017, https://www.wsj.com/articles/to-keep-up-with-ai-well -need-high-tech-brains-1509120930. More recently, a *New York Times* article described how this idea of cognitive stimulation has gained traction. See Kim Tingley, "A Better Way to Zap Our Brains," *New York Times*, February 28, 2021, https://www.nytimes .com/2021/02/24/magazine/brain-stimulation-mental-health.html.

41. According to the joint staff website, "The U.S. Department of Defense (DoD) Strategic Multilayer Assessment (SMA) program is a multidisciplinary, multi-agency portfolio of projects that studies and assesses challenging problems associated with planning and operations of DoD, military services, and government agencies. SMA is accepted and synchronized by Joint Staff/J39 Directorate for Special Activities and Operations and executed by Assistant Secretary of Defense for Research and Engineering/Rapid Fielding Directorate/Rapid Reaction Technology Office." See U.S. Joint Staff, SMA Virtual Conference, "The Mind-Tech Nexus: How Will Minds Plus Technology Win Future Wars?" January 31, 2023.

42. U.S. Joint Staff, SMA Virtual Conference, "The Quantified Warrior: Monitoring the Physiology of the Human for War," February 16, 2023.

43. Avi Goldfarb and John Lindsay, *Artificial Intelligence in War: Human Judgment as an Organizational Strength and a Strategic Liability* (Washington, DC: The Brookings Institution, November 2020), https://www.brookings.edu/research/artificial-intelli gence-in-war-human-judgment-as-an-organizational-strength-and-a-strategic-liability/.

44. Arquilla and Denning, "Automation Will Change Sea Power."

45. Recent use of the quote includes Mark Stout, "Are We Winning Yet? Led Astray by Metrics," *War on the Rocks*, October 2, 2013, https://warontherocks.com/2013/10/ are-we-winning-yet-led-astray-by-metrics/.

CHAPTER 7. IS THE GENIE OUT OF THE BOTTLE?

1. Robert Work, remarks at the Center for New American Security Defense Forum, December 14, 2015.

2. William Roper, director, Strategic Capabilities Office, Office of the Secretary of Defense, on CBS *60 Minutes*, January 8, 2017: "I've heard people say that autonomy is the biggest thing in military technology since nuclear weapons."

3. Jyoti Narayan, Kristal Hu, and Supantha Mukherjee, "Elon Musk, Others Urge an AI Pause, Citing 'Risks to Society,'" Reuters, https://www.reuters.com/technology/musk -experts-urge-pause-training-ai-systems-that-can-outperform-gpt-4-2023-03-29/.

4. In 2004 after Israel announced the sale of this system to China, the Harpy became the focus of a U.S. effort to restrict arms transfers and the sales of advanced military technology to China.

5. National Security Commission on Artificial Intelligence, *Final Report*.

6. Lloyd Austin, remarks at the Reagan National Defense Forum, December 4, 2021.

7. See, for example, Singer, *Wired for War*; Bradley Strawser and Jeff McMahan, *Killing By Remote Control: The Ethics of an Unmanned Military* (Oxford, UK: Oxford University Press, 2013); William Arkin, *Data and the Illusion of Perfect Warfare* (New York: Little Brown and Company, 2015); Larry Lewis and Diane Vavrichek, *Rethinking the Drone War* (Washington, DC: Center for Naval Analyses, 2016); Scharre, *Army of None*; and John Jackson, ed., *One Nation Under Drones* (Annapolis, MD: Naval Institute Press, 2018).

8. "Morals and the Machine," *The Economist*, June 2, 2012, https://www.economist.com/leaders/2012/06/02/morals-and-the-machine.

9. Bill Keller, "Smart Drones," *New York Times*, March 10, 2013, https://www.nytimes.com/2013/03/17/opinion/sunday/keller-smart-drones.html.

10. Alex Garland, "Alex Garland of 'Ex Machina' Talks about Artificial Intelligence," *New York Times*, April 22, 2015, https://www.nytimes.com/2015/04/26/movies/alex-garland-of-ex-machina-talks-about-artificial-intelligence.html. This heated dialogue continues among other tech titans. See, for example, Cade Metz, "Mark Zuckerberg, Elon Musk, and the Feud over Killer Robots," *New York Times*, June 9, 2018, https://www.nytimes.com/2018/06/09/technology/elon-musk-mark-zuckerberg-artificial-intelligence.html.

11. "Pause Giant AI Experiments: An Open Letter," Future of Life Institute, March 23, 2023, https://futureoflife.org/open-letter/pause-giant-ai-experiments/.

12. Tom Huddleston, "Elon Musk Wants to Pause 'Dangerous' AI Development. Bill Gates Disagrees—And He Is Not the Only One," CNBC, April 6, 2023, https://www.cnbc.com/2023/04/06/bill-gates-ai-developers-push-back-against-musk-wozniak-open-letter.html.

13. "The World Needs an International Agency for Artificial Intelligence, Say Two AI Experts," *The Economist*, April 18, 2023, https://www.economist.com/by-invitation/2023/04/18/the-world-needs-an-international-agency-for-artificial-intelligence-say-two-ai-experts.

14. See, for example, Wakabayashi and Shane, "Google Will Not Renew Pentagon Contract that Upset Employees."

15. Noah Shachtman, "Inside the Robo-Cannon Rampage," *Wired*, October 19, 2007.

16. David Sanger, "U.S. Decides to Retaliate against China's Hacking," *New York Times*, July 30, 2015, https://www.nytimes.com/2015/08/01/world/asia/us-decides-to-retaliate-against-chinas-hacking.html.

17. Dorothy Denning, "Iran's Cyber Warfare Program Is Now a Major Threat to the United States," *Newsweek*, December 12, 2017.

18. David Kushner, "The Real Story of Stuxnet," *IEEE Spectrum: Technology, Engineering, and Science News*, February 26, 2013, https://spectrum.ieee.org/the-real-story-of-stuxnet.

19. James Temperon, "When Robots Kill: Deaths by Machines Are Nothing New But AI Is About to Change Everything," *Wired*, March 17, 2017.

20. P. W. Singer, author of *Wired for War*, put it this way in an address to the AFCEA C4ISR Symposium in San Diego, April 27, 2017: "What is playing out in driverless cars is also playing out in military UxS. You will never be able to 'engineer out' all of the ethical dilemmas surrounding the use of military UxS."

21. Neal Boudette, "Tesla to Recall 362,000 Cars for Safety Flaw in Technology," *New York Times*, February 17, 2023, https://www.nytimes.com/2023/02/16/business/tesla -recall-full-self-driving.html. This article notes that between July 1, 2021, and May 15, 2022, six people died and five were seriously injured in nearly 400 accidents involving driver-assistance technologies.

22. Azim Shariff, Iyad Rahwan, and Jean-Francois Bonnefon, "Whose Life Should Your Car Save?" *New York Times*, November 6, 2016, https://www.nytimes.com/2016/11/06/ opinion/sunday/whose-life-should-your-car-save.html. See also Aaron Kessler, "Riding Down the Highway, with Tesla's Code at the Wheel," *New York Times*, October 15, 2015, https://www.nytimes.com/2015/10/16/automobiles/tesla-adds-high-speed-auto nomous-driving-to-its-bag-of-tricks.html.

23. Cade Metz, "A Warning Signal on Self-Driving Cars," *New York Times*, February 16, 2023, https://www.nytimes.com/2023/02/15/business/missy-cummings-tesla-auto pilot.html.

24. This acronym ChatGPT stands for generative pertained transformer, which is a lan- guage prediction model.

25. Kevin Roose, "Bing's Chatbot Drew Me In and Creeped Me Out," *New York Times*, February 17, 2023, https://www.nytimes.com/2023/02/16/technology/bing-chatbot -microsoft-chatgpt.html.

26. Department of Defense, "Implementing Responsible Artificial Intelligence in the Department of Defense," May 2021, https://media.defense.gov/2021/May/27/2002 730593/-1/-1/0/IMPLEMENTING-RESPONSIBLE-ARTIFICIAL-INTELLI GENCE-IN-THE-DEPARTMENT-OF-DEFENSE.PDF.

27. DoD Directive 3000.09.

28. DoD Directive 3000.09.

29. Mike Corder, "U.S. Launches Artificial Intelligence Military Use Initiative," AP News, February 16, 2023, https://apnews.com/article/russia-ukraine-technology-china-the -hague-artificial-intelligence-d49c5fb442fa825e0a7a7419d6f04469.

30. "How Drones Dogfight above Ukraine," *The Economist*, February 7, 2023, https:// www.economist.com/the-economist-explains/2023/02/07/how-drones-dogfight -above-ukraine.

31. Peter Bergen, "General David Petraeus: How the War in Ukraine Will End," CNN Live, February 14, 2023, https://www.cnn.com/2023/02/14/opinions/petraeus-how -ukraine-war-ends-bergen-ctpr.

32. Scharre, *Army of None*, 232–33.

CHAPTER 8. THE LAWS OF WAR

1. Barack H. Obama, "Remarks by the President at the National Defense University," Fort McNair, Washington, DC, May 23, 2013, https://obamawhitehouse.archives.gov/ the-press-office/2013/05/23/remarks-president-national-defense-university.

2. Congressional Research Service, *Defense Primer: U.S. Policy on Lethal Autonomous Weapons Systems*, November 14, 2022, https://crsreports.congress.gov/product/pdf/ IF/IF11150.

3. As we continue to examine this matter in more detail, it is worth looking at a companion definition of levels of autonomy simply because it is embodied in an official DoD publication and has more granularity than the triad of definitions we present here. Linell Letendre put it this way in "Lethal Autonomous Weapon Systems: Translating Geek Speak for Lawyers," *International Law Studies* 96 (2020):

> The Defense Department outlined four levels of autonomy in its *2011 Unmanned Systems Integrated Roadmap*, https://www.defensedaily.com/wp-content/uploads/post_attachment/206477.pdf. This approach focused on whether the machine or the human makes the decision. The 2011 document describes the four levels as (1) human operated (where the human makes all decisions), (2) human delegated (where the system can perform those functions allowed by the human), (3) human supervised (where the unmanned system conducts an array of activities under the supervision of a human operator, including initiating its own actions based on the machine's assessment of the environment), and (4) fully autonomous (where the system functions completely independently of a human operator other than the human setting the over-arching goals of the mission).

4. Stanley A. McChrystal, foreword to *U.S. Military Operations: Law, Policy, and Practice*, ed. Geoffrey S. Corn, Rachel E. VanLandingham, and Shane R. Reeves (New York: Oxford University Press, 2015).
5. Tate Nurkin and Stephen Rodriguez, *A Candle in the Dark: U.S. National Security Strategy for Artificial Intelligence* (Washington, DC: The Atlantic Council, 2019), https://www.atlanticcouncil.org/wp-content/uploads/2019/12/AC_CandleinDark120419_FINAL.pdf.
6. Letendre, "Lethal Autonomous Weapon Systems."
7. L. W. King, *The Code of Hammurabi* (CreateSpace, December 2, 2015).
8. Scharre, *Army of None*, 331.
9. George Galdorisi and Kevin Vienna, *Beyond the Law of the Sea: New Directions for United States Oceans Policy* (Westport, CT: Greenwood Press, 1997). See also Orde Kittrie, *Lawfare: Law as a Weapon of War* (New York: Oxford University Press, 2016), and Stephen Schiffman, "Great Power Use of Lawfare: Is the Joint Force Prepared?" *Joint Force Quarterly* 107 (4th Quarter 2022): 15–20, https://ndupress.ndu.edu/JFQ/Joint-Force-Quarterly-107/Article/Article/3197205/great-power-use-of-lawfare-is-the-joint-force-prepared/.
10. The body of international humanitarian law consists primarily of the four Geneva Conventions of 1949 and the two Additional Protocols of 1977.
11. Charles Dunlap, "Lawfare 101: A Primer," *Military Review* 97, no. 3 (May-June 2017), 8–17.
12. Scharre, *Army of None*, 258–61.

13. DARPA website, Collaborative Operations in Denied Environment (CODE), https://www.darpa.mil/program/collaborative-operations-in-denied-environment.

14. Gary Marcus and Ernest Davis, *Rebooting AI: Building Artificial Intelligence We Can Trust* (New York: Vintage Books, 2019).

15. Lewis and Vavrichek, *Rethinking the Drone War*, 64–65.

16. Lewis and Vavrichek, 86.

17. Dunlap, "Lawfare 101," 11.

18. "Five-Power Naval Limitation Treaty," Britannica Online, January 30, 2023, https://www.britannica.com/event/Five-Power-Naval-Limitation-Treaty.

19. Valerie Hopkins, "In a Blaring Celebration of the War, Russia Displays and Demands Unity," *New York Times*, February 23, 2023, https://www.nytimes.com/2023/02/22/world/europe/russia-ukraine-war-rally.html.

20. A nation-by-nation summary of national positions on fully autonomous lethal weapons systems, published by Human Rights Watch in 2020, can be found at https://www.hrw.org/report/2020/08/10/stopping-killer-robots/country-positions-banning-fully-auto nomous-weapons-and.

21. Hitoshi Nasu and David Letts, "The Legal Characterization of Lethal Autonomous Maritime Systems: Warship, Torpedo, or Naval Mine?" *International Law Studies* 96 (2020).

22. Adam Satariano, Nick Cumming-Bruce, and Rick Gladstone, "Killer Robots Aren't Science Fiction. A Push to Ban Them Is Growing," *New York Times*, December 17, 2021, https://www.nytimes.com/2021/12/17/world/robot-drone-ban.html.

23. James Kraska, "Command Accountability for AI Weapon Systems," *International Law Studies* 97 (2021), 407.

24. *Defense Primer: U.S. Policy on Lethal Autonomous Weapons Systems.*

25. Department of State, "Political Declaration on Responsible Military Use of Artificial Intelligence and Autonomy," February 2023, https://www.state.gov/political-declara tion-on-responsible-military-use-of-artificial-intelligence-and-autonomy/.

26. Patrick Tucker, "U.S. Woos Other Nations for Military-AI Ethics Pact," *Defense One*, February 16, 2023, https://www.defenseone.com/technology/2023/02/us-woos-other -nations-military-ai-ethics-pact/383024/.

27. Chris M. Ford, "Autonomous Weapons and the Law," in *One Nation Under Drones*, ed. John Jackson (Annapolis, MD: Naval Institute Press, 2018), 150–64.

28. *Defense Primer: U.S. Policy on Lethal Autonomous Weapons Systems.*

CHAPTER 9. WORLD WAR III

1. P. W. Singer and August Cole, *Ghost Fleet: A Novel of the Next World War* (New York: Houghton Mifflin Harcourt, 2015).

2. Elliot Ackerman and James G. Stavridis, *2034: A Novel of the Next World War* (New York: Penguin, 2021).

3. In 1914 the "system" was mass mobilization and the railroad networks that could move troops faster than ever before. In 1939 the system was the combination of aircrafts, tanks, and radios integrated to form the blitzkrieg.

4. The first detection of the Imperial Japanese aircraft nearing Pearl Harbor on December 7, 1941, was at 0720 local time. In the case of that attack, a radar detection warning was not reported because the operators assumed they were U.S. Army aircraft flying in from California.

5. Carl von Clausewitz, *On War*, trans. by O. J. Matthijs Jolles (New York: Random House, 1943), 280.

6. Defense Intelligence Agency, *Russia Military Power: Building a Military to Support Great Power Aspirations*, DIA-11-1704-161 (2017), 27, https://www.dia.mil/Portals/110/Images/News/Military_Powers_Publications/Russia_Military_Power_Report_2017.pdf.

7. Nicholas Thompson, "Inside the Apocalyptic Soviet Doomsday Machine," *Wired*, September 21, 2009, https://www.wired.com/2009/09/mf-deadhand/.

8. William J. Broad, "Russia Has 'Doomsday' Machine, U.S. Expert Says," *New York Times*, October 8, 1993, http://www.nytimes.com/1993/10/08/world/russia-has-doomsday -machine-us-expert-says.html.

9. Maris Goldmanis, "The Origin of Buzzer Monoliths, the Soviet Nuclear Defense System, and the Myth of the Dead Hand," Numbers Stations, January 24, 2015, http://www.numbers-stations.com/buzzer-monoliths-and-nuclear-defence-system.

10. Ron Rosenbaum, "The Return of the Doomsday Machine?" *Slate*, August 31, 2007, https://web.archive.org/web/20110907105928/http://www.slate.com/id/2173108/pagenum/all.

11. "Perimetr 15E601," Global Security.org, February 6, 2018, https://www.globalsecurity.org/wmd/world/russia/perimetr.htm.

12. Roberta Wohlstetter, *Pearl Harbor: Warning and Decision* (Stanford, CA: Stanford University Press, 1962), 348.

13. Steven E. Pelz, *Race to Pearl Harbor* (Cambridge, MA: Harvard University Press, 1974), 224.

14. For example, Adm. William A. Owens, USN, with Ed Offley, *Lifting the Fog of War* (New York: Farrar, Straus and Giroux, 2000).

15. *The United States Strategic Bombing Surveys*, reprint of summary report (Maxwell Air Force Base, AL: Air University Press, October 1987), 13.

16. John T. Correll, "Daytime Precision Bombing," *Air and Space Forces Magazine*, October 1, 2008, https://www.airandspaceforces.com/article/1008daylight/.

17. Joseph Frantiska, "The Azimuth 'Smart' Bombs of World War II," Warfare History Network, July 2013, https://warfarehistorynetwork.com/article/the-azimuth-smart -bombs-of-world-war-ii/.

CHAPTER 10. WILL WORLD WAR III EVER END?

1. Dan Robitzki, "Advanced Artificial Intelligence Could Run the World Better than Humans Ever Could," Futurism.com, August 29, 2018, https://futurism.com/advanced-artificial-intelligence-better-humans.

2. Stephen Losey, "U.S. Air Force Eyes Fleet of 1,000 Drone Wingmen as Planning Accelerates," *Defense News*, March 8, 2023, https://www.defensenews.com/air/2023/03/08/us-air-force-eyes-fleet-of-1000-drone-wingmen-as-planning-accelerates/.

3. Congressional Research Service, *Defense Primer: U.S. Defense Industrial Base*, updated April 17, 2023, 1, https://crsreports.congress.gov/product/pdf/IF/IF10548.

4. Tara Copp, "How Ukraine War Has Shaped U.S. Planning for a China Conflict," AP News, February 16, 2023, https://apnews.com/article/russia-ukraine-taiwan-politics -china-8a038605d8dd5f4baf225bdaf2c6396b.

5. Michael Sheetz, "Elon Musk's SpaceX Sent Thousands of Starlink Satellite Internet Dishes to Ukraine, Company President Says," CNBC, March 22, 2022, https://www .cnbc.com/2022/03/22/elon-musk-spacex-thousands-of-starlink-satellite-dishes -sent-to-ukraine.html.

6. An argument that nanoweapons are possible and constitute a future threat is made by Louis A. Del Monte, *Nanoweapons: A Growing Threat to Humanity* (Lincoln, NE: Potomac Books, 2017).

7. Frank Bajak, "Musk Deputy's Words on Starlink 'Weaponization' Vex Ukraine," AP News, February 9, 2023, https://apnews.com/article/russia-ukraine-elon-musk-spacex -technology-business-c79c81ff4e6a09f4a185e627dad858fa.

CHAPTER 11. TOWARD A NATIONAL DIALOGUE ON MILITARY AI

1. Amit Ray, *Compassionate Artificial Intelligence* (self-published, 2018).

2. Interview, September 29, 2022.

3. Jonathan E. Hillman, *The Digital Silk Road: China's Quest to Wire the World and Win the Future* (New York: Harper Business, 2021).

4. Fedasiuk, Melot, and Murphy, *Harnessed Lightning*, 37–39.

5. William Liscomb Borden, *There Will Be No Time: The Revolution in Strategy* (New York: Macmillan, 1946).

6. Kenneth Payne, *I, Warbot: The Dawn of Artificially Intelligent Conflict* (New York: Oxford University Press, 2021), 246–56.

CONCLUSION

1. Cade Metz, "He Warns of Risks from AI He Helped Create," *New York Times*, May 2, 2023, https://www.nytimes.com/2023/05/01/technology/ai-google-chatbot-engin eer-quits-hinton.html. The impact of Dr. Hinton's remarks is seen in the fact that his statements were carried in a wide range of national and international media—the *Christian Science Monitor*, *Forbes*, *The Guardian*, and many others, as well as many network television channels and streaming services.

2. Berber Jin and Deepa Seetharaman, "Elon Musk Tries to Direct AI—Again," *Wall Street Journal*, May 2, 2023, https://www.wsj.com/articles/elon-musk-ai-chatgpt-arti ficial-intelligence-x-69464a1.

3. Cade Metz, Ryan Mac, and Kate Conger, "Musk's Stance on AI: It's Tricky," *New York Times*, April 28, 2023, https://www.nytimes.com/2023/04/27/technology/elon -musk-ai-openai.html.

4. Kevin Roose, "Google Chief Opens Up about AI," *New York Times*, April 23, 2023, https://www.nytimes.com/2023/03/31/technology/google-pichai-ai.html.

5. Jeremy Roos, "We Don't Know What Will Happen Next," *New York Times*, April 18, 2023, https://www.nytimes.com/2023/04/18/opinion/global-crisis-future.html.
6. Sabrina Siddiqui and John McKinnon, "Biden Administration Warns of AI's Dangers: There's a Limit to What White House Can Do," *New York Times*, May 4, 2023, https://www.wsj.com/articles/white-house-warns-of-risks-as-ai-use-takes-off-d4cc217f.
7. Ryan Tracy, "U.S. Weighs Regulating AI Tools," *Wall Street Journal*, April 12, 2023, https://www.wsj.com/articles/biden-administration-weighs-possible-rules-for-ai-tools-like-chatgpt-46f8257b.
8. Lina Kahn, "The U.S. Needs to Regulate AI," *New York Times*, May 6, 2023, https://www.nytimes.com/2023/05/03/opinion/ai-lina-khan-ftc-technology.html.
9. David McCabe, "White House Pushes Tech C.E.O.s to Limit Risks of A.I.," *New York Times*, May 5, 2023, https://www.nytimes.com/2023/05/04/technology/us-ai-research-regulation.html.
10. Tracy, "U.S. Weighs Regulating AI Tools."
11. Cade Metz, "The ChatGPT King Isn't Worried, But He Knows You Might Be," *New York Times*, April 2, 2023, https://www.nytimes.com/2023/03/31/technology/sam-altman-open-ai-chatgpt.html.
12. Cade Metz, "If Some Dangers Posed by AI Are Already Here, Then What Lies Ahead?" *New York Times*, May 8, 2023, https://www.nytimes.com/2023/05/01/technology/ai-problems-danger-chatgpt.html.
13. Secretary of Defense Lloyd Austin, remarks at the Reagan National Defense Forum, December 4, 2021, https://www.defense.gov/News/Speeches/Speech/Article/2861931/remarks-by-secretary-of-defense-lloyd-j-austin-iii-at-the-reagan-national-defen/.
14. Department of Defense, DEPSECDEF Memorandum, "Accelerating Data and Artificial Intelligence for the Warfighter," June 21, 2021.
15. David Sanger, "AI's Potential on the Battlefield Alarms U.S. Defense Experts," *New York Times*, May 6, 2023, https://www.nytimes.com/2023/05/05/us/politics/ai-military-war-nuclear-weapons-russia-china.html.
16. Scharre, *Four Battlegrounds*.

INDEX

ABOUT THE AUTHORS

George Galdorisi is Director of Strategic Assessments and Technical Futures for the Naval Information Warfare Center Pacific. Prior to joining NIWC Pacific, he completed a thirty-year career as a naval aviator, culminating in fourteen years of consecutive service as executive officer, commanding officer, commodore, and chief of staff. He enjoys writing, especially speculative fiction about the future of warfare. He is the author of sixteen books, including four consecutive *New York Times* bestsellers.

Dr. Sam Tangredi is the Leidos Chair of Future Warfare Studies and Professor of National, Naval and Maritime Strategy in the Center for Naval Warfare Studies of the U.S. Naval War College. He has published six books and numerous journal articles, book chapters, and reports for government and academic organizations. He has appeared on CNN and the History Channel. Dr. Tangredi is a retired Navy captain and surface warfare officer also specializing in naval strategy. He held command at sea and directed several Department of Defense strategic planning organizations.